THE
WAY
OF
INNOVATION

**Master the Five Elements of
Change to Reinvent Your Products,
Services, and Organization**

KAIHAN KRIPPENDORFF

PLATINUM PRESS®
Avon, Massachusetts

Published by Platinum Press®, an imprint of
Adams Media, an F+W Publications Company
57 Littlefield Street, Avon, MA 02322. U.S.A.
www.adamsmedia.com

Platinum Press is a registered trademark of F+W Publications, Inc.

ISBN 10: 1-59869-379-4
ISBN 13: 978-1-59869-379-9

Printed in Canada.

J I H G F E D C B A

Library of Congress Cataloging-in-Publication Data
is available from the publisher.

This publication is designed to provide accurate and authoritative information
with regard to the subject matter covered. It is sold with the understanding
that the publisher is not engaged in rendering legal, accounting, or other
professional advice. If legal advice or other expert assistance is required, the
services of a competent professional person should be sought.
    —From a *Declaration of Principles* jointly adopted by a Committee of the
  American Bar Association and a Committee of Publishers and Associations

Many of the designations used by manufacturers and sellers to distinguish
their product are claimed as trademarks. Where those designations appear in
this book and Adams Media was aware of a trademark claim, the designations
have been printed with initial capital letters.

This book is available at quantity discounts for bulk purchases.
For information, please call 1-800-289-0963.

CONTENTS

BOOK THREE
APPLICATION
145

BOOK FOUR
CASE STUDIES
189

Acknowledgments

Over the past three years I have enjoyed innumerable conversations with extraordinary people about the source, path, and theories of innovation. This book is a syncretism of their wide-ranging philosophies and insights—I could only write it because such a diverse and thoughtful group agreed to share their time with me.

I particularly want to thank a group of extraordinary innovators, each of whom has significantly impacted the world in some way, for sharing their time and experiences: Dr. Muhammad Yunus, Kris Gopalakrishnan, Dick Hayne, Ted Leonsis, Verne Harnish, Zaki Mustafa, Elon Musk, Scott Hill, Bill Drayton, Sabrina Herrera, and Jochen Zeitz.

I owe a debt to scholars who contributed decades of knowledge. This book draws heavily on the work of my father, Klaus Krippendorff, who has spent more than thirty years exploring how humans construct reality. Steven Heine, Alan Carsrud, Malin Brannback, Katheryn Harrigan, and Michael Goussev provided invaluable guidance. Maggie Stuckey helped refine my prose.

In addition, I want to thank numerous executives from some of the world's most dynamic companies for sharing ways in which large organizations can sustain innovativeness. I thank, among others, Mariana Castro, Melinda Large, Taneli Ruda, Juan Jose Gonzalez, Jacob Peters, Bill Lombardo, Joanna Popper, and Liz Codd. This book was made richer by the insights of numerous friends and colleagues including Christina Zhu, AnaMaria Rivera, Itza Manuela Acosta, and Stephannie Wasserstein.

My agent, Laurie Harper, continues to provide me steady guidance. Of all those who contributed to this book, I owe most to my family—Pilar, Lucas, and Kaira—who provided me the encouragement and space, even during those lonely Sunday afternoons of writing, to complete a work I can be proud of.

Miami Beach, Florida

BOOK ONE

INNOVATION'S SOURCE

CHAPTER ONE

THE INNOVATION SHIFT

Innovation is not an option. It is a fundamental requisite of survival.

Throughout history, innovative societies have dominated their less-creative rivals. The first civilizations to adopt a new innovation—the first to embrace agriculture, direct rivers, learn metallurgy, or organize themselves into governments—always gained power over their neighbors, at least for some period of time. Indeed, the ability to innovate has determined life and death, dominance and subservience, winning and losing for as long as humankind has been concerned with such things.

In the same way, innovative companies dominate their competition. The companies that have created the greatest value, that outperform their peers for any meaningful time span, almost always do so by adopting an innovation more quickly and more completely than their competitors.

This has been so since the earliest days of commerce, and with the passage of time it has only increased in urgency. As our world becomes more complex, no one should expect the task of piloting innovations to become easier. Quite the reverse: The coming age will demand dynamic, flexible strategies and an ability to respond quickly to emerging threats and opportunities. It will require unleashing innovations with speed, efficiency, and flair.

Yet despite vast history to draw upon, we remain ineffective at this critical skill. Our attempts to introduce new "things"—new products, business transformations, entrepreneurial ventures, social movements—consistently fail. That poor success rate evidences that our understanding of change remains incomplete.

I believe the reason we are so ineffective at driving innovation is that we are overlooking much of our collective experience. Our modern frameworks for change are rooted in only 50, perhaps 100, years of history and limit themselves almost exclusively to corporate and technological innovation.

We tend to focus on the physical side of innovation (design, production, marketing), all the while missing another important perspective. To become more effective innovators we need to draw on a deeper and broader reservoir of experience. We need to incorporate the wisdom of older traditions—Taoist, Hindu, and Buddhist—that have been refining their theories of innovation for 5,000 years. We have been ignoring the vast, rich body of human knowledge such traditions have gathered. One goal of this book is to correct this oversight.

If we open our ancestors' notebooks, we will be treated to this important insight: The things we can easily study—the technology, the user, the community, and so forth—only effect change indirectly. The true source of innovation, these ancient sciences tell us, is something we cannot see or touch.

Innovation Begins with a Shift

The originating source of all innovation is the Shift.

I use that term as a kind of shorthand for the mental leap we make when we first fully recognize something—when a child looks at the round object in his room and for the first time sees "ball," when an engineer sees small speakers inserted in his colleague's ears and suddenly sees "headphones," or, as we will discuss later, when a caveman looks at a three-pronged stick and recognizes it as a "plow." All innovations start when someone experiences a Shift by naming something, categorizing it, or seeing a use for it in a novel way, and then convinces others to experience the same Shift. It is the aim of this book to help you understand how to cause the Shift in yourself, your organization, and your environment . . . to become a more effective innovator, better skilled at changing the world.

The Shift That Triggered Civilization

Let me start by telling you a story. Sometime around 6000 B.C. an anonymous farmer tried something new: He scratched the ground with an odd-shaped stick he had just found. He lived somewhere in the land arcing up from the Nile delta into Palestine and eastward over the hills of Anatolia, the area today known as the Fertile Crescent. With that one simple act, this innovator arguably sparked the formation of civilization. James Burke, the British science historian, describes what happened:

> At about the same time as these first attempts at irrigation, the digging stick changed its shape; it became a simple scratch plough, with a forward-curving wooden blade for cutting the soil, and a backward-curving pair of handles with which the farmer could direct the oxen. This simple implement may arguably be called the most fundamental invention in the history of man, and the innovation that brought civilization into being, because it was the instrument of surplus. It is not until [a community] can produce food which is surplus to requirements, and is therefore capable of supporting those who are not food producers, that it will flourish. This development was made possible by the plough, and it caused a radical transformation of Egyptian society.

The ability to plow made it possible to produce surplus food, which freed the Egyptians to expand. They built an empire of unprecedented reach and power. They introduced the world to a technology that freed humankind, as Burke described it, from our "total and passive dependence of the vagaries of nature" and set us on the path of innovation. The scratch plow, Burke argues, made possible all subsequent inventions with which humans began mastering their environment. This humble invention also has a great deal to teach us about the process of innovation itself.

Six Modern Views of Innovation

Our modern knowledge base of innovation, what we find in journals and books, draws on 50 to 100 years of study. Over that period, experts have examined innovation by focusing on six different parts of the whole:

- The technology
- The environment
- The innovator
- The user
- The community
- The competing technologies

We can use the scratch plow to illuminate the differences in these separate parts, and thus come closer to understanding the whole. By then asking how the Taoist, Hindu, and Buddhist traditions would explain the innovation, we will see the gap in our understanding, the missing piece that, if filled, will help us become far more effective change-makers.

The Technology. The technologist would say that the tool itself makes possible all subsequent changes. Without the three-pronged stick, humans would not have plowed their first field.

The Environment. The environmentalist points us away from the tool toward the environment and asks what it is about the environment that can spur or hinder growth. He or she might consider that first farmer's community as a prehistoric R & D lab that brought together the right mix of factors to launch a new product.

The Innovator. Other modern students of innovation direct us to the individual entrepreneur. They would ask us to analyze what combination of his or her history and character traits led the farmer who first used a stick as a plow to introduce the innovation to the world.

The User. "Innovation diffusion" studies offer useful insight about the characters of the people who first try new technologies and how less progressive users eventually decide to adopt the technology as well. The argument would be that the innovator may have shared the plow with the world, but it took 3,000 years for the scratch plow to catch on, and that to understand innovation we need to understand how users adopt new things.

The Community. A growing number of innovation experts would say we are simplifying things to an unreal level by separating innovators from users; they argue that both belong to a community and jointly develop a new technology. Users become innovators by changing the technology physically (for example, by reshaping the stick) or functionally (such as by using it to create time instead of surplus). Perhaps the scratch plow is the product of some sort of "open" or shared community innovation.

The Competing Technologies. Finally, other experts point to the alternative methods and argue that the innovation would not spread unless it overcame competing technologies. The scratch plow would not have been so widely accepted if it did not beat hunting, planting crops by hand, or other competing technologies. The scratch plow might have been a "disruptive technology" that preempted competitive resistance.

The Limitations of Modern Theories

"If we want to understand creativity, we need to understand the process of choice. How can we enhance creativity by improving the way we select and implement new ideas?"

—Mihaly Csikszentmihalyi

Together these views paint what seems like a complete picture of the plow's emergence and humankind's transformation from hunter-gatherers into farmers. In the painting we see the stick (technology) in the hand of a caveman (innovator). These are set against a background (environment) replete with all the right elements—humans training oxen, for example, which are waiting for something to pull. Beyond this first farmer are other would-be farmers (users), inspecting the new tool with their friends (community), while farther in the background we see hunters (competing technologies) letting down their spears and gathering around the first plow.

But because these views focus on just the painting, they restrict our attention. Each perspective assumes there are only two players in innovation—the physical technology and its users—and that innovation happens when a technology is built and people use it or refuse it.

But pull away from the painting and you will see that these explanations blind us to something else, a critical player we cannot capture with color or brush. That "something" is the Shift that happens in the observer's mind when the stick, without changing shape, suddenly becomes a plow. Even with the painting complete—the innovator holding a stick, the users waiting for something new, inferior competing technologies in the background, and so on—no change could begin until someone saw a stick and actually *recognized* it as a plow.

Eastern philosophers have been pointing us toward this mental layer, and away from the physical painting, for thousands of years. If we are ever to fully grasp the essence of innovation, so that we may shape it and guide it, we must understand the Shift.

The Shift Changes Perceived Options

In the villages along Lake Victoria in Uganda, AIDS has ravaged the population for the past twenty years. Lands that were once used for farming have been converted into graveyards. While the Ugandan government has made progress in reducing the death count in other areas of the country, this lakefront region remains a problem.

Ironically, many of the deaths are not directly caused by AIDS. Rather they are related to depression that overcomes the family members of people who die from AIDS. Researchers who spoke to villagers in the region estimated that about 20 percent of the population is suffering from depression. Complicating efforts to help these people is the fact that in the local language, Luganda, there is no word for "depression." Because those suffering with depression have no way to name their ailment, they have no concept that it is something others share and that they can treat. Counselors from a nongovernmental agency, World Vision, decided to help. They assembled women who seemed to be suffering from the condition and held group counseling sessions in which they talked about this "thing" called depression: its history, its causes, its treatment. The results were encouraging. When the sufferers had something to call their condition, the depression lifted. They experienced the Shift when they were able to see depression as something that was real and that existed outside of themselves. By creating the concept of "depression," counselors changed perspectives, behaviors, and lives.

The Shift Tells You What to Do

Here's another way to think about this concept of Shift. Imagine you are walking along a road and see an oddly shaped piece of wood on the ground. You pick it up and realize it is actually a small sculpture, hand-carved, in the shape of a horse's head. What do you do with it? If it exists for you as a sculpture, you might put it on display in your home and tell your friends the story of its discovery. But suppose one of your guests picks it up and then, instead of placing it back on the shelf, puts it down on a chessboard you have in your den. Seeing your sculpture of a horse's head sitting on a chessboard suddenly transforms your perspective entirely. This is no longer a sculpture; it is a chess piece, specifically a knight. What can you do with a knight? The options come immediately to mind. A knight can be moved in an "L" shape along the board, jumping two steps vertically and then one more horizontally, or jumping one step vertically and two horizontally.

In both of these examples, something happened that changed human behavior. In the first case a new concept was introduced. Before, "depression" did not exist; afterward, it did. Before, people died; afterward, more lived. In the second case the piece of wood was transformed from a sculpture into a chess piece without actually changing form at all. Nothing in the physical world changed, but something new appeared. Before, there was no knight; afterward, there was. Before, people stood around and looked at a sculpture; afterward, they moved it along a chessboard in a precise, specific manner.

Understanding the Shift

"People are not disturbed by things but by the views they take of them."

—*Epictetus, first century A.D.*

Arm & Hammer saved its core product, baking soda, from the seemingly inevitable jaws of commoditization without introducing any new technology or product innovation. By simply adding to the list of ways the product could be used, the company sold its boxes into nearly every refrigerator in the United States. Just as the ancient farmer transformed a stick into a plow, Arm & Hammer transformed a cooking ingredient into an air freshener.

Innovation begins not when something changes in the physical world but rather when our conception or understanding of that thing shifts. When a stick becomes a plow it communicates to us a new behavior and a new way of life. What moments earlier was something to walk by or burn for fire suddenly inspires us to put down our hunting tools and begin planting seeds in the ground. This shift from "stick" to "plow" is the source of innovation. All the players—innovator, community, entrepreneur, users, gatekeepers—had definite roles in the transformation of human existence. But, had they played their roles with a "stick" instead of a "plow," nothing could have changed. To understand innovation we must understand how a "stick" transforms into a "plow." Luckily we are not the first to explore this transformation. Philosophers and scientists, particularly those of ancient Asia, have been investigating this shift for millennia. Western scientists have picked up this inquiry over the last hundred years, studying how humans construct reality. Together, these two paths of inquiry offer a powerful set of tools and a framework for causing change.

CHAPTER TWO

AN ANCIENT FRAMEWORK
FOR CHANGE

Let us now fast-forward a few thousand years. The invention of the plow triggered the innovation of agriculture, which allowed people to devote time to other interests besides gathering their daily food.

By 1000 B.C., Egypt had developed unprecedented power, and was continuing its dominance over the Nile region. In Greece, philosophers accepted the liberation that agriculture afforded and invested their newly freed time into developing philosophies that would define Western civilization.

In China and India, scientists or spiritualists—at the time the two were the same, as there was no distinction between science and religion, or spirituality—put their free time toward a different investigation. They began exploring and documenting how change occurred. By 1000 B.C., Chinese and Indian philosophers, politicians, and military thinkers had been contributing to a set of evolving texts, ancient blogs if you will, that collectively attempted to understand change: why it happens and how humankind should deal with it.

Through the rises and falls of new governments, wars, and societal shifts, China's greatest thinkers documented their observations in a set of texts that now form the foundation of Chinese thought: the *I Ching* (*Book of Changes*); *Tao Te Ching*; Sun Tzu's *The Art of War*; and *The 36 Stratagems*. Over a similarly vast time period Indian philosophers memorized, added to, and passed down a set of instructional poems, called Vedas, that form the basis of Hindu and Buddhist thought. Imagine if Western thinkers did this, if Plato, Machiavelli, and Benjamin Franklin passed along an evolving set of working documents decade to decade, each editing and enhancing what the texts advise, sharing a conversation about change. The result would be a powerful playbook for causing change, for driving innovation.

If we can unwrap and synthesize these ancient Asian guides, we will have a practical, accessible tool for leading innovation.

The Mechanics of Change

The Eastern model for change offers a unique view of how innovations occur and how we can influence them. This framework eludes most in the West because it requires an uncomfortable shift in our perception of change. But it is perhaps the most tested change framework known to man.

The framework consists of four basic concepts:

- The dance between two parallel worlds—the material and immaterial—determines the direction of change.
- An endless cycle of creation and destruction fuels change.
- Three primal powers—Heaven, Earth, and Man—drive change.
- Innovations evolve through five phases of change.

The Dance of Two Parallel Worlds

The first concept in the Eastern change framework is the idea that the universe consists of two parallel worlds. One is the material world we can see and measure. The second is an immaterial world of words, thoughts, and ideas. The two worlds are linked by what can be described as rubber bands, with the material world constantly catching up to the immaterial.

Effective leaders know how to change the material world by influencing the immaterial. A CEO introduces a new vision or redrafts her company's mission to change her organization's words, stories, and beliefs. These shifts, in turn, have a delayed influence on the material world as her company's decisions and actions align with the new vision or mission.

This is the essence of the notion of the Shift—that beliefs (immaterial world) change behavior in the material world. That is why I argued that it was the plow, not the stick, that triggered agriculture. To understand and influence innovation we must operate at its source, which is the moment the immaterial world changes, when the stick converts into a plow in its user's mind and begins transforming behavior. Corporations have formally used language—the immaterial—to influence consumers' actions for several decades now.

The basic premise, that missions, visions, values, beliefs, and stories are linked to actions, is not new. Indian and Chinese thinkers arrived at this insight 3,000 years ago. While the Western world was unlocking insights about the external world, through disciplines such as physics and math, Eastern philosophers were looking internally and making breakthroughs in how our minds represent the external world. Their conclusions were both consistent with, yet radically different from those of the Western philosophers and scientists.

The Eastern view suggests that the immaterial world is as real for us as the material world. That the former defies measure, that we cannot see it, should not negate its existence or relevance. As things form in the material world, we perceive and name them in our immaterial world and these immaterial representations become what we call "real." The two—the immaterial representations and the material objects—are both real.

Shifting your perspective from "imaginary/real" to "immaterial/material" may seem minor. But, as you will learn in greater detail later, it can significantly strengthen your ability to successfully predict and influence emerging trends.

Corporate success is often compared to winning a war. No matter how you see the question morally, it is certainly true that military strategies depend on fundamental principles that can be useful in the business world, and that the collected wisdom of military leaders, which goes back many centuries, clearly shows the link between the material and immaterial worlds. That is perhaps why retired General Samuel Griffith likes to cite Sun Tzu's adage that "the primary target is the mind of the opposing commander; the victorious situation, a product of his creative imagination."

Modern military approaches are currently undergoing a significant transformation as the U.S. and other Western armies are slowly adopting "fourth generation warfare" (4GW), which is based on the play between reality and perception. 4GW is credited with delivering the United States a seemingly effortless victory during the 1991 Desert Storm campaign. Its fast-paced, asymmetrical approach is proving highly effective in the dynamic environments of modern conflict. 4GW strategists focus as much on their opponents' synapses (the mental wiring their opponents depend on to interpret their environments) as they do on troop formations. The approach argues that a mental battle occurs in parallel with the physical battle, and incorporates this mental level into the design of military strategy.

Just as winning a war requires manipulating the relationship between your opponent's environment and his interpretation of that environment, introducing an innovation requires influencing how others understand their realities. The innovator steps on the battlefield sequentially with several different types of opponents. At each stage of his campaign he must achieve a different goal. In each battle, however, he must use the linkages between reality and perception to achieve victory. Understanding how reality and perception are linked is critical to innovation.

Numerous models exist, both ancient and modern, to help us understand the connections between the material and immaterial world. I have found a Buddhist framework to be particularly powerful. The model—known as the "five aggregates"—distinguishes five linkages between the immaterial and material. By playing on these five linkages, we can more precisely understand and influence the adoption of new innovations. The five aggregates (or linkages) are explained in the following table.

The Buddhist Five Aggregates

Aggregate	Explanation	Example
1. Form	What you actually perceive of the material world. What you see, hear, smell, taste, or feel directly.	Walking through the forest, you see something move out of the corner of your eye.
2. Feeling	The primitive reaction you have to what you just sensed. You immediately have a favorable, unfavorable, or neutral reaction.	You feel immediately scared; the hair on your neck rises, your pupils dilate, and your heart rate increases.
3. Recognition	The classification and naming of what you sense—"recognizing" it according to your past experiences.	You turn to see a shape with antlers and recognize it to be a deer.
4. Mental formation	Attaching pre-existing "baggage"—associations, memories, impediments—to what you recognize. This baggage may cause you to automatically want something or push it away.	Recalling *Bambi,* you have warm feelings for the deer, so you soften your eyes and look.
5. Consciousness	The experience of being conscious of the thing you have sensed (form) and named (recognition) and of the associated feelings you have about it ("baggage").	You are aware you are looking at a deer. You remind yourself to keep quiet so as not to scare it away.

Three key lessons of this framework are repeated across almost every discipline that attempts to explain how humans understand their environments, from the ancient studies of Taoism and Hinduism to modern Western sciences such as cognitive psychology and social construction. The three lessons are:

1. While we can directly experience the real world (we can see, smell, taste, feel, or hear it), the images that we call the real world are only interpretations. When you look at a wooden

chair, for example, you are looking at light reflected off the chair. It comes to you in a spectrum corresponding with the colors of wood. Your eyes transform the light into electrical patterns that the relevant parts of your brain can interpret and recognize as several straight lines, wood, a seat, a back, and therefore a chair. There is no light in your head; only electrical patterns.

2. We react, both consciously and unconsciously, not to what we actually experience but to the name or category we give to what we experience. The chair means nothing to you—it is but a puzzle of interlocked wood—until you call it a chair and categorize it as such. Only then do you understand its intended use. Until you recognize it as a chair, you do not even think to sit in it.

3. Most of this process occurs outside of our consciousness. Your brain operates without bothering you with the details as it continuously absorbs, transforms, categorizes, names, interprets, and filters massive amounts of data. It informs your consciousness of only a small portion of these activities.

The Continual Cycle of Creation and Destruction

The second element of the Eastern framework for change is something physicists agreed on two decades ago: Things appear and disappear. The view that physical matter is temporary (that is, it can disappear) diverges fundamentally from our traditional view that matter is solid and, until acted upon, inactive.

While physicists have evolved their viewpoint, most of us remain stuck with the latter, outdated view. We prefer a static world, where things will be as they are unless acted upon, or at best a happy, dynamic world in which things are created but not destroyed. We want to build companies that last, even though we know that nothing truly lasts.

We understand that natural law dictates old foliage must die to fertilize soil and make way for new plants. We also know that this same law applies to our company. The economist Joseph Schumpeter termed this law *creative destruction*, noting that creation almost always depends on a destructive precursor. The old must step aside for the new. The AT&T monopoly had to die for the Baby Bells, Sprint, and Verizon to grow. We know this intuitively to be true but tend to resist it anyway, especially when we are on the receiving end of destruction, secretly hoping we can avoid the inevitable.

The Chinese Taoist model sees death and birth as co-dependent. This has two critical implications. First, death is both an end and a beginning. Death symbolizes accomplishment and rebirth. Great leaders accept and work with this natural law. Inferior leaders fight it.

The second implication is that what we usually term *change* is not change at all. The new order of things we seek cannot come about by modifying what exists but rather by replacing what exists with something new. The most meaningful changes are actually transformations that occur when we kill off an old belief, perspective, story, metaphor, identity, habit, or commitment and replace it with a new one.

Indian philosophers arrived at the same conclusion. The Hindu philosophy sees the world as being in a dynamic balance between creation and destruction, with the multi-armed god Shiva dancing between the two to keep creation and destruction in balance. Martin Luther King Jr. knew that his vision was inconsistent with existing beliefs and laws, and that he would need to replace them with new ones. You could say that what distinguished his approach from other civil rights movements was that he focused on removing the fear and uncertainty of this "destruction" process so that those who depended on the existing models would feel less threatened by change.

Three Primal Powers

"If you know the enemy and know yourself, your victory will not stand in doubt; if you know Heaven and know Earth, you may make your victory complete."

—Sun Tzu, The Art of War

The ancient and oft-cited Chinese text on military strategy, *The Art of War*, proposes that three forces influence all change and calls these powers Heaven, Earth, and Man. To successfully launch an innovation, you must assess your situation along these three dimensions. To skillfully manage your innovation, you must understand which forces, from these three directions, are influencing your effort by offering resistance or support.

This framework maps neatly to what modern corporate strategists use today during the strategic planning process. Correlating this modern process to the *Art of War* dimensions, we can say that you would start with Heaven: the environmental factors relatively beyond your control, such as societal trends and governmental regulation. Next you analyze the Earth dimension: activities of other players who influence your game, such as competitors, customers, suppliers, and distributors. These two steps are often termed a "situation analysis." After understanding them, you can finally assess the Man dimension, which interacts within and between the other two. The Man dimension involves inquiries such as what you wish to achieve, where you want to compete, and what winning moves you'll need to triumph.

The Three Primal Powers Applied to Business

Primal Power	Business Strategy Term	Key Variables
Heaven	Environment	Societal factors, macroeconomic trends, technological innovations, government regulation
Man	Individual and Company	Capabilities/resources, business model, product/service offering, distribution, promotion
Earth	Market Players	Customers, competitors (direct, indirect, and potential), distributors, suppliers

Innovation Evolves Through Five Phases

Just as we cannot see the ancient Nazca Lines in Peru without the perspective afforded by an airplane, seeing the patterns of innovation requires the perspective that only thousands of years of study can provide. A smaller sample set risks leading us to incorrect and overly complex conclusions about how change happens.

That our modern frameworks for change seem complex and incapable of consistently delivering successful innovations is due to their grounding in shallow soil. They are rooted in just a hundred or so years of experience. To understand and predict change, we need more data. We need to look more deeply into the past. By studying ancient frameworks for change we can derive a simple, effective, and tested tool for unleashing innovation.

We can trace the study of change among Eastern philosophies to two sources: the Taoist school, which influenced Sun Tzu; and the Hindu school, which gave birth to Buddhism. Both share compelling parallels that point us to a simple, powerful framework for causing change.

Between 900 and 600 B.C., Indian philosophers memorized and passed down poems that captured key lessons on how the universe operates. These were eventually written down and collected as a work called the Upanishads. These, along with a sister text called the *Bhagavad Gita*, form the foundation of Hindu and Buddhist philosophy.

Central to the Upanishads' explanation of how the world changes is the notion that change occurs in three phases: creating, sustaining, and destroying. Each of these is further broken down into sub-phases that detail the process through which new things come into the world.

At the same time that Indian philosophers were detailing the dynamics of change, Chinese philosophers were undertaking a parallel pursuit. Their conclusions were surprising similar: Underneath the chaotic surface of change rests a consistent pattern. Their theory is captured in what is probably the oldest text known to humankind, the *I Ching*. Like the *Bhagavad Gita*, it argues that all innovations pass through phases of evolution, but the *I Ching* identifies five phases (rather than three), each represented by a physical element: metal, water, wood, fire, and earth. These phases continually repeat to form the Wu Xing cycle.

Modern students of change have arrived at surprisingly similar findings. Joseph Schumpeter's previously mentioned theory of "creative destruction" draws on these change cycles and shows that innovative companies and industries must often destroy their predecessors. Before him the Russian economist Nikolai Kondratieff found that economies (their prices, interest rates, production) rise and fall through fifty to sixty cycles. Along the same lines as Schumpeter and Kondratieff, marketers regularly use the language of life cycles to describe the process by which products and companies come into the world and die again.

If we step back and look at modern cycles from the perspective of their ancient predecessors, we will see that modern theorists are merely repeating the older discovery. While each cycle may consist of smaller or larger steps or be marked at different breaking points, they all fit a five-stage cycle of creation and destruction. Collectively they show that all innovations must pass through each of the five phases in the proper sequence: metal into water into wood, then fire, and finally earth.

From the birth and disappearance of the ancient Greek religion and the rise and decline of Egyptian civilization, to the execution of a military campaign or the emergence of Starbucks, all innovations are born out of rigidity and discontent (the first phase) and must follow through the other four phases in sequence back into rigidity. What determines how far or fast an innovation will travel along the sequence is the subject of this book.

The framework of this book borrows the metaphors of the Wu Xing cycle, because they nicely capture each phase's character, but does not apply to the cycle literally. Rather, this book synthesizes several change cycles into one comprehensive tool.

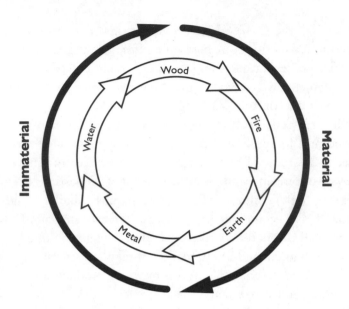

Metal: Discontent

Innovations are born when their environment is rigid and life-less. Hindu sciences called this "frozen energy" or *Tamas*—the system's energy is trapped in the bonds that hold the system motionless, incapable of freeing itself. The system is stuck in a fixed set of beliefs, assumptions, attitudes, habits, or identities so completely that an organization can only maintain the status quo; it cannot respond to threats and opportunities with sufficient speed. An organization cannot move past the Metal phase if it does not recognize that it is stuck. The only way change happens is that someone who holds a powerful commitment, vision, or aspiration realizes that the vision cannot be fulfilled under current conditions, and decides it is time to break out of existing rigidity. Only then can innovation begin.

> *"No organization is going to change in a fundamental way unless it believes there's real pain staying the way we are."*
>
> —*Louis Gerstner, former CEO, IBM*

Water: Imagination

Just as water is fluid and spontaneous, devoid of structure, an innovation begins to take shape when an individual or a small group of people realize they are stuck—are in a Metal state—and develop a plan to change the future. While most of the organization remains stuck, a pocket of water is forming. A few people are beginning to see that what was once deemed impossible can actually be achieved. They dream of alternatives and brainstorm new strategic options and, by introducing them into their organization's dialogue, begin altering the immaterial world. However, just as water will slide off the table without the structure of a glass to contain it, the leaders of the innovation risk losing their energy to the mass of nonbelievers. The innovators must begin building the structure that will propel the innovation from the immaterial world into the material one. They must turn Water into Wood.

Wood: Formation

Sun Tzu points out that power comes from formation. In this phase the innovator must grow wood and bend it into a bow; as the bow is pulled, potential energy is harnessed. But this phase requires dedication and faith because progress can be excruciatingly slow. Even as it stretches itself into a great oak, the sapling seems still. Similarly, all innovations enter a phase in which effort overshadows results—when a leader must gather resources, convince others to believe in a future, warn against slipping back into complacency—before the organization is ready to unleash its new strategy and seize a new future. Many innovators give up before their innovations take form, before their strategy resonates with the supporters they will need to advance the innovation into the Fire phase.

Fire: Breakout

Once an innovation has assembled its formation and attracted key supporters, it will cross its tipping point, at which it has attracted the critical mass needed to begin self-generating. Then the innovation is "on fire." People switch sides and want to be part of this new wave of change. The competition, which once discounted the innovation, takes notice and responds. This phase, like fire itself, is characterized by disorder and speed. Managing this phase requires an approach different from the patience the Wood phase demanded. It requires speed, creativity, and a careful calculation of competitive behavior. For those who have the skill to succeed through breakout, the opportunity exists to stay on top.

Earth: Consolidation

Your innovation will eventually mature and become like earth: stable, consistent, and reliable. With the battle over, you have time to erect walls and prolong a period of peace. What made you successful through the breakout phase will not be what keeps you successful during maturity. Before, you relied on speed and on shrewdly managing your competition. At maturity, however, you no longer enjoy the benefits of being small and fast. Your continued success depends on consistency rather than unpredictability. Your competitors now take their time to plan new strategies and, attracted to your success, are more willing than before to change their practices to win.

This cycle then repeats itself. You want to hold on to Earth as long as you can but you will eventually return to Metal, grow stiff, and be reborn. Companies that intend to last will survive not by hoping for a sustainable Earth state, but rather through reinvention. You might even say that the original company does not survive at all, but instead begins a new cycle, creates a new version of itself, when its old cycle has run its course. Sony reinvented itself from an electric blanket company into a radio company and then into a media company. Disney grew from cartoons to theme parks to movies. And GE has managed to reinvent itself at least five times in its 115 years of life.

"No one wants to die. Even people who want to go to heaven don't want to die to get there. And yet death is the destination we all share. No one has ever escaped it. And that is as it should be, because Death is very likely the single best invention of Life. It is Life's change agent. It clears out the old to make way for the new."

—Steve Jobs, commencement address to Stanford University, 2005

Each phase of innovation puts you in front of new challenges, new opponents, or new players to enroll into your innovation. You will sequentially navigate new networks of adopters, convincing each to embrace your innovation, until your immaterial vision becomes the accepted reality.

The five-phases framework lies at the heart of this book. In Book Two, which follows, each one is described in depth, in its own chapter.

Conclusion

By drawing on ancient frameworks for change, you can dramatically improve your skill at leading innovation. Adopting this new mindset requires you to make four shifts in how you understand change:

Shift 1: Working with two parallel worlds—the immaterial and material—influencing the former to change the latter.

Shift 2: Appreciating that change is grounded in an endless cycle of creation and destruction.

Shift 3: Understanding the three primal powers—Heaven, Earth, and Man—to assess which actions to take at which times.

Shift 4: Guiding your innovation through the five phases of change from Metal to Water to Wood to Fire to Earth by making the choices and taking the actions appropriate to each phase.

As you begin to master these models—two worlds, three forces, and five phases—you begin to master innovation. Your ability to drive change within your company or community multiplies.

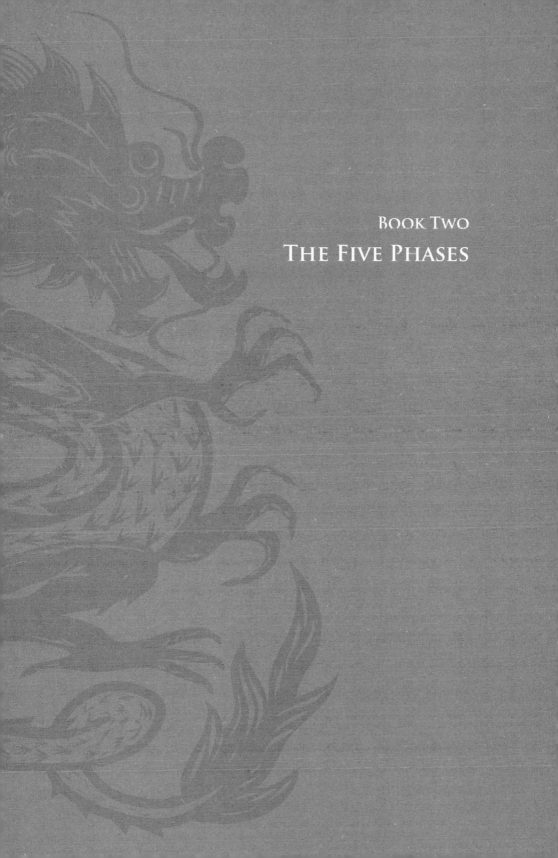

BOOK TWO
THE FIVE PHASES

CHAPTER THREE

METAL: DISCONTENT

"If you want to shrink something, you must first allow it to expand.
If you want to get rid of something, you must first allow it to flourish.
If you want to take something, you must first allow it to be given.
This is called the subtle perception of the way things are."

—*Lao Tzu,* Tao Te Ching

All great innovations emerge out of rigidity. They are born when someone recognizes that the system—the company, the industry, the country—has frozen and can no longer react to new opportunities or threats. Hindu sciences describe this state as frozen energy, like ice. The ancient Chinese framework for change calls this frozen condition Metal. Both metaphors represent something that is cold, rigid, inactive.

When this rigid state appears in the business world, what you see is a company that is stuck in an old perspective. The competition is also stuck in the old frame, and so are the industry experts, customers, distributors, and underwriters. This state persists until someone with sufficient discontent recognizes the latent energy in the frozen system.

Thus the starting point for launching an innovation is to recognize when the system has fallen so far into a state of rigidity that the time is ripe for a new order of things. Someone—you, perhaps—

challenges the rigidity with a new idea. Initially this idea will be soundly rejected; I can almost guarantee it. But if you carefully build support and remove resistance, eventually you will prove that your idea is better, one that might just change the world.

To change the world, then, you must first recognize that the system is stuck. The key condition is discontent: Someone is sufficiently discontented with the frozen system to want to take action.

Innovations Begin When the System Is Stuck

"The rush of water, to the point of tossing rocks about.
This is shih *[power].*
The strike of a hawk, at the killing snap. This is the node.
Shih *is like drawing the crossbow.*
The node is like pulling the trigger."

—*Sun Tzu,* The Art of War

Significant innovations almost always appear against a backdrop of rigidity. Business rivalries are often won on the basis of which company first recognizes the "stuck-ness."

In the early 1990s, two global footwear brands were in deep financial trouble. Puma AG had not produced a profitable quarter since it went public in 1986. Traditionally strong in the lower-end athletic shoe market, Puma was seeing its customers trade up to more expensive shoes offered by Nike and Adidas. At the same time, even lower-priced brands were attacking Puma's customer base, forcing the company to lower prices.

While Puma was battling two fronts in Europe—competition for high- and low-end buyers—Reebok was facing a similar situation in the United States. In the 1980s, Reebok had been the shoe of choice for the millions of people who trekked to gyms for aerobic and dance classes. But that craze faded, and as exercisers traded the dance floor for the free-weight area and the outdoors, Reebok's sales were stagnating.

Both companies were executing losing strategies. Both held on to outdated brands. Both had reason to change. But only Puma took meaningful action.

At first, Puma attempted to alter its strategy and push into the United States, where fewer people knew of the brand. But by 1993 it became clear that a more dramatic change was needed. The company was rapidly approaching bankruptcy. A new CEO was named but left after three months, forcing Puma to make a quick decision. The company chose thirty-year-old Jochen Zeitz as its leader.

Reebok, meanwhile, continued tweaking its strategy. Sales were flat and margins low, but neither stood out significantly from industry averages. The company was less profitable than before, but it was still profitable. It did not face the threat of bankruptcy.

Forced out of complacency, Puma began changing. Zeitz, the youngest CEO of a publicly traded European company, brought less historical baggage than a seasoned industry insider might. He was willing to challenge the rigidity of his company and his competitors with new thinking. (In the case studies section of this book, you will find a detailed analysis of Puma's subsequent history, so this section will just summarize it.)

Of the several radical changes Zeitz launched, two were especially significant. He changed the company's official language from German to English, and he reconceptualized the company as a fashion brand. This was an unprecedented shift in business model, and results showed almost immediately. Revenue rose from $275 million in 1994 to almost $2 billion ten years later. Reebok's revenues were essentially flat over the same period. Puma is producing about 25 percent profit margins, while Reebok's margins have remained stagnant at about 8 percent. That Puma's margins exceed Reebok's at all is impressive since Reebok's size (it is still twice the size of Puma) should provide it greater scale advantages and thereby higher margins. That Puma generates three times the margins Reebok does is even more significant.

By becoming soft when its competition remained rigid, Puma has far outperformed all of its publicly traded peers, including Nike. The transformation began when Puma recognized that it and its market had grown rigid in the face of changing customer needs. Because it reached a point of dissatisfaction before its rivals did, Puma seized an opportunity and transformed its business ahead of the competition.

A Side-by-Side Comparison

Reebok	Puma
1980s Situation	
Slowing revenue as traditional market (aerobics) stagnates	Losing money; being squeezed from high- and low-end competition
Level of Dissatisfaction in Early 1990s	
Medium: Slowing but not negative revenue growth; lower but not negative profit margins	High: Negative cash flow, reaching bankruptcy in 1993
Average Revenue Growth 1994–2004	
1.4 percent	21.3 percent
Average Profit Margin 1994–2004	
8.8 percent	25.1 percent

We like to believe that winning innovations run a fair race, that they offer an option that is simply better than others and that the best option wins. But few innovations that have had a significant impact on the world were born this way. Most are the result of an unfair race in which one idea takes off while others run with their legs tied. Almost any meaningful innovation emerges when someone recognizes rigidity and brings forth sufficient discontent to question the established system. This is true in every other domain of human competition. Consider some significant changes in business, politics, and sports:

Business Innovations
- Western Union nearly dies when its traditional business—the telegram—is replaced by the telephone. Its discontent drives it to repurpose its technology to transfer money, thereby creating and dominating the money transfer business.

- IBM twice recognizes it has fallen into rigidity and twice reacts with innovation, first when it transforms itself from a punch-card company into a computer company and again when it exits the computer hardware business to become a consulting services firm. Each time it revolutionizes its industry.
- Nucor Steel sees a market for producing steel with "mini-mills" at a time when incumbent players were ignoring this potential. Nucor transforms the steel industry and displaces many large players.
- Michael Dell sees that the computer industry is stuck in a retail distribution model and launches a direct-to-consumer business. From a dorm room he grows this business into one of the largest computer companies in the world.
- Fox News launches a new (and successful) cable news station in the United States at a time when industry experts believe no room existed for a new news channel.

Business Stagnations
- Greyhound has been unable to innovate itself out of the bus business. Attacked by regional airlines (such as Southwest) and the preference of U.S. travelers to drive themselves, the company is in a long, steady decline.
- Sony led innovation in the electronics industry before 1990. But for the next fifteen years it introduced few industry innovations and missed many others. This has been due at least in part to Sony holding on to its practice of trying to establish and own a closed standard, while most of its competition adopts an open, collaborative stance.

Political Innovations
- Venice recognizes and reacts effectively to an emerging foreign threat around A.D. 1000. Genoa fails to recognize the threat, resists change, experiences a revolution, and eventually stagnates.

- England's Glorious Revolution of 1688 and the American Revolution of 1776 each challenge outdated government structures that have grown rigid.
- Winston Churchill warns England and European countries of the Nazi threat for ten years before they recognize the danger.
- Nelson Mandela and his movement spend decades showing South African whites and blacks that apartheid is no longer a viable system.
- Martin Luther King Jr. sees that existing black organizing groups—the NAACP and Urban League—are stuck. They pursue only incremental change, in part because they depend heavily on whites for donations. His message, which calls for dramatic change, creates powerful resonance and following because it fills a gap created by rigidity.

Political Stagnations
- Rome rises to dominate its known world, introducing innovations in engineering, governance, and warfare. But when disparity between its citizens and its plebeian noncitizen population widens, discontent among plebs weakens Rome's societal foundation. Eventually the empire falls.
- Britain's colonial approach to ruling India no longer proves the best model. And when the British rulers refuse to rethink their practices despite growing discontent, Jawaharlal Nehru and Mahatma Gandhi lead a movement to end British rule.

Sports Innovations
- In 1932 Sonja Henie abandons traditional approaches to competing in figure skating by incorporating ballet into her performance in the 1932 Olympics, thus setting a new standard.
- Before Bill Walsh proves them wrong, football coaches and experts use running plays to set up touchdown passes.

Walsh adopts the opposite approach: He uses passing plays to set up the touchdown runs. With his new strategy, he wins three Super Bowls.

Sports Stagnation
• For years professional high-jumpers insisted on leaping erect over the measuring bar. Dick Fosbury proves the establishment has stagnated by jumping over backward. In 1968 Fosbury wins the Olympics and the "Fosbury Flop" becomes the new standard.

If you study the origins of successful innovations, you will find that these conditions were present at nearly every beginning:

The system has become rigid, unable to react to new opportunities or threats.

It holds on to beliefs that prevent it from seeing change as possible.

It lives in a story that robs it of power to act.

Someone perceives "weak signals" that the environment is changing.

That person brings to this situation a long-held commitment that requires him or her to change the system.

The System Has Become Rigid

Because the starting point of any significant innovation is a system having stagnated (stuck in Metal), the first requirement is that you be able to recognize this frozen state. Doing this is not easy. Most rigidity comes not from physical limitations but rather from mental ones that are harder to recognize and harder to dissect.

Twenty years ago companies could predict whether a competitor would react to their attack by analyzing the competitor's conflicting investments. If your competitor had recently built a major new factory in the United States, for example, he would be unlikely to abandon that factory for a less expensive one in India. He would want to hold on to U.S. production to show a positive return on his investment. This knowledge created an opportunity for you. If you built a business that depended on low-cost production in India, you could be reasonably sure that your competition would not copy you for some time. In fact, you could calculate quite accurately at what point he would abandon his U.S. factory for an Indian one. Now, however, such physical sources of rigidity are eroding. Today you can sign a short-term contract with an Indian producer and, for relatively little investment, instantly turn on immense production capacity.

The economies of scale that provided most competitive advantage over the past fifty years rarely last today. While this makes it easier for small attackers to take on established incumbents, it also complicates your ability to see when the competition is stuck enough to present you with opportunity.

You can learn to recognize this stuck-ness. Start by familiarizing yourself with the two mental dynamics that characterize the condition, and then analyze your situation to see whether one or both exists. It may be your company that exhibits these dynamics, or it may be your competition's. In either case, you need to understand what is happening.

- The system is stuck in a set of beliefs that prevent people from seeing change as possible.
- The system is living in a story that leads people to inaction.

If you or your competition is experiencing one or both of these dynamics, the current climate is ripe for innovation.

A Rigid System Can't Imagine Change
"The problem was that [IBM] couldn't move, it couldn't change."
                                        —Lou Gerstner, former CEO, IBM

We are all susceptible to a natural human tendency to become trapped in beliefs, assumptions, attitudes, identities, or habits.

Innovations begin when someone questions what others have accepted as "the way things are."

How We Unconsciously Step on the Brakes

"If you want to create you have to get rid of all conditionings; otherwise your creativity will be nothing but copying, it will be just a carbon copy."

—*Osho*

Cognitive scientists have dissected the process by which we adopt automatic responses to changes in our environment. They studied how children learn, and noticed that a baby does not respond to a popped balloon the first time she hears it. But after hearing a balloon pop enough times, the baby starts showing signs of being startled. By the time she is an adult, she responds to a popped balloon immediately and unconsciously.

Companies respond to new threats the same way. As an economy declines, a company analyzes its options and decides to pull out of the country. This decline happens again, and the company remembers what worked last time. It may do some further analysis but is almost certain to respond the same way—by pulling out. With enough experience, the "pullout" response becomes automatic.

Recognizing when responses (your competitor's or your own) have become automatic can offer valuable opportunities. If your competition is acting on autopilot, you can move against it with minimum resistance by adopting a more radical approach. If your own organization has adopted something as "the way things are," you may see ways to innovate by reconsidering whether this is the way things should be.

When any of our accepted beliefs, assumptions, attitudes, habits, or identities prove false and prevent us from realizing a goal or solving a problem, they become traps. We fall into traps when we stop questioning something and simply accept it.

Entrapment is the foundation out of which emerge many great organizations and products. Nearly every company that has produced breakthrough growth in revenues and profitability over the past decade emerged out of an industry entrapped by false beliefs. When your industry holds a consensus as a fact and stops questioning this fact, there may exist the potential to revolutionize the industry by challenging that "fact." Consider some of the better-known modern examples of companies and products that challenged accepted beliefs:

IBM PCs: There will only be demand for a few computers in the world; no individual would have use for a personal computer.

Sixt AG: Renting cars is a luxury that only the (German) upper class can afford.

Southwest Airlines: The hub-and-spoke system is the most efficient choice for transporting customers. Customers want meals and a flying experience.

Dell: Computer buyers need hands-on help from retailers before they are willing to buy.

University of Phoenix: College students are recent high-school graduates.

Smirnoff Ice: The wine cooler craze has ruined U.S. consumers' tastes for sweet, low-proof drinks.

Wikipedia: Encyclopedia readers will only trust accepted experts vetted by a well-known brand.

Apple's iPod: Music labels will never allow their music to be downloaded.

Cisco Systems: The software, not the hardware, holds the "brains" of a network.

The Cost to Seeing "Multi-verses"

Breakthroughs almost always start with the challenge of an accepted beliefs, assumptions, attitudes, identites, or habits. Innovators seem able to move fluidly between mental universes and even operate with two or more universes in mind simultaneously; they seem able to see "multi-verses."

Unfortunately, there is a cost to this ability: It can turn on itself. If your new belief works well, you begin to consider this belief to be truth and therefore knowledge. You trap yourself again.

Business Model as a Trap

To see this process, consider Xerox. In the mid-1950s the company revolutionized offices worldwide by seeing through a commonly accepted fact that had entrapped the world: Document copies had to be made one by one. Years earlier a lawyer had grown frustrated with this arduous process and had begun seeking a better solution. When Joe Wilson, president of the Haloid Corporation, met this lawyer he was fascinated by his solution. It would require significantly more research, but if it worked, it could open up a vast market.

At the time, the only copying options offered low-quality images that did not age well. Some options were wet and messy. Others were dry but crude. All required users to use special supplies. Manufacturers charged a relatively low price for a machine and then inflated prices for supplies.

Wilson saw that if he could commercialize this new technology, he could offer a much higher-quality copy at about the same per-copy price. However, his machine would probably cost more than existing technologies. This created a conceptual dilemma. Because Haloid's machine went against the dominant industry conception, he could not find partners to distribute his product. He approached IBM, Kodak, General Electric, and Arthur D. Little, but none of them were interested. The technology's value proposition of selling higher quality for higher cost was not sufficiently compelling.

The Haloid Corporation could not convince others to drop their beliefs. If the company wanted to prove its new technology superior, Haloid would have to distribute it on its own. This meant challenging the prevailing business model in which one company produced a copying machine and another distributed and serviced the machine. Forced to break free from this trap, Haloid launched an expensive effort to build its own dedicated sales force. Since Haloid's new business model was unprecedented, the company could approach the challenge creatively, unchained by existing beliefs or habits.

The results were astounding, even to Joe Wilson. Customers who installed the new machines were drawn to the dramatic improvement in copy quality. Instead of thermal paper that yellowed easily and curled, they could copy on regular office paper. They no longer worried about smudges. The copies were far sharper. As a result, customers made many more copies. Haloid had projected that customers would make 2,000 copies per month; instead, the average customer made 2,000 copies per day. Since Haloid charged users by the copy, revenues exploded. The company grew from $30 million in revenue to $2.5 billion in twelve years and changed its name to the Xerox Corporation.

Xerox challenged two beliefs the industry had accepted as truths:
1. The best business model for office machines depended on a producer partnering with an independent sales/distribution/service company.
2. Companies would not pay more for better-quality copies.

By undoing these two entrapments, Xerox transformed how businesses operate and emerged as one of the world's largest corporations.

Success, however, can quickly lead back into entrapment. Companies want to keep doing what they are doing, especially when it seems to be working. Xerox's "do it yourself" model, which was born out of the necessity to build its own sales force, grew into a habit. It not only distributed directly to consumers, but also provided its own financing, its own support, even its own paper.

Xerox's "belief," which it considered the "truth," was that the right way to grow is to do it all.

But in its success, Xerox was becoming stuck in its own beliefs, and failed to see that its business model was growing outdated. In the 1970s it invested heavily in a research lab (PARC), growing it into one of the country's largest research centers. PARC created cutting-edge technologies in digital printing and high-speed laser printing. It developed what would eventually become the computer mouse and even the first graphical computer interface.

But Xerox's focus was on how it could use these technologies to improve Xerox machines. It did not partner with companies in other industries. It viewed PARC as a captive tool for increasing the advantages of Xerox's products, not as an operation that could be profitable on its own. Many PARC researchers came to see that their inventions were not realizing their full potential because this potential lay outside of Xerox's products. Frustrated, they began leaving, and often took with them licenses to their technologies, which they had bought from Xerox for small fees.

3Com Corporation, for example, was founded when a PARC computer scientist, Robert Metcalfe, wanted to pursue new uses for the Ethernet local area network (LAN) technology he had developed. He bought nonexclusive licenses to four Xerox patents for $1,000 and began commercializing his inventions. Today 3Com generates about $800 million in revenue from its computer network infrastructure products.

Adobe Systems was founded when two PARC researchers, Charles Geschke and John Warnock, left Xerox in 1983 to pursue their invention of a page-description language. It first developed a product called PostScript, which allowed printers to print a greater variety of fonts. This product led Adobe down a path of developing even more advanced technologies for digitally transferring documents. The company developed Adobe Illustrator, became the standard in digital document transfer, and then established its flagship product, Adobe Photoshop, as the leading digital design software. Today it generates just over $2.5 billion in revenue.

The PARC inventions that produced the computer mouse and graphical interface revolutionized personal computing. Xerox played a critical role in their invention, but not in their commercialization. Instead these inventions enabled Apple Computer to introduce the first computer with a mouse and graphical interface, which established the company as a leading computer firm and set off a transformation of the PC industry. Today Apple Inc. generates nearly $19 billion in revenue.

Had Xerox not entrapped itself into a closed business model, might it have commercialized these and other technologies itself? Might it be twice the size it is today? We cannot know for certain, but it does seem clear that Xerox, once forced to undo industry traps, fell back into a trap of its own success. The Xerox story shows that success is often the greatest barrier to innovation because it blinds you from seeing that there exists a sufficient reason to challenge accepted beliefs.

The pull to remaining trapped is strong enough to topple even the most powerful, well-entrenched establishment. Industries are littered with once-dominant incumbents who held on too long to their beliefs, and eventually fell from their perch. Entrapment, or more precisely the recognition that you and your industry are trapped, is the source of innovation.

The Cost-Benefit Analysis of Entrapment

Undoing entrapment is only possible when discontent is present. Without sufficient discontent with the current state of things, the cost of challenging a belief will win. This cost is greater than you might think because it consists of several layers:

1. The cost in time of investigating your belief to validate it.
2. The potential cost of investigating other dependent beliefs if your analysis proves your original belief is wrong.
3. The uncertainty and associated discomfort you must live with as you are investigating various beliefs, not knowing what in your universe is true or not true.

Testing for traps opens the door to great uncertainty. The cost of questioning the unquestioned is so high, it is easier to keep on believing what everyone else believes. You will not jump to the challenge unless you have a compelling reason to do so. Complicating your efforts, however, is a second mental trap. If innovation begins when a cost-benefit analysis convinces you to change, and entrapment provides the cost, then the benefit of change is influenced by a story you, your organizations, your competitors, and your market are telling yourselves.

A Rigid System Has No Power to Act

The second reason a system falls into a rigid state is the story you tell about your strategic situation. The narratives we live in have a powerful, hidden hand in determining how we interpret our environment. This fact, long noted by Hindu and Buddhist traditions, is supported by an ever-growing body of scientific knowledge. Innovators seem able to recognize when the system is living a story with a dead ending, an ending that leads to inaction. They can abandon the prevailing story and enter a new one, one that empowers them to act when no one else will.

Looking at business innovations from the point of view of the stories they abandon provides a new perspective. Four specific dead-end stories prevail:

- "The market won't change."
- "The market may change, but the changes will not affect us."
- "The changes may affect us, but we will somehow survive."
- "We won't have a response and there is nothing we can do about it."

"The market won't change."

The innovators of a new industry, having no history to guide them, concern themselves with convincing nonusers to become users. They speculate about the market's potential size. But as the market matures, such inquiries fall in frequency. Analysts study the past and write detailed reports that describe what the future might provide. We can imagine a brand-new market growing to almost any size tomorrow. But a thirty-year-old market that has consistently grown at 5 percent per year is unlikely to diverge much from this rate next year. The narrative's past leads you to believe in an inevitable future.

Such a narrative presents an opportunity for the innovator willing to ignore it. When the competition starts believing that tomorrow's customer base will look similar to yesterday's, there may be an opportunity to think differently.

An example of a company capitalizing on such an opportunity is Callaway Golf. The business studied the U.S. golf market's history as carefully as did its competitors. But while the competitors' narratives led them to conclude tomorrow's golfers would look a lot like today's, and therefore growth must be had by stealing golfers from the competition, Callaway focused on nongolfers instead. It explored what might convince nongolfers to become golfers and novices to play more often. Callaway's research led it to develop a radical new golf club design, the Big Bertha, which turned would-be golfers on to the game at unexpectedly high rates, thereby expanding the entire golf market. The club became the bestseller among almost all categories of golfers.

"The market may change, but the changes will not affect us."

Another common path innovations follow is to disrupt competition by stealing a customer segment the competitors are ignoring. They first attack a low-end, low-profit customer segment the competition will not miss, indeed one the competition may even be happy to be rid of. In the absence of competitive resistance, the innovation flourishes. It collects experience, gathers a user base, and strengthens itself. The incumbent continues telling itself a happy story, ignoring the threat until its opportunities for defense run out. This innovation pattern has been documented as the transforming mechanism of numerous industries, from steel production to computer storage devices to education.

In the early 1990s, for example, established educational firms thought Apollo Group founder John Sperling was crazy. He invented a university that no self-respecting educator would want to call a competitor. His University of Phoenix offered low-priced online courses to working adults. He shunned many traditions universities had followed closely for centuries, including faculty selection, curriculum design, and course delivery. While his competition comforted themselves in a narrative of history and tradition and the noble purpose of education, Sperling's innovation grew. In 1994 the Apollo Group earned $125 million in revenue. Today it makes nearly $3 billion in educational services annually.

"The changes may affect us, but we will somehow survive."

Often the narrative provides false feedback that everything will work out okay. This kind of story follows on the heels of success, and usually sounds something like "We have been through hard times before and we have survived" or "Sure, the competition is getting traction now but they do not understand the market the way we do and they do not have the experience we have."

Most large companies fall into this losing narrative. GE is unique because despite its size, it does not. Of the twelve companies originally included in the Dow Jones Index in 1896, GE is the only one that remains. One of the keys to its success is its ability to forget its past successes. As CEO Jeff Immelt notes, "Most people inside GE learn from the past but have a healthy disrespect for history. They have an ability to live in the moment and not be burdened by the past, which is extremely important."

"We won't have a response and there is nothing we can do about it."

Ultimately every story has a perpetrator, someone at the source of the problem. There are two options in assigning roles: This perpetrator either can be you and your company, or it can be someone else. In the first case you may say, "Our underperformance is due to us missing an important trend." You could make an equally compelling argument for the second case, saying, "Our underperformance is due to macro-factors beyond our control." The differences are subtle but their implications profound—if you are not at least part of the cause of the problem you are unlikely to have the power to change it. If your organization (or your competition) is not playing a role in its story, it will be slow to react, leaving open a need (or an opportunity) for you to launch the innovation.

When Vaughn Beals was group vice president for Harley-Davidson, he blamed Japanese manufacturers for his company's poor performance. Later he joined the group that bought the company and became Harley-Davidson's CEO. When he and his colleagues looked more deeply into Harley-Davidson's problems, Beals concluded that "the problem was us [senior management]." Changing the story from one centered around Japanese attackers to one about senior management who made the wrong choices made it possible for Harley-Davidson to begin changing. The turnaround was by any measure a clear success, transforming the aging motorcycle company into a thriving lifestyle business.

In sum, to know the time is right to launch a new, meaningful innovation, look for evidence that the system is living a story of inaction.

However, simply recognizing that the system is rigid—that prevailing beliefs and stories lead to inaction—is not enough. You must recognize if that rigidity matters. If the environment is not changing, this rigid system may continue to go unchanged, remaining perfectly in tune with the environment. Being rigid does not actually matter until it prevents the system from reacting to new opportunities or threats by reaching a more optimum state. In order for the rigidity to matter, you must first sense that the world is changing in some way.

Someone Perceives "Weak Signals" That the Environment Is Changing

"Heaven signifies night and day, cold and heat, times and seasons. . . . By means of these considerations I can forecast victory or defeat."

—*Sun Tzu*, The Art of War

To recognize where an innovation has potential requires reading the heaven. "Heaven" in this case means looking from a high perspective so that you see patterns others cannot. This ability to sense the world changing has been the source of many of history's most definitive corporate battles.

In 1924, Robert E. Wood left his employer, retailer Montgomery Ward, to join the competition, Sears. At Sears, Wood saw something that his competition did not. He saw signals that the end of World War II would lead to an economic boom. He bet on this forecast while his former employer held back. By 1953, Sears was earning annual sales of $3 billion while Montgomery Ward produced just $1 billion.

The auto industry has gone through a similar case of environment capitalization. As we know, Henry Ford revolutionized the automobile industry by introducing the production line. His ability to produce cars at prices below what anyone believed possible allowed Ford to dominate the industry. But by focusing on production, Ford Motor Company failed to sense that consumers were starting to demand design, that Ford's one-model, one-color offering was going out of style. General Motors sensed this consumer trend, reacted with better designs, and by the 1930s became the world's largest automaker.

We could follow these examples with a hundred more—how Wal-Mart later outmaneuvered Sears, and how Toyota later outmaneuvered General Motors—but the necessary point has been made. Overtaking the competition requires sensing that the world is changing, which requires sensing "weak signals."

This is not simply a matter of being the first to see an opportunity and pounce on it. First-mover advantage rarely leads to sustained success. TiVo innovated the digital video recorder only to be squeezed out of the market it created by cable companies offering bundled services. Creative Technologies beat Apple's iPod to the market with a hard-drive-enabled MP3 player by years, only to be overwhelmed later.

The ability to read weak signals involves sensing that change is stirring, but more importantly it involves sensing that the system is not responding to change and is therefore stuck. Successfully using weak signals to innovate requires that you look for information where your competition does not, that you interpret it differently, and that you act early.

Look Where Your Competition Does Not

"Thus, what enables the wise sovereign and the good general to strike and conquer, and achieve things beyond the reach of ordinary men, is foreknowledge."

—*Sun Tzu*, The Art of War

We tend to believe that innovators are able to see further into the future than others. But if you speak to people who have significantly affected the world, you will not hear them claim any such skill. What makes them unique is that they paid attention to information that others were ignoring. Just as the reliability of an equation increases with the more variables you have information for, the reliability of a prediction increases with the greater the diversity of information you have to base it on. Innovators come to different conclusions about the future simply because they look for information where others do not.

For example, in 1996 John Fredriksen and his investors bought an oil freight company for $55 million. Today his company is worth over $2 billion. It grew from one of hundreds of average oil tanker owners to the largest one in the world, commanding a 25 percent market share.

At the time Fredriksen bought the company, the rest of the world thought the oil freight business was dead. For nearly twenty years oil tanker owners had been struggling under intense pricing pressure. They could barely cover their costs and were only looking to sell, not buy or build, more tankers. If you analyzed the business using the information most existing players used, you could only come to the same conclusion: The oil tanker business was one to avoid.

Fredriksen, however, looked deeper than did his peers. Instead of looking back just twenty years, he looked back further and saw that around thirty-five years earlier, oil tanker production fell dramatically. Fredriksen conducted some simple math: Since the average oil tanker has a life span of thirty years, over the next five years large numbers of aging oil tankers were going to be decommissioned.

Fredriksen also looked more broadly and saw evidence of growing global concern for the environment. He concluded that this movement would eventually touch the oil industry. He believed that oil companies would eventually be looking for double-hull tankers, which are environmentally safer, rather than the more common single-hull tankers that can more easily lead to oil spills.

These two conclusions—that oil tanker supply would begin decreasing and that demand for double-hull tankers would begin increasing—led Fredriksen to predict what others considered impossible: The oil tanker business, at least the double-hull oil tanker business, would soon become profitable again. He began buying and consolidating oil tanker companies, focusing on the more environmentally friendly double-hull tankers. His prognostication proved right. Today, Fredriksen's Frontline LTD is the largest, most profitable, and fastest-growing publicly traded oil tanker company in the world.

Foresight to capitalize on the competitions' Metal phase comes from looking at information that others are ignoring. This is complicated by the fact that our conscious brains hide information from us that we do not recognize. Other oil experts, for example, may not have even noticed the environmental trend that Fredriksen did because they did not deem this information relevant. This happens at a subconscious level. But you can overcome the barriers and begin seeing information that others do not see by simply forcing yourself to look more deeply and broadly and to consider how this information could affect your innovation or industry even if its relevance is not immediately obvious.

Interpret the Information Differently

"Here the success of everything depends on . . . seeing things in a way which afterwards proves to be true, even though it cannot be established at the moment."

—*Joseph A. Schumpeter,* The Theory of Economic Development

Once you have gathered information others are ignoring, you must process it to arrive at a conclusion others do not see. The key challenge to this is to recognize the role of intuition and logic.

Transforming "weak signals" into insights requires intuition. The work is too complicated for logic alone. Logic is useful in navigating through established industries, playing games that have been played before; it is not useful in new situations. Innovators, who play the early game, not the end game, must rely on intuition to understand their environments.

The problem with arriving at conclusions with intuition is that, since people are not consciously aware of its inner workings, they have difficulty defending their intuitively derived answer. Under the pressure of scrutiny, they often give up their answer for something more logical. Successful innovators show an ability to switch comfortably between intuition and logic, appreciating logic's role as a communication tool for building support for their idea. If you ask those who had a great insight why they are right, they are likely to explain themselves with simple, clear logic. But if you ask them how they came to their conclusion, the answer, if they can give you one at all, is rarely grounded in logic.

React to Weak Signals with Small Bets

We hold a romantic view of how innovators react to weak signals of change. A lone pioneer sees a possibility no one else believes in and makes a big bet, risking everything to prove he or she is right. When music fans began illegally downloading and sharing digital music online, most industry players fought back. The response of the hard-rock band Metallica was representative of the whole. Metallica sued Napster, the major music-sharing site at the time, and even threatened fans. U2, another rock band, adopted an unorthodox response. It legally released all of its songs online in a huge compilation package. Even though it was the first of its kind and the digital bundle had a high price tag of $149, the package sold well. U2 also agreed to appear in TV advertisements for Apple's iTunes online music store and iPod digital music player without compensation. In addition, the band partnered with Apple to release a special red and black U2 co-branded iPod. As the band's manager Paul McGuinness said about the digital music revolution, "We thought it was an opportunity to be taken with both hands."

However, such bold bets usually happen only after an innovation is already gaining momentum. U2 jumped in earlier than other bands, but by that time music downloading had already gained broad acceptance. Early in an innovation's emergence, the key seems to be to make small, incremental bets.

Intel, for example, transformed itself from a memory-chip maker into a microprocessor inventor and manufacturer, saving itself from the jaws of low-cost Asian competitors, by making small, incremental bets on microprocessors. Intel production managers were told to allocate capacity according to rules that stipulated making decisions based on margin per square inch of silicon wafer. Following this goal, and without a directive from above, production managers began shifting production from memory-chips to microprocessors simply because microprocessors were starting to command higher margins and to experience higher demand. It was not until microprocessor production represented 90 percent of Intel's output that management officially ratified Intel as a microprocessor manufacturer.

Aligning to the Universe

The ultimate payoff of being able to sense and respond to "weak signals" is that your innovation may have the potential to last. Innovations that are aligned with environmental and societal dynamics have the potential to survive for a longer time and to have a bigger impact.

Unstable Innovation: not aligned with society/environment

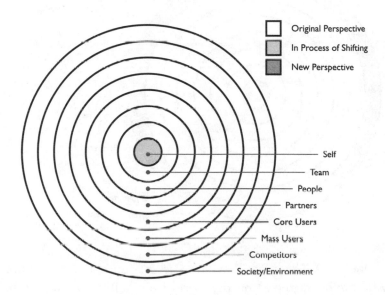

Think of your innovation as a movement that must win over several layers of communities as it expands. You must first overcome your own mind and its barriers to seeing something new. Your new idea must then win over your team, who will come to believe in your innovation. You and your team must then overcome the resistance of your organization and your partners (suppliers and distributors), then win over customers, then angle yourself and your innovation in order to convince your competitors to resist competing against you. But ultimately your innovation will only endure if it is aligned with society and the broad environment. You must be able to sense the weak signals that society and the environment are giving you.

Stable Innovation: aligned with society/environment

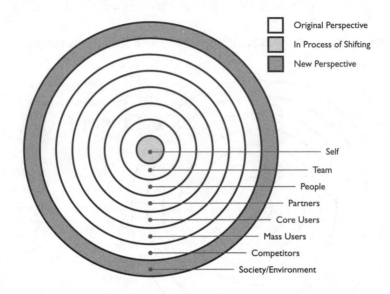

One of the defining characteristics of innovators who have had a profound impact on the world is an ability to sense weak signals that society or the environment are changing. As John Adams wrote about the American Revolution, "The Revolution was effected before the war commenced. The Revolution was in the hearts and minds of the people. . . . This radical change in the principles, opinions, sentiments and affections of the people was the real American Revolution." Or as the *I Ching* suggested 3,000 years prior, leaders must awaken what is already in the hearts of the people.

Weak signals can help you test whether the system is stuck. If the system is not responding to changes, potential energy is building, the bow is bending, the potential is emerging for change. But the bow at this point is only partly drawn. To draw it completely, to build sufficient discontent to trigger change, requires one more thing to be true. Someone must walk into this situation with a sufficiently strong commitment to change.

A Long-Held Commitment Mandates Change

"Until one is committed, there is hesitancy, the chance to draw back. Concerning all acts of initiative (and creation), there is one elementary truth, the ignorance of which kills countless ideas and splendid plans: that the moment one definitely commits oneself, then Providence moves too."

—*Johann Wolfgang von Goethe*

Research into how innovations are adopted shows that there are generally two types of people: people who recognize a need for an innovation once they see it (people who suddenly want a flashy new car when they spot it on the dealer's lot) and people who feel a need for an innovation before they know it exists (people who know they want a flashy new car so they begin surfing the Internet to research their options). Diffusion theory shows that, particularly in the early stages of an innovation's life cycle, users must first find a need to gather more information about the new thing before they reach a phase in which they are willing to try it.

In order to be an innovator, you must fall into the second category—those who feel a need for innovation before it's set clearly in front of them. They bring to the situation a deep-seated commitment that urges them to seek a solution and, if a solution does not exist, to invent one.

Researchers trying to understand what drives an entrepreneur to start a business have established that intention begins at a young age. Intention—a pre-existing commitment—precedes the passion, self-belief, and mindset required to start a business.

The commitment tells you what to focus on. Subconsciously, you look for opportunities to fulfill the commitment. The regions in your neocortex pass information into your consciousness about new opportunities to fulfill your commitment; without the commitment, this information would be filtered away. Your consciousness, then, actually sees things that it would otherwise not see.

When your commitment recognizes a ripe moment—when it sees weak signals that an opportunity exists and notices that the system is stuck and will not seize the opportunity—the magic occurs. Innovators can usually remember this moment vividly and describe it almost as a supernatural experience. It is the moment when suddenly they see a vision that proves something is possible that moments ago seemed impossible.

A New Vision Is Introduced

"Without the vision of a goal, a man cannot manage his own life, much less the lives of others."

—*Genghis Khan*

After college, Scott Hill took a job selling newspaper ads. He was a star, a natural salesman, winning awards and promotions none would expect of someone so young. One of his innovative tactics was to sell advertising inserts to car dealerships and outsource the printing.

One day his boss asked Scott to explain why the car dealer insert business was performing so poorly and why Scott continued to push it. The boss had read a report showing the margin on car inserts was extremely low. This was only so because of accounting practices, Scott explained. Since the newspaper was used to printing its own inserts and did not assign the printing cost to jobs when they did so, they were not accurately accounting for printing costs. Scott could have the inserts printed in-house; this would show a better accounting margin. But the margin would simply not be real, because it ignored printing costs altogether. Scott estimated that in-house printing costs were actually higher than outsourcing to external printers.

Scott's boss was not convinced. He asked Scott to write a report explaining why he had pursued this low-margin business for so long. That night, after his sales day was complete, Scott sat down at his desk and began his report.

He had been frustrated with the slow pace of newspaper advertising for many months now. It operated using outdated processes. It refused new ideas. It resisted change. This current task was just further evidence of the growing discontent in Scott's heart.

It took Scott two hours to prepare his report. But midway through he forgot about time. He stopped writing for his boss and instead found himself pounding at his keyboard for himself. He was analyzing why this car dealer insert business actually made sense. When he was finished, Scott leaned back and looked at what he had produced and realized he hadn't written a report; he had written a business plan.

At that moment, Scott decided that he would pursue this business on his own. As he left the newspaper building that night, Scott was smiling. When he got home he called his longtime best friend and told him he was going to start a business and wanted his friend to join him. He couldn't sleep that night. The power of his vision kept him awake with excitement.

Today, Scott's company, CIK Enterprises, is one of the fastest-growing private companies in the country. Its revenues broke through $20 million in 2006, and it was ranked as the best company to work for in Indianapolis.

Though Scott admits to no passion for the car dealership business itself, his vision of creating something new—a company that people would love to work for, that would challenge the status quo—opened up the possibility for Scott to innovate in an area that had stagnated into rigidity.

This is the final step of the Metal phase, when a system that is rigid steps onto the path of change because someone brings commitment and vision to this stagnant environment. This commitment and vision create a powerful counter to the stagnant system.

Once you move into a state of discontent, you have established yourself in the Metal phase. You have created a gap between where things are headed and where you want them to be headed. There are two ways to close this gap. First, you can reduce your vision so that it becomes your trajectory. This is the easiest and most common approach. Second, you can undertake the creativity and effort required to change your trajectory so that it is the same as your vision. This will begin to change the world as you know it.

CHAPTER FOUR

WATER: IMAGINATION

In 1983, Ted Leonsis was speeding through the air on an Eastern Airlines flight when he heard the announcement we all dread. The airplane had lost its ability to move its wing flaps and landing gear. It could not steer and, even if it did somehow get to a runway, could not lower its wheels to land. While flight attendants scurried to prepare the plane and passengers for a crash landing, Leonsis began thinking about what he would do if he survived. "I promised myself," he recalls today, "that if I didn't die, I'd play offense for the rest of my life."

While Leonsis surely used a different adjective to describe his situation, you could say he recognized he was in a profound state of Metal. He was not dissatisfied in the way most people would be in such a dilemma, facing the very real possibility of imminent death. Instead, Leonsis felt a keen dissatisfaction with his life's trajectory.

By most measures Leonsis had to that point lived a remarkably colorful life. He worked at Wang Laboratories after college. At age twenty-four he conceived of an idea for a computer magazine, pitched it to IBM, raised $1 million, and launched a successful media business. But in that dramatic moment, Leonsis realized there was a gap between the life he was living and the life he wished to live. He decided from that point on to live life more fully.

The nature of a gap is to be filled. As we saw at the end of the last chapter, there are two ways to fill a gap: You can reduce your aspirations, as most companies do, or you can raise your trajectory. When Leonsis's plane miraculously landed safely, it would not have been surprising for Leonsis's gap to evaporate. He could have wiped his brow, thanked a higher power, and returned to his old life. The discontent that draws the bow of urgency is easily dissipated by complacency.

But Leonsis stepped beyond the Metal state because he imagined a compelling future and had detailed a plan to realize it. He developed a list of 101 things he would do before he died, and then got to work.

In the twenty-four years since his plane nearly crashed, Leonsis has checked off many of these things, including fall in love and get married (no. 1), have a healthy son and healthy daughter (nos. 2 and 3), generate a net worth of $100 million, after taxes (no. 14), conduct an IPO on a company he founded (no. 21), and buy a sports franchise (no. 40). At the moment, he has just twenty-eight to go, including travel into outer space (no. 84) and sailing around the world with his family (no. 100).

Most of us would probably stop with the commitment to live life to the fullest, and then eventually that commitment would fade, just in the way that the mission and vision of companies fade with time. How did Leonsis avoid this fate? What did he do to ensure that the momentum he built on that plane actually redirected his trajectory and began changing his world? The link between discontent (Metal) and strategy (Water) is in what Sun Tzu calls "laying plans."

Water: enrolling a team with a plan

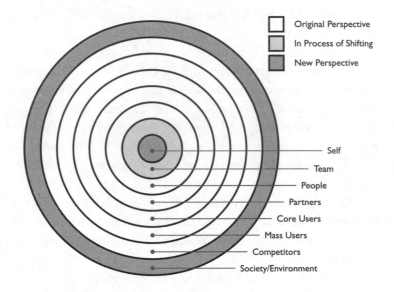

Original Perspective

In Process of Shifting

New Perspective

Self
Team
People
Partners
Core Users
Mass Users
Competitors
Society/Environment

The Role of Water

While Metal is cold, rigid, and void of possibility, it lays the foundation for Water to form. Water transforms the rigid into the fluid; structure into spontaneity. To ensure that the gap you have created does not close again into complacency, it is important to develop a plan that shows you and a group of believers how to convert the immaterial (vision) into the material (action). The outcome of the Water phase will be a strategy composed of a holistic list of choices and priorities (perhaps not as long as Leonsis's 101) that will guide you and your team toward coordinated action. The risk of not creating such a plan is that you, your team, or your organization will remain in discontent or, worse yet, denial.

When introducing a new innovation, you can make good use of the innate human tendency to want what we fantasize about. You do this by creating a compelling vision. Then you must link this vision to a plan of action so people can see that even though your vision seems distant from current reality, you have a plan to get there. By specifying things like your mission, vision, measures for success, obstacles you may face, and the strategic priorities that will give you victory, your plan says, "We are on the path. We will achieve our vision even if we have not achieved it yet."

The Elements of a Winning Strategy

Innovations that reach significant scale adopt strategies with two characteristics:

1. They describe openings, not the end game.
2. They move you away from the pack.

Traditional strategy-development methods rarely work well for young innovations because they are designed for managing a mature state of a game—the end game—when moves and countermoves lead to a manageable number of possibilities. During the Water phase, however, we must design strategies during great uncertainty.

The human mind can process but a few options per minute. Some measurements show that chess players, for instance, consider on average four options per minute. If you were to use logic during the opening of a chess game, even if you were to think forward only a few moves, you would need to stare at the board for hours before calculating the best response. Great chess players, then, cannot be using logic to design their openings.

This dependence on logic is why many large, established companies—which are designed to operate in the predictable state of an end game—are rarely behind meaningful innovations. A new innovation means giving up logic, at least temporarily, and designing a strategy that is flexible.

An opening needs improvisation. The first move you make does not commit you to one, specific tactic five moves later. Instead it positions you to choose from several. It produces options rather than limiting them.

So the strategy you develop out of this phase will be composed of several choices or priorities. Those choices will paint a somewhat "fuzzy" picture of what must happen. They will not lock you into one direction.

Another way of looking at this is that you are designing a "grand strategy" that creates sufficient flexibility for you to adapt to emerging conditions as you learn more about the market. You do not want to jump into the bush without first knowing that a snake lives there.

Consider Whole Foods Market, the fastest-growing, most profitable publicly traded grocery store chain in the country. The company has delivered unprecedented performance while facing minimal competitive resistance. In an industry growing at just 6 percent per year, Whole Foods is growing at 25 percent. While competitors squeeze out 4.5 percent profit margins, Whole Foods, with far less scale, manages 8 percent. Whole Foods is clear on its mission, vision, measures, obstacles, and grand strategy. More important, it left sufficient flexibility in its grand strategy to allow for dynamic adaptation in how that strategy is realized.

The mission, vision, measures, obstacles, and grand strategy of Whole Foods are outlined in its "Declaration of Interdependence," which I have summarized as follows:

1. Mission: "We are a mission-driven company that aims to set the standards of excellence for food retailers. We are building a business in which high standards permeate all aspects of our company. Quality is a state of mind at Whole Foods Market."

2. Vision: "Whole Foods Market is a dynamic leader in the quality food business." Measures include "customer satisfaction, team member excellence and happiness, return on capital investment, improvement in the state of the environment, and local and larger community support."

3. Obstacles: potential conflicts between stakeholders. These "must be mediated and win-win solutions found. Creating and nurturing this community of stakeholders is critical to the long-term success of our company."

4. Grand strategy: to realize its vision, Whole Foods outlines five main priorities:

- Sell the highest-quality natural and organic products available.
- Satisfy and delight our customers.
- Support team member excellence and happiness. [Note: Whole Foods uses "team member" instead of "employee"]
- Create wealth through profits and growth.
- Promote environmental stewardship.

While Whole Foods' strategy distinguishes it clearly from the competition, it does not limit the innumerable other innovations that managers and employees have deployed to further complicate competitor efforts to copy Whole Foods. For example, Whole Foods decided to share such detailed financial information with employees so that all of its employees are classified as insiders by the SEC. The company set a CEO salary cap at eight times the average Whole Foods employee's salary. These and numerous other strategic thrusts make it difficult for traditional supermarkets to resist Whole Foods. These strategic thrusts align with the company's grand strategy but are not dictated by it. The strategy unlocks, rather than limits, new possibilities.

Step Away from the Pack

A well-known Zen koan points out that if a bird and a fish try to achieve their ends but abandon their natural means, the bird will drown and the fish will suffocate. In the winter, their aims are the same: They both wish to stay warm. But to achieve those aims, the bird flies up and away and the fish swims deep to avoid ice. In the same way, your strategy should reflect your inherent nature; it should be a unique expression of who you are.

The best strategies avoid competition. If you race a horse in the pack you are always a little bit ahead or a little bit behind. You may launch the newest product but six months later your competition has copied you. So you reduce your costs a few percentage points and then your competition soon follows and erases your lead. Running in the pack requires great effort. The alternative is nearly effortless but requires courage.

All innovations replace something. Therefore all innovations face some form of resistance. This may not come from direct competition but from other players who make decisions that limit your innovation's ability to take root.

So even if your innovation does not have an obvious competitor, consider that there is some behavior that it must replace. It is critical therefore that you launch your innovation with a grand strategy that pre-empts competitive resistance. It will then achieve what Sun Tzu terms the pinnacle of advantage: You make your competition obsolete.

Sun Tzu's Levels of Strategy

Level	Sun Tzu's Insight	Implication
1	"The highest form of generalship is to balk the enemy's plans."	Choose a strategy that your competition will choose not to resist.
2	"The next best is to prevent the junction of the enemy's forces."	Hinder your competitor's ability to attack (for example, cut off their supply lines).
3	"Next in order is to attack the enemy's army in the field."	Attack a competitor small enough that you can outmuscle them.
4	"The worst policy of all is to besiege walled cities."	Attack a large, entrenched competitor.

Mahatma Gandhi and Martin Luther King Jr. both subdued resistance by carefully avoiding direct conflict. Similarly, companies who have transformed industries always push into "soft" zones, the empty spaces of the market, choosing targets and strategies that would preclude resistance. Home Depot originally targeted contractors, who were too fragmented to organize a defense. Apple launched the precise MP3 player that Sony, fearing piracy, would have the most difficulty introducing. Porsche targeted a segment between luxury and super-luxury that no automaker was interested in defending.

Many great companies achieve dominance by attacking competitors who will not respond. But the highest form of strategy, and the one that has led to the world's most dominant firms, is to choose an "attack" that the competition will actually embrace. Microsoft's MS-DOS, for example, became the de facto standard because everyone—IBM, Intel, and the worldwide community of independent software programmers—wanted one, common platform on which to base their businesses. Google became the leading search firm by adopting a strategy that its would-be competitors initially embraced. Yahoo!, for example, helped Google become the leading search engine because Google initially only focused on the boring search work Yahoo! was eager to outsource.

When your competition no longer sees you as a threat, they will stop racing against you. You will no longer be one of the pack, but will be running your own race free from resistance. By the time your adversaries realize your unique race (operating systems, Internet search) is worth running, you may have created a lead no one can close.

Strategy as Action

"Those who excel as warriors are not martial.
Those who excel in combat do not get angry.
Those who excel in conquering the enemy do not do battle."

—*Lao Tzu,* Tao Te Ching

Strategy is often looked upon with disdain, considered a soft, weak, abstract sibling to the more tangible "real work" of managing an organization: hiring people, setting operations, following up on action plans, measuring performance, and so on. The "gap," people argue, lies not in creating strategy but in executing it. Execution translates plans into action, they say; that is where value is actually created.

Critics of strategy wield statistics to support their claim. Execution, they say, adds 90 percent of value to strategy's 10 percent. But these statistics—like the well-accepted, but indisputably incorrect belief that 90 percent of all businesses fail in the first few years—

are folklore. Separating strategy from execution to weigh the value of each is as difficult as separating the heart from a body to see which contributes more to life.

But the criticisms do underscore an important point: Strategy is too often a hollow activity with no impact on the material world of action, performance, or results. The process of developing a strategy often produces little more than words on paper. A strategy document is written, printed, bound, placed on a bookshelf, and not seen again until the end of the year. Should we be surprised that it induces no change?

But to throw out strategy and focus on just execution is a naive answer to an important question. How do you make your strategies happen? How do you convert your plans into reality?

This gap between strategy and action arises when people hold a simplified understanding of what strategy is. They see it as a promise, a description of something they will do. Or they confuse strategy with importance. But being important doesn't make a decision strategic. It is important for supermarkets to offer low prices; however, since everyone (except Whole Foods) offers low prices, that will not differentiate you from others. Low prices are important but not strategic.

To create powerful strategies that actually change things, you should consider a new way of looking at and creating strategy.

As an analogy, consider the role of language. Most people believe that language exists to describe what is already true (it describes what happened) or what will be true (for example, to make promises). Most statements do fill this role: "Jane is a woman" or "I will marry Jane."

But some statements serve a different kind of function. They do not describe or promise anything; instead, they actually do something. By speaking or writing certain statements you actually change things. For example, when you say "I do" in response to a priest asking if you will take Jane to be your wife, you are not saying that you have already married her or promising that you will. By making the statement "I do" you are actually performing the action of marrying Jane. You have changed reality because a moment ago you were her fiancé and now you are her husband.

Such statements are called "performatives" because they perform a function and so are considered actions. Performatives do more than state what is so; they actually change reality. In that way they are far more powerful for creating strategy than are the types of statements usually used to document strategies. The key to creating a powerful strategy, therefore, is to make the strategy performative, as something that actually changes reality.

Turn Strategy into Action

The power of a strategic statement depends, as do all performative statements, as much on its context as on its content. Following traditional approaches, most strategy or product development processes are performed by a few, isolated people or departments. These people gather ideas, and then test, build, validate, and introduce them to the rest of the world. The approach segments the "thinkers" and the "doers."

But this segmented approach is crumbling. Strategy design is becoming a collaborative process, very much like what is happening with new-product development.

The practice of "open innovation," in which customers collaborate to develop new products, is now well established. It can be seen in the practice (common with Google, for one) of launching new products as "beta" versions that are not yet considered complete. Many of Google's most popular products have remained in beta state seemingly endlessly as the company gathers user experiences and suggestions and incorporates them into new versions. The beta strategy makes users feel like a part of the design process. They feel they are helping to create something. Since people are usually more loyal to what they themselves create, the strategy can lead not just to better products but to ones with a more loyal customer base. Strategy design is due for a similar revolution.

Happily, strategy is starting to move out of the boardroom. GE pioneered the approach of engaging employees broadly in problem-solving with what they called "work outs." Large groups of front-line GE employees would lock themselves in a room together off-site, and brainstorm ways to reduce costs, increase sales, or improve efficiency. Today, strategists like W. Chan Kim and Renée Mauborgne of INSEAD advise companies to involve a broad, diverse group of employees formally in the strategy development process.

I have found the approach particularly powerful. When I opened up the strategy process in a way that allowed nearly 100 managers of a pharmaceutical company to participate in brainstorming and selecting ideas, we not only created many more options to choose from—the group generated more than 200 ideas for growing faster—but also, when the strategy was finally written down, it was immediately adopted as their own.

As you can see from these examples, strategic planning is being turned on its head. Instead of the historical top-down approach, wherein the CEO and senior managers decide what is important and dictate priorities down below, the most flexible companies are reversing the flow of insights. By generating a volume of ideas from the front line and funneling them upward to look for patterns with which to form a holistic strategy, you can become more adaptive and creative innovators. By turning the process of creating strategy into a collaborative one that involves a broad base of people, you transform the process into a new model, one in which strategy becomes action. When the process is collaborative, you can build strategies as performative statements that directly change the world.

To visualize that depth of collaboration, you might think of strategy as language. At the base level are letters. At the next level, words; then sentences, then paragraphs. Allow people to create the "letters," then combine them with the letters of others to create "words." See what sense you can make out of the words and form "sentences." Then synthesize everything into a "paragraph" that captures your strategic intent holistically yet shows why each individual letter is critical.

Be aware, however, that when you gather a group of people to co-create a strategy, you run the risk of adopting the predictable, obvious options. To ensure that the group develops something unique requires arming them with new viewpoints, new metaphors.

Change Your Metaphor

"Creativity is just connecting things. When you ask creative peo-
ple how they did something, they feel a little guilty because they
didn't really do it, they just saw something. It seemed obvious
to them after a while. That's because they were able to connect
experiences they've had and synthesize new things. And the reason
they were able to do that was that they've had more experiences
than other people."

—Steve Jobs

Metaphors are often at the source of innovation. They perform two functions. First, they help the problem-solver see a new solution by viewing the challenge from a new perspective. They then help this innovator efficiently transfer the new answer to others—investors, customers, partners, suppliers, and so on—so that others see the innovator's new solution as possible.

Metaphors and Possibilities

Standing in a restaurant parking lot, Andrea Kilpatrick felt her life unexpectedly change course. She remembers the moment clearly. She had just finished having brunch with her boyfriend and his sister when, as they stood chatting, the sister complained that the after-school program where she taught was a waste of children's time. They sat at desks, talked with each other, organized games amongst themselves. The program offered supervision but nothing in the way of activities. It was nothing more than a school-based baby-sitting service.

That complaint opened a door in Andrea's mind. For nearly two decades she had held on to a discontent—sat in the Metal state—without knowing how to realize a desire.

Andrea was raised in a family that put great store by education. Her great-grandfather was a slave. Her grandfather, who only completed eighth grade, saw to it that all his children attended college. Andrea's father continued the tradition. She herself dreamed of starting a school, and even as her life unfolded in slightly different directions—degrees from Princeton, Harvard Law School, and Oxford University, followed by a position at McKinsey & Company—the dream never died. Andrea was collecting the skills and credentials to realize her dream. But she learned the hard way that her degrees and commitment would not make up for lack of experience in education. She would need to invest many years as a full-time educator, putting in time as a teacher, a principal, an administrator, working her way into the system, before she had any hope of making her dream a reality.

Then, one day in 2001, in a parking lot in Miramar, Florida, Andrea's perspective shifted. With the comment by her boyfriend's sister, suddenly it occurred to Andrea that perhaps she need not wait for the credibility to start a school after all. Perhaps she could create an after-school program.

The prevailing conception was that after-school programs were a substitute for baby-sitting. But what if they were instead an extension of school? This would allow Andrea to create a "mini-school." She could realize her goal with few complications. She could overcome the experience barrier that had kept her dream stuck on the shelf.

This shift in perspective—from "after-school is baby-sitting" to "after-school is school continuation"—made possible what a moment earlier had seemed impossible. The effect worked first on Andrea. She decided to pursue her new vision. She validated her idea with facts and wrote a business plan using her management consulting skills. The new metaphor then began working with others. It helped donors and school administrators change their perspectives too.

Today Andrea's organization operates after-school programs throughout South Florida. It also led to a tutoring program that in just two years has grown into operations across four states (Florida, Georgia, Tennessee, and Alabama) and is still expanding.

The changing of a metaphor unlocks possibilities. In that Florida parking lot, Andrea looked at her desire and an opportunity from a different perspective and suddenly saw as possible what before was not. This *"aha"* moment, as we will see, involves predictable mechanics. When intention and a new metaphor come together, new possibilities are born. That mixture has sparked history's most significant corporations and innovations.

The Origin of Insight

Numerous groundbreaking businesses were born when their originators applied a new metaphor:

- In 1993 the consumer electronics retailer Circuit City took investors by surprise when it announced it was entering the used-car business. It seemed to be a daring diversion into an unrelated market. But Circuit City showed that the new business closely matched its experience in consumer electronics. The company entered a fragmented market (consumer electronics, used cars) with a poor reputation (stereo salespeople, used-car salespeople) and won by redefining the shopping experience (in both cases hassle-free, commission-free sales). Circuit City's used car business, CarMax, disrupted competitors and relatively quickly became the only used-car superstore chain in the United States.
- When Howard Schultz returned to Seattle from an Italian vacation he brought with him a new metaphor. He saw that in Europe people spent their time in three "places": their home, their work, and cafés. The café played an important role in people's lives. It was a place to talk with friends, to think, to watch people. But the United States was missing the café culture. People lived in just two places: home and work. So Schultz saw an opportunity to create "the third place," somewhere Americans could spend time away from the other two. This conception of Starbucks as the third place has guided the company's growth from one coffee shop to thousands.
- When Charlie Merrill decided to enter the financial services business, he drew on his experience in supermarkets to offer a fresh perspective on an old business. He conceived of his company as a shopping center where customers could pick and choose from a full selection of financial products.

His innovation is today Merrill Lynch, one of the world's largest financial services companies.

- Toys "R" Us was similarly conceived using a supermarket metaphor. When Charles Lazarus founded the company in the 1950s, his vision was to transform toy-store shopping, at the time dominated by small, local toy stores, into a supermarket experience. This implied big aisles, large inventories, broad selection, and low prices.

- When Cirque du Soleil decided to rethink the circus, it introduced a new metaphor: the circus as theater. Taking this view made it obvious that certain common circus elements should be discarded, including concessions, three rings, and animals. Removing these low-value, high-cost elements not only transformed the circus experience; it transformed cost structure. Cirque du Soleil distinguished itself from its competition and began growing rapidly, opening temporary and permanent "tents" in major cities throughout the world.

- When Infosys saw computer programming as manufacturing, it became easy for customers to see that outsourcing parts of the programming process would make sense. This sparked a growth in IT outsourcing that has transformed both India and the IT sector worldwide (see "Infosys and the Rise of Software Outsourcing" in Chapter 10).

New metaphors unlock innovations at two levels. They reveal a new possibility to the innovator, and they help that innovator sell his or her idea to key stakeholders. Metaphors are powerful because they tap a fundamental structure in human thought.

Metaphors as Problem-Framing Tools

A group of managers from a leading computer manufacturer gathered one afternoon to strategize. They ran the financing division of their company and gave loans to companies that bought hardware. They wanted to significantly accelerate their growth the next year but were not sure what options they had to do so.

Their ability to drive growth was, to a great extent, limited to indirect influence. Most of their company's computers were sold through independent "partners," primarily IT consulting firms. Companies typically chose the financing option that their IT consulting firm recommended, and those consultants didn't care much about the choice of the financing source. They were more concerned with technical specifications and project plans.

How could this financing group increase its influence over partners and thereby the market? They had implemented many of the standard tactics other financing groups use to attract more customers. They had worked on customer service, rates, and marketing materials. These efforts were increasing their loan base but not fast enough to meet aggressive growth targets.

In working with this group I encouraged them to look at their challenge through a set of new metaphors, drawn from an ancient collection of Chinese warfare tactics. We chose five metaphors to work with, and one in particular—"exchange a brick for a jade"—triggered a compelling new strategy.

The "exchange a brick for a jade" tactic plays on the fact that value is relative. What you may value highly (i.e., what you consider a jade), your customer may not perceive as valuable, and vice versa. By playing on these differences, companies can often transform their customer relationship from a dependent one, in which a company depends on its customers, into a co-dependent one, in which the customer depends equally on the company.

The group first decided that the "jade" in this metaphor should represent the loyalty of its IT partners. Having a loyal—better yet, a captive—IT consulting firm as a partner represents immense value because this loyalty would funnel a long-term flow of business from the customers of the IT firm.

If loyalty was the "jade," then what was the "brick?" What did they have somewhere in their company that seemed of low value to them but could be of high value to their partners? We brainstormed this for several minutes, and then one of the managers had an idea. "We know when people bought hardware. This might be valuable to partners."

Suddenly a new strategy emerged. Knowing when people had bought hardware and when it might need to be replaced would help IT consulting firms target potential customers who were likely to need new computers. They could spend their sales efforts on high-potential leads and thereby multiply their sales.

They had defined the "jade" and the "brick." What was left of the metaphor was the "exchange." How could they link the brick and jade so they did not just give away bricks? To do this, the group decided to create a special program that gave loyal partners special status. By being loyal to this financing arm, an IT consulting firm would gain access to sales leads. The new program was first launched regionally. It proved so successful that within a year similar programs were adopted globally.

Metaphors are powerful tools for helping people see new strategic options. They operate by forcing people to look at areas of their situation that they would otherwise overlook.

Consider how a new metaphor can reveal new solutions:

1. An underlying metaphor already exists for the problem. This metaphor may be obvious (shallow) or hidden (deep).
2. You replace this metaphor (say A = B) with a new metaphor (say A = C).
3. A and C are different things, but they share common elements. These common elements are called their grounding. First you look for commonalities; for example, you equate the "jade" with "loyalty."
4. Then you look to complete the metaphor by "mapping" the other elements of C onto A. These areas may be less obvious. They create tension between A and B, and thereby force you to look at areas of A you might have overlooked. You force yourself to ask "What 'bricks' do we have?" and "How might we 'exchange' these bricks for jades?"
5. When you look at elements you previously ignored, you see solutions to which you were previously blind.

In each of the preceding corporate examples, a new metaphor revealed to an innovator or entrepreneur a new way to approach a problem. The next function of the metaphor is to help other people see the new solution. You must help coworkers, partners, investors, suppliers, distributors, and other key stakeholders see the problem from your new perspective and see a new possibility. Metaphors are powerful tools for achieving this second challenge.

Metaphors as Transfer Tools

The word *metaphor* derives from the Greek *metapherein* which means "transfer." Metaphors, then, are tools for transferring information (including knowledge, perspectives, and possibilities) efficiently from one person to another. By mastering their use you can become a more powerful influencer.

To see how metaphors efficiently transfer knowledge, consider this statement: "Fred is an angel." Most people would not interpret that statement literally (unless Fred is actually growing wings), but would understand that you mean that Fred is a nice person who cares about others.

Why not simply say "Fred is a nice person who cares about others"? For one thing, that's less efficient; it requires more than double the syllables and words. More important, it also conveys less information. By comparing Fred to an angel you are linking him to a vast body of associations built over years of communication already stored in your listener's mind. An angel, for example, is not only nice and caring but also pure of heart, someone who actively seeks to help or protect others, and of another world beyond the experience of most human beings. The thought of an angel brings up associations of light, and life after death, and the twists and turns of the human struggle. You could take the time to say all of these things you wish to assign to Fred, or you could simply assign him the name *angel*. This lets your listener immediately tap from his memory all that the word invokes.

A metaphor, then, is a vehicle that transfers large "chunks" of information efficiently. By saying "A is B" you are saying that the characteristics and meaning you currently assign to "B" also apply to "A." This precludes the need to speak or otherwise reiterate everything that "B" means to your listener.

Metaphors also help others understand an innovation by linking the innovation to existing knowledge. Many new scientific discoveries have emerged from obscurity into accepted fact because they effectively built on existing metaphors. Explaining an odd, hypothetical special anomaly as a "worm hole," for example, helps others understand what might otherwise require too long of a leap in conception. People understand what a worm hole looks like on earth. They can then project this image into space and thereby immediately have a conception of what physicists believe may exist.

Expanding the Game Board

Another powerful barrier to innovative thinking is the limits we impose on our game. When Steve Jobs introduced the iPod he worked outside of the sandbox his predecessors confined themselves to. Others who had attempted to launch digital music players took for granted that music companies would resist the digital downloading of their songs. This is why the first digital music services and devices were either illegal or boring. Illegal services such as Napster and Kazaa allowed listeners to share and download songs with other people from across the world. But they failed to profit from their innovations because they conflicted with existing law, and had no plans to reconcile that conflict. Such innovations eventually disappear. Legal alternatives, like Sony's MP3 Walkman, were boring. They dramatically limited what you could do with your music. Listeners had to "check" music out of their computers to play it on their devices and then "check" it back in to play it on their computer.

Steve Jobs viewed the game board as stretching beyond the boundaries defined by music labels. He saw music labels as just another player to convince. He would need to enroll them in his innovation just as he needed to enroll customers into buying his product, and retailers into carrying it. He used the mounting threat illegal services were wielding to move music labels into action. By deconstructing what others accepted, Jobs was able to drive an innovation where no one else had: the creation of an exciting, legal digital music listening experience.

Consider the Crazy

"If we want to understand creativity, we need to understand the process of choice. How can we enhance creativity by improving the way we select and implement new ideas?"

—*Mihaly Csikszentmihalyi*

Even if you are able to introduce a new metaphor to create a new idea, your innovation will confront its next obstacle. It will necessarily seem illogical. All innovative ideas do. If they were consistent with prevailing logic, they would not be innovative. This Catch-22 is one that innovators have struggled with since the beginning of time. Joseph Schumpeter, the German economist who invented the study of entrepreneurship, pointed out this dilemma 200 years ago. As mentioned earlier, he wrote, "Here the success of everything depends on seeing things in a way which afterwards proves to be true, even though it cannot be established at the moment."

About 150 years ago, when Carl Friedrich Gauss was an elementary student, his teacher gave the class busywork, hoping to occupy their time for a while: Add up all the numbers from 1 to 100. The tradition at the time was that the first student to finish the problem would place his tablet face down on a table, then the second student would place his down on top of the first one, and so on. The teacher was shocked when after just a few minutes young Gauss had placed his tablet down. Gauss waited quietly for an hour while the other students worked.

The teacher thought Gauss had cheated. When all the students were done and the teacher pulled Gauss's tablet from the bottom of the pile, his suspicion seemed correct. While the other students listed each figure from 1 to 100, Gauss's tablet contained just one number—the answer, 5,050.

Gauss defended his work and explained his method. By adding the first and last numbers in the series you always get 101 (1 + 100 = 2 + 99 = 3 + 98 = 101). Since there are only 50 such pairs, the answer must be 50 × 101 = 5,050. With this insight Gauss was able to solve in minutes what took the rest of his classmates an hour. Though Gauss's solution was right, the reaction to his discovery was common: disbelief. Great ideas are almost always rejected initially.

Imagine for a moment that Michael Dell was born four years earlier than he actually was. He completes his college degree and, since he is interested in computers, takes a job at Hewlett-Packard. Then, while at HP, he has an insight: There is an opportunity to sell computers directly to consumers. In this alternative reality, however, Michael Dell is not in the safe seclusion of his dorm room. Instead he is sitting at a conference table in the harsh, logical, serious reality of corporate America. How will his colleagues respond? They would almost certainly discount his idea as impossible.

Dissecting this reaction is critical because it is perhaps the most costly barrier to innovation that infects corporations. Let's analyze it using the Buddhist five aggregates framework:

Aggregate	Explanation	The Dell Hypothetical
1. Form	What you actually perceive of the material world. What you see, hear, smell, taste, or feel directly.	Michael Dell's boss (let's call him Jim) hears sounds leave Michael's mouth.
2. Feeling	The primitive reaction you have to what you just sensed. You immediately have a favorable, unfavorable, or neutral reaction.	Jim hears words all day and has no opinion regarding them either way, so his reaction is neutral.
3. Recognition	The classification and naming of what you sense. Then "re-cognizing" it according to your past experiences.	He translates the words, interprets their meaning, and categorizes the idea as something he's never thought of before. But he remembers a moment in the past when they tried something completely novel and recognizes this as a similar situation.

Aggregate	Explanation	The Dell Hypothetical
4. Mental formation	The attachment of pre-existing "baggage"—associations, memories, impediments—to what you recognize. You automatically want something or push it away.	Jim is immediately fearful as the past attempt to try something novel turned out poorly and led to a tough, uncomfortable meeting with his superior.
5. Consciousness	The experience of being conscious of the thing you have sensed (form), named (recognition), and attached pre-existing feelings to (mental formation).	He knows he has heard something like this before and it leaves a bad taste in his mouth. He is not sure why but begins to come up with logical reasons why this is a bad idea, like retailers will revolt and customers need face-to-face support.

The process leaves Jim looking for the reason behind his negative reaction. He wants to be open to new ideas, because this is a value he believes he holds, so he decides to think it through consciously. He asks himself, "Can I see this working?" This leads him to another question, "Have I seen this work before?" Because he has not seen this before, he concludes it is not an idea that would work.

All of this happens in an instant. Buddha said that we have seventeen thoughts in a moment, and Jim has just had about as many. Most of this happened subconsciously, and now Jim must look for reason or logic. He thinks he is using logic to test the idea, but his mind is already made up. Jim is actually using logic to support his belief that the idea is a bad one. He can think of many reasons.

The biggest problem Jim sees is that consumers need their hands held when buying something complicated like a computer. Another problem is that retailers will retaliate. Another is that the company does not have the distribution capabilities to ship single computers. Jim can think of a hundred more.

So in a matter of a few minutes Dell's idea is killed. Jim, Michael, and their colleagues turn to more pressing issues, like how they might reduce the cost of hard drives by a few percentage points.

A Brief Summary of the Water Phase

"Well, we allow people to be creative. We set a direction, we set the vision, we set the strategy, but within that framework we allow our people to be as creative as they want to be. There's no one idea that can be crazy enough. We just allow that."

—Jochen Zeitz, CEO, Puma

Innovation and evolution require three stages to grow: variation, selection, and transmission. Studies of creativity address the issue of variation. Studies of customer adoption address transmission. But the barrier to the Water phase often lies in selection—specifically, which ideas the people with the power to select ideas (the gatekeepers) will select and which they will kill off. It is important to choose carefully in which context you will generate your strategic ideas. The context in which they are conceived can be more important to their success than the virtue of the idea itself.

CHAPTER FIVE

WOOD: FORMATION

"There is nothing more difficult to take in hand, more perilous to conduct, than to take a lead in the introduction of a new order of things, because the innovation has for enemies all those who have done well under the old conditions and lukewarm defenders in those who may do well under the new."

—*Niccolo Machiavelli,* The Prince

Even if an innovation survives the Water phase, it remains a dream because it exists only in the imaginations and words of a few people. You and your team have agreed on a vision and defined a strategy, but you have not yet changed behavior in a significant way. The next step is to move your innovation from idea into reality—a major shift. This means you must take what you and a few close colleagues have in your heads and enroll a larger group of supporters so that your ideas actually change behavior and begin making a measurable impact on the world.

This phase, the Wood phase, seems to be the most critical of all. Most new ideas fail its long, thankless test. The great energy being invested into the innovation yields little encouragement. Sales are not growing; customers are not buying; newspapers are not covering your innovation. Without such feedback you may want to quit, and in fact, many innovators do.

But progress is being made, even though it may not be readily apparent. Just as a growing tree stretches too slowly for us to notice, during the Wood phase an innovation is growing but in a manner you cannot perceive. Consider the following example of a simple innovation with the potential to save thousands of lives that fought for 150 years in the Wood phase before finally reaching adoption.

In the fifteenth and sixteenth centuries, scurvy regularly killed large numbers of sailors. Of the 160 men who sailed with Vasco da Gama around the Cape of Good Hope in 1497, for instance, 100 died of scurvy.

Fed up with this problem (reaching the discontent of the Metal phase), a British captain, James Lancaster, decided to conduct an experiment in 1601. Earlier sea captains had demonstrated the connection between citrus fruits and general health, and Lancaster had the idea to test the impact of citrus on scurvy. He was then commanding four ships under sail to India, and chose one of these ships as a test sample. All sailors on that one ship were given three teaspoons of lemon juice daily; the others received none.

The sailors who were served lemon juice survived the voyage in good health. The 278 sailors on the other ships did not. Halfway through the journey, 110 of those 278 sailors had already died.

The results of this test were compelling: Lemons saved lives, and at quite minimal cost. With such a dramatic outcome, we might expect the British Navy to quickly grab on to this innovation and make daily citrus rations a requirement. But the idea hit the Wood phase. The British Navy did not adopt the practice until 1795, nearly 200 years after Captain Lancaster's experiment.

All innovations must journey through the long, plodding, thankless Wood phase—the period when effort outweighs results. With few exceptions, every company that has produced breakthrough growth and profitability has done so only after a distinct, and often protracted, period of formation. Take the following companies and concepts for example:

- Sony executive Ken Kutaragi saw the potential of video games in the 1980s, but it took him nearly a decade to convince

his employer to enter the video game business. The result
was the phenomenally successful PlayStation game console,
first released in 1994.

- In 1974, Muhammad Yunus (see profile in Chapter 15)
proved that banks could affordably lend money in small
amounts to the poor. He visited banks throughout his home
country of Bangladesh and continued building evidence that
repayment rates were above 90 percent. Despite his proof, it
took over three decades for the world to embrace his "microcredit" concept.

- The cofounders of Infosys, one of the world's leading software firms, spent more than a decade building critical skills,
reputation, and a client base before they could begin growing in a major way. (See profile in Chapter 10.)

- The founders of Urban Outfitters, one of the world's fastest-
growing, most profitable retail chains, invested more than
fifteen years refining their store concept before they could
secure the funding to fuel rapid expansion. (See profile in
Chapter 11.)

- Today FedEx is the leading international package delivery company in China, generating more revenue from that
country than do UPS or DHL. But its success only came
after twenty-two years of laying a foundation. As CEO Fred
Smith explains, "It's a fast-growing market for us now, but it
took a lot of hard work and diplomacy to get this far."

Why must innovations pass through the Wood phase, and why
do most innovators give up when their innovations reach it? As
before, we can answer these questions from a diverse set of perspectives. Modern scientists who study expertise (such as studies
into how chess players think), cognition, social construction, and
innovation diffusion have collected findings that together paint a
fairly clear picture of this problematic Wood phase. The picture
is surprisingly similar to what the ancient philosophies about
change—from Buddhism to Taoism—began describing several
thousand years prior.

A Platform for Growth

Buddhist philosophy says that before you can enjoy fruit, first a seed must sprout. From the sprout comes a sapling, then a trunk, then a branch, then a flower, and finally fruit. Similarly, for innovations to bear fruit, you must lay down an adequate foundation. This means you must sow several seeds and patiently help them grow. If you only measure your innovation in terms of fruit, you appear to be making no progress because while your seeds grow into saplings and trees, your fruit count remains zero. Unless you understand the progress you are making, you will give up.

Let's return to Ted Leonsis and his list of 101 things to do before he died. Checking off this list eventually led Leonsis to America Online (AOL), where he became vice chairman. During his tenure at AOL he has been credited with leading a profound transformation.

Early on, Leonsis saw that AOL's role as an Internet service provider offered no future and that to survive, the company needed to reconceptualize itself (Metal). He led AOL on a strategy to become a media company and adopt the channel format that distinguishes the AOL experience from that of its competitors today (Water).

While Leonsis's vision and strategy were clear, AOL remained far from reaching the goal he set. It already had a head start as an ISP, with a strong brand and major investments in hardware; switching emphasis to a media company would require capabilities and assets that AOL was missing. Under Leonsis's influence, AOL began putting the critical pieces in place. The company invested in a series of companies to fill in its picture as a media company, including MovieFone, MapQuest, and ICQ. Assembling the pieces took a while, and their impact on revenue came with a significant lag time. But as AOL's new configuration formed, these additions unlocked impressive growth. When Leonsis joined AOL, the company was generating under $100 million in revenue. Today it earns $2 billion each year.

Innovators operate well in these "fuzzy" states, where the pieces are not in place. Others cannot yet see what is going to happen, but innovators have a clear image of the strategy. As Sun Tzu said, "All men can see the tactics whereby I conquer, but what none can see is the strategy out of which victory is evolved."

When Steve Case, the founder of AOL, left that company and decided to start a new one in the wellness field, he gathered a grand vision that few could fully comprehend. He formed a company called Revolution Health Care and began putting critical pieces into formation. He assembled a powerful and eclectic board of directors, including former secretary of state Colin Powell, former *Fortune* 500 CEOs Jim Barksdale, Frank Raines, Carly Fiorina, and Steve Wiggins, and high-profile venture capitalists/financiers Miles Gilburne, Jeff Zients, John Delaney, and David Golden.

The new company began an aggressive program of acquisitions. Some were in the medical arena: companies that operate medical clinics, provide online health information, sell software to help patients manage their health-care spending, and help companies provide individualized health benefits to employees. Others were less obvious: real estate companies, hotel operators, and spas.

Like dots on a blank canvas, when looked at one at a time, these acquisitions make little sense. But as Revolution adds more dots, more companies, a picture begins to emerge. The company's goal is to "transform how people improve their health by putting consumers at the center of the health system, with better choices, more convenience and more control."

The company recognizes that when pursuing big visions—like transforming health care—innovations must survive a very long, drawn-out period in the Wood phase as the innovation incubates. Revolution constantly reinforces this fact to set proper expectations. As company CEO John Pleasants said, "With these acquisitions we've got some great pieces, . . . but there is still much work to be done."

When Nick Negroponte, the former head of MIT's Media Lab, set out on the quest to build a $100 laptop and make these available to poor children around the world, his first step was to assemble the needed pieces. He used his influence to gain buy-in from Google, AMD, Microsoft, and Brazil's president, "Lula" da Silva. He convinced high-powered executives to leave better-paying jobs to help him solve the technical and social challenge his project presents. His effort faces numerous challenges. The costs of a computer's components—battery, screen, processor, and so on—simply add up to more than $100, leading many experts to skepticism. But as Negroponte patiently assembles the pieces, expert opinion is shifting. People are beginning to see a $100 computer as possible.

This is the nature of the Wood phase. Others may not see your vision clearly and, even if they think they do, may not believe it viable. But as you methodically assemble the pieces, you transform a vision (which exists in the immaterial world) into reality (the material world). The Shift takes on great significance.

If you can navigate through this phase, you have the potential to realize your vision. But the challenges are severe, and perseverance alone is not the answer. The deeper problem is that few can understand your strategy, and yet you need their support. To configure your innovation, you must enroll three critical networks of support: users, colleagues, and partners.

The Mechanics of Wood

"You can't plant a tree and see it grow in a year."

—Jeff Immelt, CEO, General Electric

Most people who have studied the innovation process are familiar with the taxonomy developed by scientists investigating how innovations diffuse throughout society. First come the "innovators," people who introduce something new. Then "early adopters" try out an innovation. If these people are popular social leaders, they will spread the innovation to the "early majority." Once the innovation is widespread, members of the more skeptical "late majority" step in. Finally the "laggards" catch on, egged on by their friends and encouraged by what has now become mainstream.

But merely knowing the sequence isn't much help, because innovators usually face a multifront war. They must convince users—early adopters and the early majority—to buy in, but first they must enroll two other networks of stakeholders: colleagues and partners. All told, it means a battle on three fronts.

The Three-Front Battle

1. Organization: Convincing your colleagues and organization to embrace your innovation, and, if you cannot, seeking or creating a different organization that will.
2. Partners: Convincing critical partners, including manufacturers, suppliers, and distributors, to cooperate with introducing and supporting your innovation.
3. Users: Convincing customers to adopt and spread your innovation.

Wood: enrolling resources

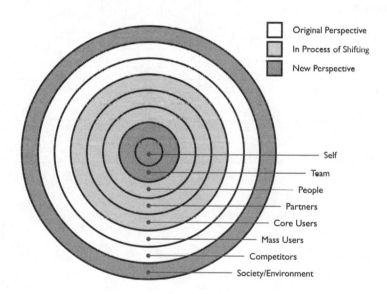

As I have argued in each chapter so far, the battles you must wage are mental, not physical. You can force any of these players to cooperate, but such efforts will be short-lived. To transform people's behavior, you must transform their will. You must change their minds.

Successful innovations operate on a mental level to break through the resistance latent in all three networks—the organization, partners, and users. To reduce resistance and maximize support, your innovation must enhance what is harmonious in their minds and defuse what is dissonant. This means using seven tools to deconstruct and reconstruct what might pose resistance to your desired change. To usher innovations through the Wood phase successfully, you must identify where in the following matrix you may face resistance, and then deconstruct and reconstruct that which is in your way.

Tools

	Organization	Partners	Users
Beliefs			
Logic			
Accountabilities			
Distinctions			
Stories			
Metaphors			
Incentives			

Seven Tools to Build Resonance for Your Innovation

You may know these tools by different names. But the concepts are identical across all of these domains.

Beliefs

"What convinces is conviction. Believe in the argument you're advancing. If you don't you're as good as dead. The other person will sense that something isn't there, and no chain of reasoning, no matter how logical or elegant or brilliant, will win your case for you."

—Lyndon B. Johnson

What social constructionists call entrapment, cognitive scientists (and, increasingly, business academics) call mental models, and Buddhists call shraddha, we will call beliefs.

Because human beings naturally seek harmony between beliefs and actions to avoid the distress of cognitive dissonance, beliefs play a powerful role in our actions. If the beliefs of your colleagues, partners, and potential users are inconsistent with actions demanded by your innovation, your innovation will likely fail.

The easiest way to overcome this is to change your innovation so that dissonance is not created with prevailing beliefs. If this is not possible, then the next best thing is to replace beliefs (just as Martin Luther King Jr. adopted a brilliant strategy to show whites it was safe to abandon beliefs inconsistent with equality). If you cannot change people's beliefs, you can change the people themselves (as corporate turnaround experts do by firing the old guard). Each approach attempts the same thing: to remove the resistance that arises from incongruent beliefs.

Logic

"Innovation is not the product of logical thought, although the result is tied to logical structure."

—Albert Einstein

Grounding an idea in rigorous logic can help you make bold moves with confidence. By proving your ideas with facts, you think you can convince yourself and your colleagues, partners, and users that the innovation is the answer.

However, logic alone won't get you there. Numerous cognitive experiments have shown that logic is actually a poor tool for changing the minds of others. People do not look at the logic and then make their decision. Instead, they make their decision and then see if it can be supported by logic.

This has important implications for how you use logic to drive the adoption of your innovations. First, you should recognize that you must provide a logical proof that your innovation is sound. Your partners and colleagues in particular will require this. If you can convince them that you are right—with nonlogical means—you must immediately support their new belief with logic. You must validate your ideas with carefully crafted, fact-based analysis.

But you must also choose a logic that generates manageable dissonance with prevailing logic. Every innovative idea, if truly innovative, will have some inconsistency with prevailing logic. All major scientific advances, for example, disprove some prevailing belief or understanding. As Francis Bacon wrote: "Logic is useless; it is creation that is science." So your idea will unavoidably find itself in conflict with prevailing logic.

You can minimize this resistance by forming your proof creatively so that it steers clear of closely held prevailing logic. If you can craft your argument in a way that allows people to hold on to their models, you will generate less resistance.

Logic, then, is critical because it serves three purposes:

1. To test that you are not proposing something entirely foolish.
2. To give others a reason to believe what you, using nonlogical means, have just warmed them up to considering.
3. To work out your plans in greater detail.

Accountabilities

Accountabilities are a necessary ingredient of a functioning society. They regulate or constrain behaviors so that things work. But this constraining function can also hinder your ability to drive adoption of your innovation if it requires people to act in ways that conflict with prevailing accountabilities.

Your innovations must be congruent with or must replace three levels of accountability:

1. Individual: Promises people make to others (for example, their bosses), such as promising to get to work by 9 A.M.
2. Organizational: Commitments people make when they choose to join the organization. Innovations that conflict with any of these are unlikely to be embraced.
3. Societal: We operate in a network of social accountabilities that we have implicitly accepted by belonging to our communities. By living in Miami, for example, I have accepted that people will often speak to me in Spanish before trying English.

People can remove their accountability by explaining away their actions, of course. They can provide excuses, claim they had no choice, or argue that breaking an accountability was justified. But if your innovation is to stick, you must eventually change, or fit in with, the web of accountabilities that hold together your organization, partners, and users.

The best innovations are those that supersede existing accountabilities. They elicit no contention because they invoke accountabilities that are of a higher order.

Distinctions
"When beauty is discovered
Then ugliness emerges;
When good is discovered
Then evil emerges."

"So alive and dead are distinguished from nature,
Difficult and easy from progress,
Long and short from contrast,
High and low from depth,
Song and speech from melody,
After and before from sequence."

—Lao Tzu, Tao Te Ching

What Lao Tzu calls "introducing distinctions," modern political strategists call "framing the debate." The principle is the same: The discussion your colleagues, partners, and users have is influenced by the topic introduced. That's exactly what Apple did by focusing on aesthetics, thus shifting the computer conversation away from processor speed and instead to design, an area in which Apple could claim a clear advantage.

The ability to strategically create a new distinction is a powerful tool for encouraging others to embrace your innovation. The U.S. Republican Party gained significant national support by introducing the distinction of "family values," which had the intended effect of directing the dialogue to what was and what was not a family value. On news programs and in households throughout the United States, the conversation shifted away from more political, less Republican-dominated topics toward an area in which Republicans believed they held an advantage.

When you face organized opposition to your innovation, your attempt to frame the debate around a new distinction may raise a challenge. For example, people opposed to abortion want the debate to center around "life," while their opposition wants the debate to center around "choice." But in general, I have found that innovators with ideas that could potentially improve the world rarely face such strong, structured opposition. They can introduce a distinction and shift the conversation to a more helpful one without inviting a unified response.

Stories

Stories are important because they tell your colleagues, partners, and potential users what to focus on and what to expect in the future. Like turning the rudder of a ship, you can change the future they anticipate by retelling the past.

This requires far greater effort than you might think. Communicating your version of the past and future—your vision—demands repeatedly delivering it to your audience using creative methods to remind them, to keep them convinced.

In 2007, Michael Dell took back the reins of his company. The company that had revolutionized the computer industry by introducing a direct-to-consumer model was in serious trouble as competitors began copying that model. With its stock sinking, the company turned to its founder for help.

In trying to craft a turnaround, Michael Dell has played on the story, as all turnaround experts do. He repeatedly says that "this is a defining moment in our history and in our relationships with customers." The first part of his message is a wake-up call: The future that Dell employees and partners are imagining is not the right one because the old direct model is no longer unique. He then paints a future of promise: "We know our competitors drive complexity and needless cost into consumers' environments. . . .We intend to break this cycle." In other words, he is arguing that the competition is stuck (in Metal) and that this represents an opportunity for his company.

Every leadership book underscores the importance of maintaining a long-term vision in the minds of your people. This vision, however, is a product of the past, of the story people tell themselves about what has happened and therefore what to expect in the future. For your innovations to succeed you must usually revise, edit, and rewrite prevailing stories.

Metaphors

Our sixth tool is the metaphor. This was covered in some detail in Chapter 3, so we need only touch on it here to emphasize that you must wrap your innovation in compelling metaphors if your colleagues, partners, and users are to embrace it.

Consider Vonage, a company that revolutionized voice-over-Internet protocol (VoIP). The company's founder, Jeffrey Citron, saw that the natural owners of this new technology, major telephone companies, were stuck in a Metal state and would not seize the opportunity. So he decided to act in this gap. He created a technology company that made it easy for average people to adopt VoIP. Around the same time, another company, Skype, formed with a similar mission. It offered free VoIP service to people who were willing to download and install a program on their computers.

Vonage has become a broadly recognized brand with 2.2 million users and millions in revenue. Skype, which is free, has more users than Vonage, but it was bought out by eBay and remains an unprofitable service used almost exclusively by the technologically savvy. Vonage was able to break out profitably into the mainstream. Skype has not. While history tells us Vonage will likely fall to cable and telephone companies, unable to ground its innovation, to date Vonage has been more successful than Skype.

The primary difference between the two is that Vonage offers a clearer metaphor. It created a device that looks a lot like a regular home telephone. It plugs into a router instead of the wall jack, but otherwise the Vonage phone looks identical to the home phone you have bought in the past. Skype, on the other hand, requires users to sit in front of a computer terminal wearing a headset. Vonage invokes a "phone" metaphor; Skype invokes a "computer" metaphor.

Creating a metaphor that resonates works equally well with employees. Steve Jobs eggs his people on with metaphors such as "we will leave a dent on the universe." General Electric focuses the managers of its hundreds of companies on two priorities—creativity and ecologically stable solutions—by adopting the word *ecomagination*. It's a metaphor that resonates yet creates something new.

Incentives

Much has already been written about incentives and how to set them. For our purposes, the key point to remember is that incentives, like logic, usually provide enforcing power. They are more useful for reinforcing newly adopted behaviors than actually changing them. It's a matter of timing. In the corporate context, innovators generally must wait a year or more to change incentives (such as restructuring bonus calculations), while their innovations must propagate more quickly.

Enrolling the Critical Networks

With these seven tools you can deconstruct sources of resistance and reconstitute them to create pull for your change. Now we will look at how to use these tools to enroll your three critical networks—your organization, your partners, and your users—into your innovation.

The Organization: Building Shih

"One skilled at employing the military takes them by the hand as if leading a single person. They cannot hold back."

—*Sun Tzu*, The Art of War

The first challenge most innovators face during this phase is how to align all the elements of their organization so as to establish firmness or integrity. When each person is making decisions in pursuit of a common goal, their efforts multiply and create a crescendo of power, or as Sun Tzu calls it, *shih*.

Wal-Mart does not boast about its track record with international acquisitions. In 1997, the company entered Germany with two acquisitions: a chain of 21 hypermarkets and then a 74-store chain. With a base of nearly 100 stores, Wal-Mart seemed poised to mount a serious challenge to European retailers, who had never had to contend with Wal-Mart's infamously aggressive everyday low-price strategy.

Ten years later, Wal-Mart gave up. It announced it was selling all of its German stores to its rival Metro, losing $1 billion on the deal. Countless analysts have weighed in on why Wal-Mart failed so dramatically in Germany. The reasons are manifold, but nearly all center around Wal-Mart's inability to fully enroll its new German employees into the Wal-Mart way. As a result could not deliver on its customer promises of everyday low prices and friendly service.

As Wal-Mart was pulling out of Germany, it was pushing into Latin America. The company had enjoyed great success in Mexico and had footholds in Argentina and Brazil. It decided to learn from its failures in Europe and launch an aggressive acquisition strategy in fast-growing Latin American markets.

The contrast is stark. In Germany the company lost its reputation of invincibility and billions of dollars; in Latin America, it is thriving. What is Wal-Mart doing differently? The answer points to the criticality of building organizational *shih*.

The first expansion plan was for Brazil. Wal-Mart operations in the country had been limited to a few stores in one city, Brazil's most populated, São Paolo. Wal-Mart set acquisition targets in northern Brazil and decided on one Brazilian retailer, Bompreço, a 118-store supermarket chain. Thinking strategically about how to avoid repeating its German fiasco, Wal-Mart made several unique choices regarding Bompreço. They center around the principle that if the employees do not choose to embrace the Wal-Mart way, the acquisition cannot achieve its potential.

Letting People Choose Accountability

Accountability—allowing another person to judge your actions—is most powerful when it is chosen by the person held accountable. Wal-Mart was careful to give its new Bompreço employees as much of a choice as possible. Rather than indoctrinate them into the Wal-Mart way, the company invested a longer period of time in inviting the new members into the family.

The president of Wal-Mart Latin America made a concerted effort to repeatedly recount the company's three basic beliefs, originally defined by Sam Walton in 1962:

1. Respect for the individual
2. Service to our customers
3. Strive for excellence

The change in approach is subtle, but the results profoundly different. Whereas in the past Wal-Mart essentially dictated acceptance—"these are our beliefs, believe them"—with Bompreço, the company's president kept repeating the beliefs and inviting Bompreço employees to choose them.

If you can get people to choose your innovation—your beliefs, your strategy, your vision, and so on—they will feel an accountability to helping you transform your idea into reality. The beliefs become their own.

Notice that Wal-Mart's three core beliefs are so universal they create no conflict with prevailing beliefs. Their resonance may be strong or weak with different cultures, but their message will not require others to give up their belief system. In this way, they offer the chance for what Sun Tzu calls "taking whole." Your opponents—in this case employees who might resist your innovation—find no reason to oppose you. They open the door and invite you in.

Winning Over Internal Networks

Marketing experts spend a great deal of time understanding how to segment customers to identify which types will be most interested in a new innovation, be it a new product or new service, and what message will move them into action. The same approach works internally.

The head of strategy for one of the world's largest mobile phone manufacturers once explained to me that most of his work involved identifying which people inside his company he needs support from, whether it be research and development (R & D), purchasing, marketing, operations, or others. He invests a great deal of time courting the right people to understand their interests and concerns. This helps him assess which battles to jump into and which to avoid. If R & D is overworked, for example, he is unlikely to get a big new phone idea through their process.

Almost all of the innovators I interviewed think strategically about the internal networks within their organizations. They identify who they need support from, what their chances are of gaining such support (is that person strongly supportive, negatively inclined, or indifferent?), and who that person has influence over or is influenced by. This mapping of the playing field helps find weak points—what Taoists would call the points of least effort—for introducing new innovations.

Wal-Mart in Brazil did two things to win internal networks. First, it conducted an analysis of the acquisition target's culture to measure how close it was to Wal-Mart's culture. Potential targets with very different cultures were unlikely to buy in to the Wal-Mart way. Bompreço, however, was already very close. So in asking Bompreço employees to align with Wal-Mart, the company was not asking them to take much of a leap.

Wal-Mart then focused on identifying Bompreço's opinion makers. This traditionally means the top team, those who can, with their excitement or concern, sway the opinions of all others. But often, influence does not depend on a title. Wal-Mart focused first on gaining the support of Bompreço early adopters—the influential managers who would be naturally open to the Wal-Mart way. They in turn brought on board the others, the early majority, the late majority, and eventually the laggards, until the entire Bompreço organization was ready to choose to be Wal-Mart.

Using an Inclusive Metaphor

Because Wal-Mart did not force people to accept beliefs that would conflict with their prevailing belief systems, it allowed Bompreço to maintain an identity. When you shop at one of the various Bompreço stores—a supermarket, hypermarket, or mini-market—you may not even know you are shopping at a Wal-Mart. There is just a small tag at the bottom of the Bompreço logo that reads "Part of the Wal-Mart Family."

Replicating Vital Organs

Finally, Wal-Mart supported its new foray into northern Brazil in a way it had not done before. Traditionally the company managed its foreign operations centrally, out of Wal-Mart headquarters in Bentonville, Arkansas. After experiencing the flaws of having someone in Bentonville make decisions about human resources in Europe, Wal-Mart decided to move critical support functions closer to Latin America.

The metaphor it used for describing this decision is that the organization is an organism. As the head of People for Latin

America explains, in Latin America Wal-Mart was growing "a new organism." If it was to function independently, the new organism needed its own vital organs. Wal-Mart defined three critical organs—People, Finance, and Operations—and positioned them in a new Latin American regional unit.

In true Wal-Mart fashion this regional unit is small and understated. In the far corner of a small office park you will find an unmarked door, behind which sit seven people who together support Wal-Mart operations in all of Latin America. This small team helps ensure that Wal-Mart Latin America can make quick, customized choices. Field people no longer have to wait for the home office in Arkansas to make critical decisions.

If there is one compelling lesson to learn from Wal-Mart's misstep in Germany and subsequent success in Brazil, it is that you must build organizational *shih*, or what modern-day organizational design experts would call organizational alignment. This requires creating an opportunity for key networks in your organization to choose your innovation, and also crafting your innovation in a way that helps them make the right choice. With the organization aligned, you can now begin turning outward, to the distributors, suppliers, and other partners you will depend on to realize your idea.

Partners—Infecting Their Minds

Even with an organization aligned to an innovation, the dispersed, fragmented, competitive environment you must increasingly play in demands you also enroll partners. As the cost of coordinating resources globally continues to drop, companies are looking less like organizations and more like networks. Succeeding today increasingly demands an ability to orchestrate partners outside of your organization into a coordinated formation that collectively achieves what no one company could manage alone. But your would-be partners will have the same natural response to a new idea that your organization does. They will fight it like a virus.

It is a natural human tendency to seek stability and resist change. It took Compaq years to realize that Dell's business model—selling directly to consumers—was superior. With evidence mounting that they were losing ground to the young innovator, Compaq's people finally built the discontent (Metal) to plan a new strategy (Water). They may even have built organizational *shih*, convincing enough Compaq managers of the need for change. But when the company attempted to launch its copycat innovation, it met opposition from CompUSA, Best Buy, and other retailers who saw that they would become obsolete if Compaq adopted Dell's direct model.

Unfortunately for Compaq, a transformation from a retail model to a direct one would take time—time during which the company still needed to sell computers, which, in turn, depended on the support of their retailers. Unable to give partners a reason to accept their intended change, Compaq failed to adapt and could not make it through the Wood phase. It watched with hands tied as Dell stole market share to become the largest computer company in the world. Failing to enroll partners can mean death to even good strategic moves.

Contrast Compaq's failure with the success of a man I'll call Nick. He had spent nearly twenty years in banking, moving through various specialties until he came upon derivatives—financial instruments that derive their values from other underlying securities. Nick enjoyed the complexity and possibilities of derivatives, so he decided to focus on this relatively young market.

Eventually Nick was brought in to one of the world's largest financial institutions to launch a new business selling hybrids of derivatives, or what are known as structured products: complex, engineered securities that derive their value from interest rates, exchange rates, or movements in other financial measures. The first year, Nick was a team of one. He sat at a lone trading terminal in a large, open space, surrounded by blinking Bloomberg terminals and hundreds of frantic traders working in other arenas.

To grow his structured products business, Nick first began building organizational *shih*. He identified the key capabilities his business would need to succeed and began enrolling people with the contacts and skills to fill the gaps. For example, he needed people who could assemble new products, who knew the market, could manage complex projects, and understood a diversity of financial instruments that they might combine and package. He also needed distribution into key geographies—the eastern United States, western United States, Europe, Asia, and Latin America. Distributing such complex products directly to consumers would be inefficient. Nick needed people who could reach customer relations managers in bank branches and show them how to sell his products.

Over the first few years, Nick built the internal organization he needed. He could not afford to hire people outright, so instead he focused on convincing others inside his company to add his products to their offerings. In a few more years, Nick's business grew to $350 million in revenue. He had two full-time employees on his team.

This early success proved to Nick's organization that structured products had potential. They were willing to invest. But Nick knew that he needed more than an internal team. To make his business a significant success, he needed to enroll partners, particularly bank officers who worked in the branches and spoke directly to customers. If he could convince them to adopt structured products on a large scale, he could expand his business many times over. If he failed to enroll his bank partners, he would likely end up with a minor practice in an obscure area of finance.

The obvious way to convince banking partners was to train them to understand the tangible advantages of structured products. This involved proving that his products could provide a higher return relative to risk than did other options or could more closely match the unique beliefs of customers. Customers who believed, for example, that the Japanese yen would fall against the dollar could buy a special security that paid out money when the yen fell.

But Nick decided to appeal to his partners with a far less complicated approach. He introduced a simple coding system composed of three colors: blue for safety and protection; yellow for opportunity; and green, the most aggressive, for performance. When customers entered a bank branch looking for something conservative, Nick's bankers would immediately think "blue." Customers looking to place some of their excess assets in more risky investments simply needed more "green."

The results have been outstanding. Over the past eight years Nick's business has grown from nothing to $4 billion in annual revenue, larger than some major corporations.

Nick credits his success to his and his team's ability to enroll partners through simplicity. His team of salespeople is constantly looking for new "concepts," such as clients asking about income or growth. During weekly meetings they share these concepts, looking for broad themes that the product development people can use to build new offerings. A theme, in Nick's experience, will resonate with his banker partners for about two to three years before the market changes and new themes are needed. The underlying product need not change significantly.

Successful innovators show an unnatural ability to enroll partners in their ideas, using a variety of techniques. Logic may work when partners are logical and their needs align neatly with your own. More often, though, successfully assembling a cohort of strong partners requires wielding other tools. Stories, metaphors, and distinctions can help you more quickly get partners on your side.

Users—Shift Them Inches Over to Your Side

Innovations by definition must be accepted by users, otherwise we cannot call them anything more than a new idea. Creativity becomes innovation only when users embrace its offering.

Find the Influential Players

The concert was to have started at 8 P.M. But by 9 P.M. we had nothing more to enjoy than a stadium packed with fidgeting fans. After sixty minutes of waiting, everyone had reached a state of discontent (Metal). Itching to do something, to organize some sort of complaint that might urge our performer to step onto the stage, we collectively could think of just one option (Water): We need to start a wave. For those unfamiliar with stadium etiquette, a wave begins when a sufficiently large mass of people suddenly stand up from their seats, raise their hands over their heads, and

then quickly sit down. This triggers the neighboring section to follow suit, which triggers the next one, and so on, until the entire
stadium exhibits a wave of up-down humanity.

From my vantage point I watched two people try to start the
wave. The first was a man in a dark shirt who suddenly rose and
encouraged five of his friends to do the same. His wave fizzled out.
The next was a woman, dressed in a bright green shirt, who turned
to a group of about twenty people, signaled to them it was time,
then raised her hands. Her loyal group of twenty followed her lead,
then the neighboring section of about fifty people caught on. They
too stood up, leading the next section, of about a hundred people,
to stand up in unison. And so the wave grew as it spread around
the stadium. Three minutes later every fan was participating in this
joint act as the wave circled around and around.

Why the woman was able to mobilize thousands of music fans
but the man was not is a question that has drawn the attention of
innovation students and marketers for decades. It depends on what
we now call the tipping point, that magic moment when an idea
suddenly, serendipitously, seems to take off. The apparent power of
consumers to self-organize and move an innovation past its tipping
point seems to hold the answer to how we collectively can change
the world. If you can engineer such tipping points, you can drive
the massive adoption of new ideas.

Unlock the Gate

*"Innovation is the whim of an elite before it becomes a need of
the public."*

Ludwig von Mises

Successful innovators are able to unlock the gate to their innovation earlier than others because they identify and focus in on the
critical gatekeeper.

Simon Cowell was already a successful British record executive
when he developed a reality television program with Simon Fuller,
another major player in the British music scene. The proposed
program would follow a group of contestants through a talent

competition. The show was already successful in the United Kingdom, and Cowell and Fuller decided to try their luck in the United
States. Though they offered the elements of a promising project—
they were experienced entertainment executives with a format that
had already been successful abroad—they hit a wall pitching to
U.S. television producers. They met with UPN, a smaller television network that should have been more open to unusual ideas
than were the more conservative leaders, but the meeting went
nowhere. UPN passed on the show. They approached Fox, but the
talks dragged on. In the meantime they tried ABC, which showed
some interest but ultimately passed as well.

Cowell and Fuller persisted through the cold responses and
eventually arrived at a new strategy. They knew that Elisabeth
Murdoch, daughter of Rupert Murdoch, founder and CEO of
News Corporation, which owns Fox TV, had seen the show in the
United Kingdom and liked it. They asked if she might be willing
to help them break through. Ms. Murdoch agreed. She called her
father and told him that the show was growing into a big success
in the United Kingdom and that she loved it. The next day Mr.
Murdoch called Peter Chernin, a top decision-maker at Fox, and
asked why Fox was taking so long to purchase the rights to the
show. "We're still looking at it," Chernin explained. "Don't look at
it," Murdoch snapped. "Buy it! Right now."

So Fox bought the show and adapted it for a U.S. audience.
Over the past six seasons *American Idol* has earned top ratings,
often attracting more viewers than any other show in its time slot.

Convincing core users to adopt your innovation requires you
to convince just one influential decision-maker to believe in your
idea. Whether this is the woman with the green shirt and twenty
friends (instead of the man with the dark shirt and five) or the
daughter of Rupert Murdoch, knowing who holds the gate keys
can help you quickly unlock progress.

The challenge of this dynamic is that you always seem far away
until you are already a breakthrough success. In 1955, for example, Boeing had been struggling for more than a decade against a
powerful competitor, Douglas. Both fought hard for each sale,

with neither proving the clear victor. That year, however, Boeing broke through with one critical deal. By promising American Airlines it would expand the width of its jet by four inches, thereby making it wider than Douglas's offering, Boeing won the carrier's order, setting the company on a path to domination. Even in the complex world of aviation, a breakthrough in customer adoption can be just inches away.

Knowing which influential customer to target and then crafting an offering that moves that customer to adopt your innovation are fundamental. Nearly every one of the fastest-growing, most profitable companies studied here unlocked their growth by winning a large, influential client.

How to Create or Seek Out Pull

Just as it is easier to raise a sail than to row a boat, it requires less effort to introduce innovations that resonate with prevailing beliefs, tastes, and conceptions of would-be users than to work against them. To watch how a master predicts such currents, let me introduce you to Bill.

Bill runs a company that makes flavorings. He develops and bottles the syrups that coffeehouses and restaurants use to spice up their drinks. When you order a mango iced tea, for example, you'll probably get a regular iced tea into which your barista has stirred mango-flavored syrup.

Bill's world depends on predicting what flavors will become popular. It's not easy, since our tastes for particular flavorings wax and wane. Five years ago, for example, few people knew what chai tea was. Today, not only is this Indian-inspired spiced tea one of Starbucks' most popular drinks; you can buy it in teabags at your local grocery store, and the name is recognized broadly enough to be mainstream. The mango flavor had an equally significant, though less dramatic, rise. Ten years ago in the United States, almost nothing was flavored with mango. But today you can order it or find it premixed into anything from iced tea crystals to martinis.

Large restaurant chains throughout the United States depend on Bill's predictions. If he is right, it translates immediately into margins and profitability. The problem with predicting flavor tastes is that, as with nearly all new innovations, customer focus groups do not work. Inside the focus group room, consumers often respond confidently about what they like at that moment. But they simply cannot accurately assess how they will make up their minds out in the world, when the full field of influences—what their friends say, what their girlfriend thinks is cool, and on and on—are unleashed on them.

Somehow Bill is able to predict emerging flavor trends. He does this by looking where others do not. Though he must protect his methodology to some degree, he does offer a glimpse into its mechanics. Most food trends are driven by what people are exposed to in restaurants. If people are ordering more spicy foods, for example, then packaged goods companies will begin selling more spicy options in grocery stores. If diners start looking for more organic choices from restaurants, you can expect to find more and more organic vegetables eventually popping up in grocery stores.

But flavors, for some reason, work in reverse. People are first exposed to new flavors "off premises" in grocery or other retail stores, and through that exposure grow more open to trying the flavor "on premises," in restaurants and bars. You may be ordering a vanilla vodka martini because you tried vanilla Coke from the grocery store last week.

So Bill is able to more accurately predict what new flavors consumers will be interested in partly because he tracks which flavors are growing and slowing in grocery stores. This leading indicator tells him what new flavors may resonate with consumers, which in turn makes him a valuable partner to restaurant chains.

A Brief Summary of the Wood Phase

Though vast amounts have been written about how to enroll customers in a new innovation, in the end the findings bring us back to the basics. First, you target influential users. Second, you look for "pull," or latent needs, and craft an offering and message that will resonate with them. Third, you move these influential customers over to your side. Fourth, you encourage and empower them to tell their friends. Following through on these four steps will help your innovation strengthen, survive, and succeed in the Wood phase.

Whether you are enrolling the influential people or have already done so and are helping them win over their friends, they may be just inches away. But as their decision comes not in degrees but in a more decisive "Yes, I will adopt your innovation" or "No, not yet," you cannot judge your progress fairly by sales, market share, or other traditional measures.

To shift their viewpoints and move them into adoption, you can use the seven tools:

1. Change their beliefs so they see your innovation as the best choice.
2. Provide them with logic that helps them hold on to the conviction in your idea.
3. Speak so as to resonate with their accountabilities (such as their moral codes, their societal roles).
4. Introduce distinctions that will focus their conversations on characteristics that give you an advantage.
5. Establish metaphors to give them something to envision that links to what they already know.
6. Retell their stories so that adopting your innovation seems a natural progression of the past.
7. Structure incentives so that they feel better off adopting what you have to offer.

In order for your vision to become an innovation, your idea to become reality, you must transform behavior. The Wood phase lays down a long, seemingly thankless challenge that many innovators fail to accept and conquer. But you can triumph by applying the above concepts and transforming perceptions, increasing your odds at reaching the other side: the Fire, or breakout, phase.

CHAPTER SIX

FIRE: BREAKOUT

"We were very, very, lucky. But then chance favors the prepared mind and we were preparing ourselves for this day for a long time, almost 11 years, and when it happened, we seized it with both hands."

—N. R. Narayana Murthy, cofounder, Infosys Technologies

In 1989, the cofounders of a software firm called Infosys gathered to assess their situation. In the first eight years, their company had grown from the original seven cofounders to almost fifty employees. From their initial investment of 10,000 rupees, they now owned a company that generated 25 million rupees in annual revenue (1.5 million USD), with offices in India and the United States.

Though they were clearly making progress, the founders were troubled. The company's growth had been steady but slower than they had hoped. They were spending more time far from home, working at client locations, than they wanted. At the time, India was not known for its engineering talent and had no significant technology sector. The founders wondered whether their dream was feasible, whether their model was working, whether they should abandon their venture entirely.

Further frustration for the founders came from an antiquated web of regulations the Indian government had imposed on the importation of computers and other technology. It could take nine months just to secure an import license for a new computer. Large Indian companies hired entire departments of lobbyists to get imports through the Indian governmental bureaucracy. Infosys, too small to afford such an investment, struggled constantly to do its work efficiently. Its staff was forced to spend most of its time working on clients' computers in the clients' offices.

On that day in 1989, six of the seven cofounders took part in the debate, reviewing their goals and exploring their options. The seventh, N. R. Narayana Murthy, who had led the company as its CEO, remained quiet. He let his colleagues express their frustrations and watched them wind down to their conclusion: They would fold the company.

Finally Murthy spoke. He expressed his conviction that the company could succeed and, as a sign of this, offered to buy out each of his colleagues if that's what they wanted. But he invited them instead to recommit to the company and with him build it into one of the world's leading information technology companies. The other founders had followed Murthy for eight years and their belief in him persisted. They agreed to continue their fight.

Less than three years later, the decision to persist suddenly paid off. In 1992 the Indian government issued a series of groundbreaking reforms that liberated the technology sector. By the end of that year the Indian economy began adjusting to its freedom—importing hardware, assembling high-tech backbones, modernizing corporations, and using technology to modernize entire sectors of the economy. Infosys, which had spent the decade assembling everything else it needed, was perfectly poised to participate. It was as if the final piece of a slowly evolving puzzle had appeared.

Infosys's profits more than doubled that year and continued to grow at an astounding pace for more than a decade. The company, which revolutionized the way software customization is done worldwide, emerged as one of the world's leading technology companies with offices spread across India, Australia, China, Hong Kong, Japan, Mauritius, the United Arab Emirates, Canada, the United States, and Europe.

The Trigger

"After our sixth store opened, our competitors came after us. We had underestimated how aggressively they would come, especially AutoNation."

—Austin Ligon, CEO, CarMax

The plot twist of the sort that launched Infosys's miraculous growth is a common one among great innovations. After a long period of high effort and slow progress, when innovators are disheartened nearly to the point of giving up, without warning the final missing piece of the puzzle moves into position and triggers sudden growth. The picture is now complete. Revenues take off, customers flock in, partners want to join, and, unfortunately, competitors take notice.

The trigger that creates the shift from Wood to Fire occurs abruptly. Unlike what you might imagine, the Wood does not catch Fire gradually; it remains unchanged until the final piece is in place and everything happens in an instant. Infosys had assembled proprietary technology, a team of engineers, project management experience, a roster of international clients, and processes and best practices for running IT projects. But none of this was sufficient to trigger a takeoff. Not until the final piece appeared—when the government reformed technology regulations—did the company's assets begin producing in a meaningful way.

This trigger is one kind of tipping point. Most of those whose study of innovation focuses on the notion of the tipping point consider only customer adoption. They look at how successful innovators convince that critical, influential customer base to adopt the innovation and then tell their friends about it so that adoption takes off, in the cycle described in Chapter 5. But this is focusing on just one piece of the puzzle. Many innovations—Infosys, Post-it Notes, digital video recorders, to name a few—reach the tipping point not because of customer adoption but rather because some other player—a CEO, the government, a partner—suddenly made possible what was not possible before.

To trigger an innovation's takeoff requires understanding the overall system, rather than focusing on just users or consumers, because the blockage to growth may exist somewhere else.

When Wood shifts to Fire, innovators find themselves in a fundamentally different type of game. The patient persistence that made them successful during the plodding period is precisely what would have them fail during the Fire phase. The game has shifted from slow to fast, from predictable to fluid, requiring the innovator to adopt new tactics. As Sun Tzu wrote, "Do not repeat the tactics which have gained you one victory, but let your methods be regulated by the infinite variety of circumstances." The innovator must adjust to a new game, one that rewards rapid reaction rather than slow determination, that is won with tactics rather than grand strategy, and that draws on intuition more than calculation.

> *"Energy may be likened to the bending of a crossbow; decision, to the releasing of a trigger."*
>
> —*Sun Tzu*, The Art of War

Fire: managing competitive response

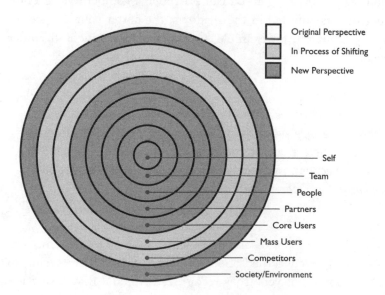

- Original Perspective
- In Process of Shifting
- New Perspective

- Self
- Team
- People
- Partners
- Core Users
- Mass Users
- Competitors
- Society/Environment

Those who have dedicated themselves to understanding the Fire phase have arrived at surprisingly consistent findings. Specifically, they advise adopting six principles:

1. Postpone competitive response
2. Shift from strategy to tactics
3. Play the mental and moral games of conflict
4. Get inside the opponent's decision cycle
5. Unleash a variety of unorthodox tactics
6. Seize the unexpected

Postpone Competitive Response

"No enterprise is more likely to succeed than one concealed from the enemy until it is ripe for execution."

—Niccolo Machiavelli

Companies that successfully topple their industry's leaders experience a consistent sequence of challenges. First, they work through all the challenges to launching a new competitive action; then they manage customer reaction; then, if they are successful, the competition reacts. The longer you can postpone a competitive reaction and grow uncontested in the shadows, the better your chances of success. Contrast, for example, the cases of Gatorade and Under Armour.

Gatorade

"The spot where we intend to fight must not be made known; for then the enemy will have to prepare against a possible attack at several different points; and his forces being thus distributed in many directions, the numbers we shall have to face at any given point will be proportionately few."

—Sun Tzu, The Art of War

In 1965, four professors at the University of Florida medical school became concerned about the injuries they were seeing in the UF football players (they recognized Metal). They tested the players during a practice and found that their electrolyte and blood sugar levels were remarkably low. The solution was obvious: They needed a way to replace those substances and rehydrate players sweating under the Florida sun more quickly than did water and other current options. They formulated a beverage that blended salt, to replace the salt lost in sweat, with a carefully calculated amount of sugar. They added lemon flavoring for taste, and named the drink after the team's nickname, "The Gators."

The first on-field tests of this drink came during a now-legendary scrimmage between UF's B team and UF freshmen. As Robert Cade, one of the drink's inventors, recalled, "At the end of the first half, the B team was ahead 13–0. They pushed the freshmen around pretty good. In the third period, the freshmen, who had been given the solution, came out and began pushing the B team around. They scored two or three touchdowns in the third period and five or six more in the fourth period." This evidence convinced UF's coach to provide Gatorade to his players.

The product worked well, so the academics began building the pieces they needed to make Gatorade a success (Wood). They found a company that could manufacture their formula and convinced the University of Florida football team to adopt Gatorade as its official drink.

As the 1960s were coming to a close, so was Gatorade's Wood phase. In 1967, the UF football team won its first Orange Bowl title. When reporters asked the coach of the opposing team, Georgia Tech, to explain his loss, he said Gatorade made the difference. His team did not have it; UF's team did. Two years later, the Kansas City Chiefs won the Super Bowl and gave part of the credit to Gatorade.

With two national victories credited to Gatorade, the drink took off. Teams across the country, across sports (football, soccer, and volleyball among them), and across levels (from pee-wee to college to professional leagues) began serving Gatorade to their players.

What happened next was perhaps the most critical dynamic of the Gatorade story. An innovation's success often hinges on who responds first—the competition or the mass market. In the case of Gatorade, it was the mass market.

Gatorade enjoyed a meteoric rise in popularity, but always as a pure sports drink. We saw it on the sidelines of football fields, or being dumped over the head of the victorious team's coach, but it didn't make it onto supermarket shelves or into consumers' refrigerators. So the competitors, who should have seen Gatorade as a threat, did not notice what was happening. Coca-Cola, Pepsi, and Kool-Aid were all well positioned to launch competing drinks. They could have used their superior marketing muscle and access to shelf space to squeeze Gatorade out. But because Gatorade seemed to be a niche beverage purchased almost exclusively by sports organizations, the competition was slow to catch on.

In the absence of competitive resistance, Gatorade continued to grow quickly. Soon everyday consumers were looking for sports drinks to consume between tennis matches or after working out. By the time competitors realized that Gatorade had created a new class of beverage, Gatorade had already established a superior brand.

Competitors tried to copy Gatorade's innovation but could not gain share against the drink that the Super Bowl winners preferred. Today Gatorade is still the leading sports drink brand in the world.

Under Armour

In 1996, under conditions not unlike those of Gatorade's birth, Kevin Plank, a former football player, founded a company called Under Armour. While he was playing ball he had to change his undershirt several times during every game or practice. He knew other players dealt with the same inconvenience, so he decided to look for a solution (he recognized Metal). He developed a T-shirt made of an innovative fabric that could wick sweat away from the body, promoting evaporation and cooling body temperature, essentially allowing sweat to perform the duty it was naturally intended to do. He raised about $300,000 in funding and started a company around his invention.

In just one year, he was able to convince twelve college football teams and ten NFL teams to begin wearing his Under Armour products. Over the following three years, he notched several business deals that propelled Under Armour into national awareness. He got his products into the hit football movie *Any Given Sunday*, he expanded distribution into retail stores (eventually reaching 2,500 stores by 2002), and he launched a national print and television advertising campaign. An IPO issued in November 2005 raised $133 million. The company's stock jumped from a $13 offer to close at $25 on the first day of trading, and continued to rise to about $50 by 2007.

By many measures, the Under Armour innovation is a success. It is certainly one any entrepreneur would be proud of. However, the test of Fire is often what separates the highly successful from the industry-transforming. Both these innovations created new categories: the sports drink, and high-performance sports apparel. However, Under Armour's rapid and very public rise attracted the attention of competitors much earlier than Gatorade did, and so it enjoyed a far shorter period of uncontested growth. Nike, Reebok, and other large athletic apparel companies responded aggressively with copycat brands.

After nearly three decades of competition, Gatorade still dominates the sports drink market, commanding an 80 percent market share. After just one decade of competition, Under Armour has reached parity with its larger competitors, capturing about 31 percent of the athletic apparel market. To maintain its position against its deeper-pocket rivals it will need to invest heavily in brand recognition, with expensive print and television ads.

This is not a story of success versus failure but rather one of degree. Innovations that can postpone competitive response have the potential to dominate their markets. Those who must manage the competition early face worse odds. When the wave of competition rises, you want your stance firmly planted.

Luckily, the game does not automatically end when the competition wakes up. There are methods for dealing with the competition so that you can successfully navigate the Fire phase.

Shift from Strategy to Tactics

"Good tactics can save even the worst strategy. Bad tactics will destroy even the best strategy."

—*General George S. Patton*

During the Water phase you set your grand strategy. During the Wood phase you secure your key positions and resources. During the Fire phase you move into tactics. That means you may have to deviate from the original strategy as you adapt to emerging circumstances.

It is this ability to adjust that often separates successful innovations from well-planned dreams. Xerox, for example, invented the laser printer, Ethernet, the graphical computer interface, and the computer mouse but commercialized none of them. The company was an outstanding innovator but proved unable for many years to light its ideas on fire. The small decisions that your teammates make every day can kill or make your strategic intent.

So we must peek into the mind of the tactician, the creative, flexible individual who can keep focused on the vision, mission, and grand strategy while at the same time adjusting quickly and intuitively to rapidly emerging changes. No one has invested more time in understanding how master tacticians think than Colonel John Boyd.

Forty-Second Boyd

Boyd was born in Erie, Pennsylvania, on January 23, 1927. After earning two bachelor's degrees, one in economics and one in industrial engineering, he joined the army and eventually moved on to the U.S. Air Force, where he proved himself to be to air-to-air combat what Michael Jordan was to basketball.

During the Korean War he was promoted to tactical instructor for his squadron. He had a tough challenge: The American fighter pilots flew F86 aircraft; their opponents flew Russian-built MiGs that accelerated faster and had greater firepower. By introducing his tactical principles, Boyd trained his pilots to dominate their better-equipped opponents. For every U.S. plane shot down, U.S. pilots shot down ten MiGs.

Throughout Boyd's life he held a standing bet: He would fly against any opponent and within forty seconds have that person locked in his sights. John Boyd never lost that bet.

As his reputation grew and he progressed from fighter pilot to tactical trainer to strategist, the U.S. military asked him to formally analyze his success as a pilot and tactician. He studied dogfights to understand why one pilot beats another. He studied historical battles to distinguish what makes one army successful over another. After several years of research, he synthesized his findings into a philosophy of strategy that emphasized tactical maneuvers. He arrived at a set of conclusions that are remarkably consistent with a military genius who embarked on a similar challenge to understand conflict 2,500 years earlier: Sun Tzu.

Both John Boyd and Sun Tzu agree on several principles for skillfully managing conflict. They both emphasize, for example, that physical conflict is the least efficient option. They believe that states should turn to the military only after less costly means, including diplomacy, prove inadequate. They both argue that even when physical conflict is inevitable, the most skilled tacticians first attack their opponents' minds and moral stamina before attacking their person.

They both found that size does not predict outcome. Small armies regularly defeat large ones just as small companies regularly topple incumbents (for example: the Mongols versus China in the 1200s; the American Colonies versus Great Britain in the revolution; Algeria versus France in the early 1950s; Chad versus Libya in 1987). Analyzing historical conflicts showed Boyd that focus, agility, speed, and unpredictability are far more important than size or resources. Study the history of any great company—all of which at some point overcame a larger, better-financed competitor—and you find the same.

Boyd's findings form the foundation of what military strategists now call "fourth generation warfare" (4GW). His theories, as we shall see, encapsulate succinctly what it takes for an innovation to win over competitive resistance.

Play the Mental and Moral Games of Conflict

"Things pass for what they seem, not for what they are."

—Baltasar Gracián,
The Art of Worldly Wisdom, *Maxim #99*

Boyd's theories are rooted in his view that conflict occurs on three levels: physical, mental, and moral. Physical warfare is the one we can see on television. It involves tanks, bombs, and guns. It is the one that those less skilled at conflict focus on because it is the one they can see.

Mental warfare occurs in your opponent's mind and involves how he perceives his environment and situation. Moral warfare is waged higher still, and involves the belief structures held by you, your opponent, and society in general. If you ignore the higher levels of conflict you risk losing or creating unsustainable victories.

This hierarchical framework bears a remarkable similarity to the conclusions arrived at by others who have studied change. It is no coincidence that they describe a similar concept of conflicts operating on multiple levels, with the physical one occupying a lower rung.

Physical Conflict

Physical warfare is becoming increasingly difficult to wage. Military theorists point out that warfare no longer occurs on open fields across clearly demarcated lines. 4GW battles involve enemies that are difficult to isolate physically because they embed themselves among the population. Laser-guided smart bombs increase our accuracy, but even technologies such as this are insufficient.

Corporate competition is experiencing a similar evolution. As communication across long distances becomes easy to achieve, consumers are identifying themselves less and less by geography. Whereas before you could market differently to Americans than you did to Indians, today Indian consumers are but a mouse-click away from knowing what product you are selling in the United States.

It has become increasingly difficult to physically isolate customers, and even competitors. The next level of conflict must come into play.

Mental Conflict

The mental level of conflict involves manipulating your opponent's perception. While you want your users—customers, partners—to understand your innovation, you do not want your competitors to understand it.

It's an ancient principle. Sun Tzu believed "all warfare is deception" and spent much of his life cataloging the various ways one could employ this strategy on the battlefield. For his part, John Boyd dove into the fundamental source of perception—the human brain—to pinpoint the strings one might use to manipulate perception. He recognized that human beings create mental images that seem to match up with what they observe and use these to explain what is going on around them. Boyd and Sun Tzu used this fundamental wiring of the human brain to disrupt resistance.

For example, Gatorade postponed competitive resistance because it prevented (perhaps unintentionally) its competition from understanding the product or its potential. Competitors saw a distinction between sports drinks and nonsports drinks, between what serious athletes needed and what recreational athletes would want. The Gatorade people shrewdly took advantage of this.

Had Gatorade's competitors called Gatorade a soft drink instead of a sports drink, they may have responded earlier and with greater force. Had IBM called the processor the brain of the computer and not just another component, it may not have given it away to Intel. Had Yahoo! called Google an Internet company and not a search service, it may not have given Google the leg up it needed to dominate advertising.

Instead, what happened? Google convinced Yahoo! it had no interest in selling advertising so it posed no threat. Intel convinced IBM it would make its technology broadly available so IBM need not fear depending on one microchip provider. Gatorade convinced large beverage companies it would remain a niche brand focused on sporting organizations rather than everyday consumers. All these innovators were playing on the mental level of conflict. They deflated resistance and expanded unchallenged.

Moral Conflict

"Preserve or build up our moral authority while compromising that of our adversaries in order to pump up our resolve, drain away adversaries' resolve, and attract them as well as others to our cause and way of life."

—Colonel John Boyd

One level above mental conflict lie the morals that guide our actions and perceived options. Boyd found that successful armies are able to use moral rules to isolate their opponents from their allies. Isolating your enemy from its supporters not only robs it of needed power but also demoralizes its people.

If during the Water phase an innovation adopts a purpose of superior moral grounds, there exists a possibility to wield this moral shield now, in the face of the competition, to deflate resistance. When your competitors find no moral grounds on which to oppose you, their resistance will grow weak. The inconsistency between morals and actions must be resolved. The opposition must either deny its guiding codes of conduct or it must drop its resistance to your innovation.

Get Inside the Opponent's Decision Cycle

"In battle, this ability to rapidly pass through the observation-orientation-decision-action loop (the Boyd cycle) gave American pilots a slight time advantage. If one views a dogfight as a series of Boyd cycles, one sees that the Americans would repeatedly gain a time advantage each cycle, until the enemy's actions became totally inappropriate for the changing situations."

—Robert Leonhard, The Art of Maneuver

When Boyd studied how highly successful air tacticians outmaneuver their opponents, he found that they pass through a four-
step decision cycle (Boyd's OODA loop):

1. Observe the environment.
2. Orient themselves to what is happening around them.
3. Decide the best course of action.
4. Act quickly to execute this decision.

Winners of tactical bouts cycle through these four steps more
quickly than do losers. Each time they do so, they increase their lead
over their adversary, each time creating a gap in their adversary's
mind between what he observes and what is actually happening.
This gap grows with each cycle until the opponent's observations
and actions are based so deeply in the past, no longer relevant, that
the opponent collapses. This is like using an old computer that is
too slow to keep up with your clicks and key taps. You hit a button
and while the computer is responding you are clicking on the next
button. As the computer opens its pop-up window, it realizes you
have already clicked that window. By the time it figures out what
to do next you are already onto the third and fourth click. Eventually your computer falls into such confusion that it crashes. Great
tacticians make their opponents feel like outdated computers.

Boyd's principle has been at work for millennia, determining
winners and losers on battlefields and in corporate conflicts. We
find evidence that the time required for decision cycles determined
competitiveness in business as early as the turn of the nineteenth
century. In the early 1800s Hudson's Bay, a trading company, was
facing collapse because a competitor, North West Company, with
a more flexible, decentralized management structure, had adopted
a new distribution strategy, locating its trading posts closer to customers. Hudson's Bay's centralized bureaucracy hindered its reaction time, and by 1809 the company seemed destined to close. In
that year, however, Hudson's Bay's ownership changed hands. The
new leadership quickly copied its rival's approach, moving trading
posts closer to customers and decentralizing operations.

By reacting quickly to a changing environment, the new owners saved their company. Hudson's Bay beat its rival, merging with it ten years later, and survived as the Hudson's Bay Company, the oldest commercial enterprise in Canada.

What Hudson's Bay realized was that its opponent had gotten inside Hudson's Bay's decision cycle or OODA loop. This happens when an innovator adopts a pace that is simply faster than the opposition so that not only can it respond more quickly but it disrupts its opponent's OODA loop.

We can mathematically represent the principle with the following equations:

- **IC** = industry cycle time, or the frequency with which the industry experiences significant macro-changes
- **DCa** = decision cycle time for company "a," or the amount of time it takes company "a" to launch a significant new tactic or strategy
- **DCb** = decision cycle time for company "b"
- **If IC < DCa and DCb,** both companies fail to respond to changes in the environment and risk dying out during the next industry shock.
- **If DCa < IC < DCb,** company "a" will survive the next shock and company "b" will die out.
- **If DCa < DCb < IC,** both companies are equipped to survive industry changes but company "a" will outmaneuver company "b," seize opportunities first, and eventually dance around its competitor until company "b" falls.

Some industries have adopted extremely short decision cycles. Consider cruise lines. Unlike most industries, which make pricing changes once per season, cruise lines employ teams of people who analyze purchasing behaviors and reset prices four times per day. These "revenue management" experts might, for example, observe that interior rooms are filling up more quickly than exterior rooms and so they would slightly raise prices on interior rooms. They spend the next hour observing changes and then notice that rooms with balconies are selling too quickly, indicating they may be able to raise prices for those rooms. Now imagine what it would be like to be the first in your industry to adopt revenue management. While your competition resets prices once per year, you reset them five times a day. You manage to get inside their price-setting cycle and leave them disoriented.

During the Fire phase this ability to cycle quickly becomes even more critical. Adjusting tactics more quickly enables you to get inside your opponent's OODA loop. But using this principle to its full potential also means looking at the variety and creativity of the new tactics you launch.

Unleash a Variety of Unorthodox Tactics

"The skillful tactician may be likened to the shuaijan. Now the shuaijan is a snake that is found in the Chung mountains. Strike at its head, and you will be attacked by its tail; strike at its tail, and you will be attacked by its head; strike at its middle, and you will be attacked by head and tail both."

—*Sun Tzu,* The Art of War

To further quell opposition it helps to put your opponent in unfamiliar situations. Inviting your opponents into an environment they have never navigated will make them hesitate. Their hesitation leaves openings for you to advance with less effort.

Conflicts are a matter of the play between the orthodox and extraordinary. If you can learn to recognize the orthodox and respond with the extraordinary, you can minimize opposition. Reducing resistance to your innovation during the Fire phase involves playing with the constantly evolving cycle of orthodox and extraordinary. As Sun Tzu wrote, "use the orthodox to engage, use the extraordinary to attain victory."

When the British Army lined up soldiers to battle the American revolutionaries, they presented a bold, red, overpowering front. But the line they expected to appear before them never materialized. Instead the enemy hid behind trees, shooting at the British from dark corners. This is the form that successful innovators seem to take. They fluster their opposition with a rapid sequence of tactics that fragments the opposition's expectations and leaves them paralyzed with a bag of useless operating procedures and best practices, unsure of how to respond.

During the Fire phase, innovators similarly launch a set of new tactics that put their opposition in unfamiliar situations that in turn slow or even paralyze resistance. Recall from the Water chapter that Whole Foods is disrupting its competition with a strategy that big supermarket chains resist copying. It sells only natural foods and sells them above market prices. It executes this grand strategy with several smaller tactics, each of which slows competitive response:

- It launched its own label, "Whole Trade Guarantee," that works like the Free Trade Certification program. Foods that carry the label are proven to be grown on farms that adopt sound environmental practices. By setting and owning the standard, Whole Foods is able to expand its brand and increase its appeal to growers.
- Its buyers focus on sourcing local products. Large chains, which fight for every point of their small operating margins, are on a constant search for scale, which leads them to prefer large national suppliers.

At Whole Foods, this list of tactics is constantly growing. Each week people from throughout the organization conceive new, creative ways to lengthen the company's lead over the competition.

Infosys provides another example. When government changes allowed the company to finally take off, it had to contend with new competitors from all directions. Other Indian IT firms were eager to capitalize on the new world order, in which India would become the technology outsourcing home for the world. United States and European technology firms wanted to defend their long-held dominance of technology services. To help immunize itself from competition, Infosys adopted a stream of innovative tactics that kept the competition constantly facing unfamiliar challenges:

- It was one of the first Indian firms to adopt the concept of sweat equity, in which employees can earn equity in the company not through cash investments but as reward for their time and effort.
- Recognizing that the majority of the company's value comes not from hard assets (such as factories and inventory) but rather from its people; Infosys was the first to measure the value of its human capital and list it as an asset on its balance sheet.
- It was the first Indian company to adopt a code of transparency that gave investors clear insight into the company's financials.
- It was the first Indian company to offer stock options to employees.

Map these and Infosys's numerous other "firsts" onto a time line, and we clearly see why such innovators overwhelmed their competition: They unleashed unpredictable moves at a rapid pace, flustering the opposition, pushing resistors into constant reaction mode.

Patterns of Competition

The need to unleash unorthodox tactics raises the question of how people become able to conceive of such innovative moves.

Scientists who have studied the cognitive workings of creativity have discovered that human brains create new ideas by combining and translating patterns. Unlike computers, human brains are not designed to act or create using logic. We are excellent pattern-recognition machines and we create by using what Einstein called "signs or images" and combining them in new ways. Patterns are fundamental to our ability to conceive new, unorthodox tactics.

The Thirty-Six Stratagems

"There are just thirty-six strategies under the sun."

—Chinese saying

Following this finding, I have spent the past decade applying a set of thirty-six strategic patterns, captured in a set of Chinese metaphors, to the creation of business strategy. There is a list of these patterns in Appendix A of this book. You can read full descriptions of each in my earlier book, *The Art of the Advantage,* and learn how they are enacted in my follow-up, *Hide a Dagger Behind a Smile.*

In following the stories of about four hundred competitive rivalries, I have found these thirty-six moves to be a powerful set of tools for explaining, predicting, and designing competitiveness. By stocking your people's reservoirs with new patterns, you help them expand their abilities to see new strategic options. They can then better apply their strategic creativity to autonomously seize advantages that your competition leaves open. Your organization becomes like the snake Sun Tzu described. Your tail and your head, acting as if independent, fluster your opponents into confusion and then inaction.

Many hold the view that we make strategy and then execute it. But there is no formal line between strategy and execution; rather, the two are linked by a stretch of gray. Decisions made every day, across every dimension of a company—how purchases are made, how mail is delivered, how prices are set, what behavior is rewarded—all have the potential to put the competition off-guard. Collectively they determine whether the initial strategy will succeed at all or smash against the wall of competition.

Seize the Unexpected

"There are rules of luck and the wise do not leave it all to chance. Luck can be assisted by care. Some content themselves with placing themselves confidently at the gate of fortune, waiting till she opens it. Others do better, and press forward and profit by their clever boldness, reaching the goddess and winning her favor on the wings of their virtue and valor. But a true philosophy has no other umpire than virtue and insight—for there is no good or bad luck except wisdom and foolishness."

—Baltasar Gracián, The Art of Worldly Wisdom, *Maxim #21*

The innovator's success depends on reacting to conditions that are in constant change, on recognizing momentary and unexpected opportunities as they arise. You cannot plan for them. You cannot save them for future use.

The dynamism of the Fire stage may make success look like arbitrary luck. We could say, for example, that Starbucks lucked into the coffee craze that was about to hit the United States, that Logitech lucked into producing computer mice just as the PC was taking off. We could say that both companies have come to dominate their industries by simply being at the right place at the right time.

But analyze truly innovative companies and the "luck" explanation fails. It does not explain how Starbucks later "lucked" into food retailing and music publishing, or how Logitech happened to again be in the right place when webcams started taking off.

How do such companies create their luck? The answer lies in their tactics. With Wood you created options; through Fire you shift them, when they are ripe, into value.

Success during Fire, then, requires abandoning the cause-and-effect mindset that dominates most of the discourse about modern business strategy. Succeeding during Fire is not about predicting, but rather about seizing the unpredictable. By shifting from hard to soft to hard, from rigid to fluid to rigid, and doing so more quickly than others, you can prepare yourself to lengthen your lead with every flux in the market.

Preparing for Earth

The day after Hurricane Katrina pulled apart New Orleans, leaving buildings without roofs and people without homes, the city's mayor declared the city had survived. The hurricane slowed as it approached the city, hitting its buildings with less force than anticipated. So structural damage, while significant, was not what it could have been and the death count promised to be less than people feared. The city had faced the Fire and survived.

Then the levees that kept New Orleans from being swallowed by the rivers and lakes that hover above its below-sea-level location broke. Water flooded into the city's poorest areas, wiping away houses that had just recently withstood hurricane-force winds. Many who had survived the battering of Katrina and thought they were lucky suddenly realized that the threat's form had changed but was still far from gone.

While we will debate for many years the premature declaration that the city had survived, it underscores a common failure among innovators who attempt to navigate through the Fire phase. They let up too soon. They want to celebrate their victory before the victory is secure. They forget that the competitor they must first overcome is often followed by another, more threatening one.

In the excitement of the Fire, the rush of rapid progress, you will be tempted to declare victory too soon. Countless innovations, as we will see shortly, have fallen victim to this natural response. You have beaten the competition, emerged victorious from the Fire, and now want to celebrate your success. But as you sit on your throne, your castle's foundations, built on shifting sands, are eroding. If you do not take seriously the important job of consolidating your gains—firming your innovation's foundation into hard Earth—the competition will swallow you up. The next chapter looks at how innovators sustain their efforts.

CHAPTER SEVEN

EARTH: CONSOLIDATION

"After crossing a river you should move far away from it."

—*Sun Tzu,* The Art of War

In 1897 Great Britain orchestrated one of history's grandest cel-ebrations, Queen Victoria's Diamond Jubilee. Some 46,000 troops gathered with eleven colonial prime ministers to pay homage to the longest reigning British monarch, and tens of thousands cheered the queen along her procession. In Australia, Canada, New Zea-land, South Africa, and other British territories around the globe, people gathered in similarly grand parades to celebrate the queen's sixty-year reign.

At the time, Victoria ruled over one-fourth of the world's pop-ulation. The Jubilee symbolized to the world that the United King-dom had achieved power of historic proportions, a standing that the *New York Times* reinforced in reporting the occasion: "We are a part . . . of the Greater Britain which seems plainly destined to dominate this planet."

By all known measures, Great Britain had changed the world and firmly consolidated its power. Yet now from our viewpoint of a century later, we can see that history treated Great Britain as it did other powers it lent dominance to. It gave Great Britain dominance for a while and then, as it did for Egypt, the Ottomans, Athens, and Rome, took it away.

Earth: consolidating your gains

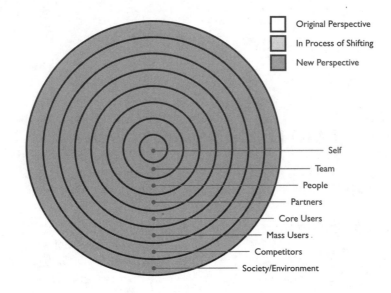

Slowing Down History

Dominance inevitably attracts competition. This is as true in business as it is in governance. Philips, the Dutch electronics company, for example, changed the world when it developed and introduced the CD-ROM. The company's research and development efforts produced a novel technology that enabled us to store unprecedented amounts of music and data on thin, round discs—a dramatic leap in performance over the prevailing technology. Because the company was smart in how it commercialized its invention, Philips's CDs took off. It transformed entire industries. Computer rooms filled with walls of spinning magnetic tape reels are out and PCs with small CD burners are in. VHS tapes are out and DVDs are in. The entire music industry has migrated from selling cassettes to CDs; today artists release "disks" rather than "albums." Though the Philips CD was by many measures a huge success, the invention eventually drew imitators who eroded Philips's profits. Copycat manufacturers popped up throughout Asia, ready to churn out CDs at commodity prices. Unable to defend its profits, Philips was pulled into the brawl, fighting for each inch of margin. Though still the innovator, today Philips generates little value from its world-changing innovation.

Companies that make it through Fire but fail at Earth succeed in driving adoption of their innovation, then lose their ownership. But companies that fail to navigate Fire just trigger adoption and the competition eats them up while users are starting to adopt. When customers adopt on a large scale and then competition enters, you have made it through Fire. But when the competition enters while only a small percentage of users have adopted, you have not successfully managed the Fire phase. Philips held off the competition during the Fire phase as companies and computer users embraced CDs. As a result, Philips reached the top and was crowned king of CD hill, the inventor of the CD. But after making it through Fire, Philips's hill eroded under its heels.

What happened to Philips is the too-common story of innovators who successfully see an opportunity (Metal), design a strategy (Water), build the resources (Wood), navigate through early competition (Fire), and then eventually stumble. Many innovators, even after years of success, are unable to protect their gains.

How do you prevent your innovation from running away from you or, worse yet, letting others steal it away? How can you avoid the fate of ideas like the personal computer, which IBM invented but the most valuable components of which it then gave away to Microsoft and Intel? Or direct current (DC), which gained acceptance but lost out to alternating current (AC)? Or Betamax, the videocassette recording standard that lost out to the inferior VHS alternative?

If innovation is to last, you must consolidate your gains. This requires yet another major shift: from the fast-paced, unorthodox movement of Fire into an entirely opposite stance. Until now you have been focused on unraveling resistance to change. Now that your innovation has won out, you want to slow down the corrosive threat of change. Before, you fought rigidity; now you want it.

Before, you sought to deconstruct the barriers to change; now you want to construct them. In order for your innovation to succeed, you must enter the Earth phase.

Replace the Source of Your Advantage

Most companies grow into greatness through creativity. They make counterintuitive choices that slow competitive reaction or, better yet, convince the competition to drop their resistance. But these types of advantages eventually erode because their success inevitably attracts imitators. The competition eventually grows impatient with losing market share or grows hungry enough to step off the sidelines to try to take what you have.

There is much debate between sustainable and temporary advantages: Which is more important? Which do competitive companies really use? But the debate assumes a simplified, static world in which strategy is a fixed thing that either works or does not work. Look more deeply into the histories of great companies and you will see that their strategies experience a fundamental shift at maturity. Just as a child gives up crawling and instead starts to walk, companies evolve new methods to move forward.

The approaches that the innovation depended on to grow must give way to a fundamentally different mindset if the innovation is to sustain. Innovations grow by choosing what the competition will not choose; but to consolidate their gains they must raise their walls one layer further and be able to do what the competition cannot do. The "choose" advantage helps you grow. The "cannot" advantage sustains your position.

Wal-Mart, for example, grew relatively unchallenged for over a decade. Its much larger competitors, Sears and JCPenney, were focused on building stores just outside of major cities. Through luck, necessity, or foresight, Sam Walton avoided the cities and began building discount stores in rural towns that Sears and JCPenney were ignoring. For years, Walton steadily grew his base of stores, expanding town by town, while the competition remained locked in on selling to city shoppers.

During Wal-Mart's Fire stage, revenue growth rode up its steep curve while the company perfected its brand and built customer loyalty. Wal-Mart's primary advantage during this period was that the competition chose not to attack. Because the competition held off year after year, Wal-Mart grew unchallenged in the seemingly unimportant rural areas of the United States.

Eventually Sears and JCPenney woke up. They realized that a major redistribution was underway, with the U.S. population moving out of the large cities into suburban and rural areas in massive numbers. By the time the leading retailers took notice of Wal-Mart, it had solidified its wall. The wall was too high for Sears to surmount it.

What made Wal-Mart competitive (targeting the rural areas that competitors ignored) was different from what kept the company competitive over subsequent years. While Wal-Mart was building its chain in rural America, it was also building a tightly knit distribution network. Many believe Wal-Mart uses size to negotiate lower prices from suppliers. But there is no meaningful evidence to support this view. What is clear, however, is that Wal-Mart can deliver its goods to its stores at a lower cost than the competition can.

When Sears decided to start building new rural stores, its trucks had to make long, expensive trips to supply these stores with goods. Wal-Mart had built close clusters of stores in the same rural area. This allowed Wal-Mart trucks to stop at a good number of stores with each trip, while Sears trucks stopped at just a few. The difference may seem minor, but it affords two critical advantages. First, Wal-Mart can replenish its stores more often. This means the stores have fresher merchandise and can respond more quickly when they discover that a particular product is selling well. Second, Wal-Mart can create a significant cost advantage over its competition.

Because each Wal-Mart truck is visiting multiple stores, it travels with empty space less often. Since stores can count on replenishing stock more often, they need to carry less inventory.

Multiply this across the entire system and you create a hard-to-copy advantage.

This new advantage has little to do with Wal-Mart's original one (a focus on rural areas the competition was ignoring). This shift in tactics is a key characteristic of the Earth phase. Some tactics are good for seizing new ground but inappropriate for protecting it. To hold your ground you must change your weapons. You must build walls.

Sustaining an innovation requires slowing the erosion of time. It involves erecting new defenses.

While there are innumerable ways to build walls around your innovation, three repeatedly appear as the most important sources of long-term competitive advantage. You have to:

1. Lock in clients
2. Lock out competition
3. Lock up resources

Lock in Clients

Many sociological studies show that we tend to shift our behavior to match that of those around us. We may temporarily adopt a stronger work ethic or exercise more or act out in anger less, but the people in our community pull us like gravity back toward the status quo.

The pull of assimilation is strong. It pulls on your people and your customers. You may convince your customers to prefer your product for a time, but if you do not lock in this new behavior they will eventually return to what they did before. To sustain your innovation, you must make those behavior changes permanent.

Companies that sustain their innovation do three things well: They reprogram customers, build dependent identities, and remove the risk of changing customer behavior.

Reprogram Customers

Mardi Gras is the greatest carnival in the United States. Every year thousands flock from around the country onto the crowded streets of New Orleans to cheer the parades. The social rules of Mardi Gras are somewhat complex. Various social clubs compete each year to put on the best parade. They select a king and queen, they decide on a theme, they spend months constructing elaborate floats, each member buys a large stash of plastic beads, and over the course of a few hours, they parade the floats along a predetermined route, throwing beads to screaming spectators.

For most onlookers, the goal of Mardi Gras is to get those beads—the more, the bigger, the more unique the better. Over the week of Mardi Gras the currency of New Orleans practically transforms from dollars to beads. But there is one float that confounds first-time visitors. When the "King Kong" float appears, the flow of beads suddenly reverses. Spectators lift beads off their neck, ball them into their palms, and throw them at the float. The costumed people on the float become, instead of the usual bead throwers, bead catchers, and dodgers, almost unable to get beads off their float.

Why do people throw beads at the King Kong float? Underpinning this reversal of behavior lies the key to locking in customers.

Years ago someone decided to build a float that was completely covered in a display of King Kong. The construction was so large there was no room on the float for bead throwers. When the King Kong float first wound through New Orleans' streets, people were unsure what to do. Since there was no platform for bead throwers, there was no chance of getting beads and so no reason to cheer. Instead, someone in the crowd impulsively threw a string of beads at the King Kong float. Someone else saw this, thought it was a good idea, and joined in. Eventually spectators' behavior all along the parade route changed.

Today the King Kong float has been redesigned so that it can carry bead catchers rather than throwers, since the practice of throwing beads at King Kong, trying to snag the beads on his head and arms, continues. It has become a tradition. It shows the power of repetition.

If you can get someone to repeat something enough, they stop thinking about it and continue doing it automatically. Martial artists share a saying that "a thinking man is a dead man." They repeat moves over and over again until they become automatic, no time-wasting thinking required. This is the state you want your customers to adopt. You want them to throw beads at your King Kong float over and over again until they stop thinking and do it automatically.

Getting your customers to automate their purchases can be more powerful than you might imagine. Scientists who have conducted brain scans on people who repeat activities have found that the repetition actually changes the physiology of their brains. Flute players, for example, have brains that are overdeveloped in areas that control the fingers and tongue. Repetition, then, actually reprograms your customers' brains physically and thereby makes their abandonment of you unlikely.

The Buddhist system of five aggregates explains the mechanics of building customer dependence. It would say that to lock in customers involves reprogramming them in three phases.

1. Conscious Choice of Innovation

When people first try an innovation, a Starbucks coffee, for example, they are fully conscious of their choice. They observe the details as they walk into the store: the green logo hanging from the window, the music, the round tables, the curved counter, and the smile of the barista.

To change behaviors first requires penetrating the conscious level in order to give your users the opportunity to try something new. If you do not penetrate this level, customers will continue doing what they did the day before. They will, say, make coffee at home or drive to a Dunkin' Donuts. If you can provide a meaningful enough experience the first time, the customer will return the next day, and then the next. Each time customers return to Starbucks, the associations they have with the Starbucks experience are being reinforced.

2. Automatic Choice of Innovation

With each visit, you are programming your customers. Somewhere beyond their consciousness they are learning, for example, that "green Starbucks logo = Starbucks = good coffee." You are giving them signs they can recognize ("re-cognize") and packing their mental baggage with positive associations. With enough visits and programming, you can direct your customers' behavior before it reaches their consciousness. They begin automatically choosing, or at least desiring, a coffee when they see a Starbucks store. They may catch themselves turning to cross the street automatically when they see a Starbucks logo or find themselves standing in line without really remembering how they decided to get there. Their minds are recognizing the signs of a Starbucks store and guiding their bodies accordingly.

Branding is simply achieving this level of programming. The goal of branding efforts is to create recognition and desirable associations with that recognition.

3. Subconscious Choice of Innovation

Though achieving an automatic response may be sufficient, some innovations are able to move even deeper into customers' minds by reprogramming the primitive associations people have with the colors, smells, sounds, feelings, or tastes. In the 1990s, for example, Nike was able to build within teenagers an association between the color blue—specifically sky blue—and Nike products. If you showed the color sky blue to a teenager, many would automatically think "Nike." For many Americans, the color brown means UPS, red Coca-Cola, and yellow 3M Post-it Notes. These associations work deeper than brand or logo associations because they do not require people to recognize or name something.

The human brain is designed to save effort. It tries new things only when necessary. When something works well enough, the brain stops asking "why" or "what else is out there." It rests comfortably in a field of beliefs, associations, and habits.

When you first launched your innovation, you had to fight hard to overcome consumers' established habits so they would try your product. Now that same habit-making tendency becomes your protector against competing innovations.

Your customers are lulled into automatic use because you keep them in familiar situations. That keeps the habit in place. Confusing your customers, for example, by changing the color of your logo, will force them to rethink their choice consciously, which gives your competitor a chance to steal them away.

You can lock in your customers by programming them to return again and again. You can link your innovations into their minds through association and thereby prevent them from making conscious choices. In this way they return to you automatically. They stop considering, or even noticing, the competition.

Reprogramming Users

		Conscious Choice of Innovation	**Automatic Choice of Innovation**	**Automatic Choice of Innovation's Form**
		User consciously considers and chooses your innovation	User recognizes your innovation and chooses it without conscious thought	User immediately chooses the color/sound/smell of your innovation without recognition
Five Aggregates				
Consciousness	The experience of being conscious of the thing you have sensed (form) and named (recognition) and the associated feelings you have about it.	▨	☐	☐
Mental Formation	The attachment of pre-existing "baggage" – associations, meaning, liking/hating – to what you recognize. You automatically want something or push it away.	▨	▨	☐
Recognition	The classification and naming of what you have. The "recognizing" it according to your past experiences.	▨	▨	☐
Feeling	The primitive reaction you have to what you sensed. You immediately have favorable, unfavorable, or neutral reaction.	▨	▨	▨
Form	What you actually perceive of the material world. What you see, hear, smell, taste, or feel directly.	▨	▨	▨

Build an Identity

Innovations that are able to build in their users a strong enough identity can block out competitive threats. Apple, for example, is uniquely effective at creating an "Apple user" identity among its customers. It is not uncommon for people to proclaim with some pride that they are Apple users. But you might exhaust yourself looking for people who would label themselves Toshiba users or Dell users. Being an "Apple user" matters because with those two words someone can efficiently express many desirable traits about themselves. It means they are different, they care about design, they are on the cutting edge; they are, in a word, cool. When people see someone open up an Apple laptop, they automatically see that person in a way he or she wants to be seen. Opening up a Toshiba, however, says little about the person.

By creating a desirable identity, linking this to your innovation, and inviting users to join in this identity, innovations become like magnets. People want to be associated with your innovation. In the 1960s, when the Western world was growing tired of war and governments, a new character appeared that was everything we wanted to be. While U.S. car makers were building behemoths, Volkswagen introduced the Bug. The physical characteristics of the car were important—it was small, reliable, and required less gas than the alternatives—but it was its character and personality that made it an innovation the world wanted to adopt. The car epitomized a persona that represented what most people in the West wanted to be. By the end of 1972, the VW Bug had surpassed the Ford Model T as the most popular car of all time.

Adopt a De-risking Strategy

These mental techniques—reprogramming and building identity—are powerful tools for locking in customers, but you should not ignore the more obvious, physical sources of protection.

You can, for instance, build in financial costs to abandonment, making it too expensive for customers to leave you. One familiar technique is to make users commit to future use when they are first ready to buy. Mobile phone service providers are good at this. They give customers one-time rebates on mobile phones in exchange for long-term service contracts. The result is that when customers later want to abandon the provider, they must pay a cancellation fee, which is set high enough so that most customers will prefer to stick with their original provider. This is the same reason that Gillette makes little profit on razors but in exchange gets a customer who is committed to buying higher-margin cartridges.

To further protect yourself from the risk of customers leaving, you can simply reduce your dependence. By 1995, for example, Infosys had established itself as one of India's leading technology firms. It had secured many of the world's largest corporations as clients, but it depended heavily on one particular client, GE, which represented 20 percent of Infosys's revenue and 8 percent of its profits. When the two companies could not agree on terms for a contract extension, Infosys lost GE to a competitor.

The experience convinced Infosys to immediately launch a "de-risking" process. It worked to diversify its revenue sources so that it depended very little on any one client. The percentage of revenue or profit that came from the largest client needed to fall so that Infosys could rely on a more secure revenue stream. A more predictable revenue stream is worth more than an erratic one, so by de-risking you create value. De-risking is a critical step in the Earth phase of innovation.

Innovators further de-risk by creating new rigidity in their environment. They convince governments to pass new laws or change regulations in a way that protect their innovations. Since governments and laws change slowly, they help protect against erosion.

Lock Out the Competition

Beyond doing what you can to lock in customers, it is worthwhile exploring how to further consolidate your innovation by locking out the competition. Choosing the best approach depends on where you start, which "ground" your innovation now occupies. A framework defined by Sun Tzu 2,500 years ago still applies today. He believed there were six types of ground (see table on pages 138–139).

Following Sun Tzu's principles, the first step is to identify which ground your innovation now occupies. Then you can decide whether the potential even exists to lock out the competition and take the appropriate steps to solidify your defenses.

Climb to "Precipitous Heights"

"If Wal-Mart invests a billion dollars and others invest $100 million, Wal-Mart is going to grow more. So if we invest $2 billion a year over many years and others invest $500 (million) or $100 million, it's illogical for them to have the same size as us."

—*Carlos Slim Helú, ranked the wealthiest man in the world by*
Fortune *magazine in August 2007*

My research into the most competitive companies of the decade shows that the ability to lock out the competition is almost always derived from numbers 4 and 5 in the following list. Consider, for example, International Game Technology (IGT), the world's leading designer and manufacturer of slot machines and video gaming machines. IGT controls two-thirds of its market, and has maintained a 15 percent annual growth rate while producing 30 percent profit margins (earnings before interest and taxes).

The company was founded by William S. Redd, the son of a Mississippi sharecropper who, at the age of eighteen, bought a used pinball machine and convinced a local hamburger shop to put the game in its space in exchange for 50 percent of the profits. This early venture led Redd on a lifelong path of gaming. He worked as a distributor for jukeboxes in New England, then for a distributor of slot machines in Nevada.

Redd saw that the gaming-machine business had latent demand that competitors were not adequately responding to (he realized Metal) and conceived a business that would capitalize on this rigidity (Water). He invested his money and the strong relationships he had built with suppliers and buyers into creating his own business (Wood), which he named A-1 Supply.

Ground	Sun Tzu's Advice	Modern Advice for Those on Such Ground	Potential for Sustainable Advantage
1. Accessible ground/ new market space	Enter first, secure the high ground (the choice positions), and carefully protect your supply lines.	If you are the first to attack a new market space, recognize that your first-mover status will not guarantee a sustainable advantage, so gather the resources to compete (for example, be ready to drop prices).	Low
2. Entangling ground/ market space your competition has abandoned	If your competition has abandoned such ground, it will be easy to defeat them. But think carefully before abandoning such ground yourself.	Test for compelling reasons that your competition will not return to what it has abandoned (for example, they have invested in next-generation technology) and if you find good reasons, take this territory (in this example, use abandoned technology) but stick to what has been abandoned; resist adopting the "new" thing yourself.	Medium
3. Temporizing ground/ market space without barriers to entry	Avoid the temptation to enter. Instead retreat and wait for the competition to enter first.	Exit such ground even if you have been successful so far because the competition will follow you and you have no advantage for being first. Retreat to a niche or take your gains and invest them somewhere else.	None

Ground	Sun Tzu's Advice	Modern Advice for Those on Such Ground	Potential for Sustainable Advantage
4. Narrow passes/market niche	If you can seize the niche first, do so quickly. If you are not first, then avoid attack.	If you are first, then build a dominant market share. If not, exit.	High
5. Precipitous heights/market space with high barriers to entry	If you can climb first, then do so and wait for your competition. If your competition has already started climbing, then retreat and try to lure them down.	Build economies of scale by investing heavily in areas like R & D, so that your competition cannot catch up. If your competition is investing more than you can afford to, then focus your investments in higher risk/higher payoff opportunities. Otherwise exit.	High
6. Positions at great distance from the enemy/market space of little interest to you or the competition	You will gain nothing by entering.	Exit. Use whatever you have gained in entering such ground and invest it somewhere else.	None

Because Redd was early to market and also was a naturally gifted salesman, his company soon reached the critical mass of customers he needed to take off (Fire). He could have been one of many other distribution companies that grew quickly, made their founders rich, and then disappeared. But Redd was able to translate his first-mover advantage into a sustainable one. He did that by recognizing the opportunity to climb what Sun Tzu would call "precipitous heights."

Redd accomplished this by allotting an unusually large amount of his resources to research and development. The result was that A-1 Supply developed a series of innovative new products, including video poker, blackjack, and keno machines. Whenever casino operators throughout Nevada and Atlantic City were looking for innovative new machines, they turned to A-1.

In October 1981, Redd's company, now renamed International Game Technology, went public on the NASDAQ exchange. By then the company had about $60 million in sales, and controlled 90 percent of the Nevada market in video machines. But rather than settle into a groove, IGT branched out.

It began a system for running lottery games and became one of the country's top providers of such technology. In 1997, it developed a new betting system called "MegaSports" that allowed players to make specialized bets on sporting events. It developed technology to help casinos track the activity and payouts of every gaming machine in real time. These investments further expanded IGT's revenue base, which allowed it to invest even more in R & D.

With each step in growth and R & D spending, IGT was moving further up the "precipitous ground." It was investing more than its three largest competitors combined. Between 1994 and 2004, IGT grew from $630 million in revenue to $2.5 billion while remaining consistently profitable, producing margins ranging from 25 percent to 40 percent.

What gave IGT its early success, enabling it to work its way through Fire, is not what gave it sustaining success. It was early to the market and excelled at selling. But to consolidate its gains,

IGT built a wall around itself in the form of abnormally high R & D investments that competitors would have great difficulty matching. And that strategy continues. Each year as IGT grows in revenue it increases its R & D investment, and raises its walls still higher. This is how an innovator builds a wall.

Not all markets offer "precipitous heights." Some innovations appear to attain early success only to give away the lead when the competition enters. Philips Electronics's introduction of the CD is an example. In the beginning, it was reasonable to assume that producing CDs would be difficult for others to copy. But Philips climbed as high as it could and found the ground still too low to turn away copycats. A CD production plant's economies of scale peak at just 2 million disks per year, so anyone who can sell 2 million disks can reach the same heights as Philips. IGT's gaming business or Cisco's router business or Microsoft's software business have peaks that reach to the billions of dollars. At such heights, they can easily lock out competition.

Seek "Narrow Passes"

When we find no "precipitous heights" to climb, we might turn to the second common way to sustain an innovation: Seek out and dominate "narrow passes."

Imagine a town so small that it can support only one shoe store. If you can be the only shoe store in that town, you have the potential to enjoy a long, comfortable life without the threat of competition. Any intelligent competitor who wishes to enter should quickly figure out that the market is not large enough to support two shoe stores, so it would be better off launching in a different town or selling something other than shoes.

By looking for these small towns (closed markets, customer niches) and building a dominant position there, you can preempt the competition from attacking. General Electric has guided itself by this principle for decades. It does not measure the potential of its businesses by revenues but instead looks for the relevant market share it controls in the particular market it serves. It looks for relative strength rather than overall size. When it finds that it cannot secure a top position in its market niche, it moves on and seeks to build advantage somewhere else.

Lock Up Resources

The last of the three most powerful advantages you can use to sustain an innovation is to own a critical source of necessary supplies so that you limit your competitor's ability to access it. The competition for resources is perhaps the oldest arena of competition known to living creatures; it has been the defining arena of evolution. It is no wonder, then, that innovations sustain or die by their ability to secure resources.

Reliance Industries, for example, has created a $20 billion annual revenue conglomerate by locking up resources. Reliance began as a small textile distributor in India. Because the company's founder had difficulty securing raw supplies he decided to look back upstream. This led him to create a textile manufacturer that would supply his distribution company. Then, because many of his textiles were polyester and therefore depended on chemicals, he decided to move upstream again, and started a petrochemicals company that would give him preferential access to the raw materials he needed.

The petrochemicals business in turn depended on further raw supplies, particularly petroleum-based products. So, again, Reliance decided to strengthen its defensive wall by getting into the petroleum refining business. It founded Reliance Refineries Private Ltd. and built a gas distribution business, assembling a network of 1,000 gas stations. When the Indian government later liberalized the oil industry and allowed private companies to produce and import oil, Reliance was well positioned to move still deeper into its supply chain. It won a large share of the government's bids to explore new fields, many of which proved unexpectedly large, including the largest natural gas field discovered in India in decades.

By locking up resources you reduce the risk that competitors will pull the legs out from under your success. This is why new products are so often built around key technologies only the innovator can control. The world of intellectual property rights, trademarks, mining rights, oilfields, and supply chains offers a rich source of competitive advantage.

A Brief Summary of the Earth Phase

Your innovations become sustainable when you build up your defensive walls and enter the Earth phase. In business this means becoming immune to time's erosion by locking in clients, locking out competition, and locking up resources. The tools to do so are often the same ones you used to create space for your innovation—the mental rules of entrapment and repetition, for example. However, whereas before rigidity was an enemy to overcome, now it is a close friend. It provides predictability and enables you to sustain your innovation in the Earth phase.

BOOK THREE

APPLICATION

CHAPTER EIGHT

LEADING INNOVATION

"That is how entrepreneurs work. Having decided that the world must change in some important way, they simply find and build highways that lead inexorably to that result. Where others see barriers, they delight in finding solutions and in turning them into society's new and concrete patterns."

—Bill Drayton, founder of Ashoka

"Entrepreneurs are simply those who understand that there is little difference between obstacle and opportunity and are able to turn both to their advantage."

—Niccolo Machiavelli

We all change the world. Your choices, actions, and words influence, to some degree, the path and future of your companies, organizations, or communities. As the marketing director you may be concerned with a particular campaign or your summer sales numbers. As a business leader you may be concerned with where your product is in its path of evolution and what you must do to grow market share or reinvent your business. As a parent your interest may center on your child's school district and the quality of its education.

The nature and scope of your innovation may differ from those of your neighbors and colleagues. But the fundamental principles by which you realize the change you wish to see in the world are constant:

- You must first experience a mental shift that reveals a new perspective, path, or set of possibilities.
- You must then propagate this shift through a sequence of communities (a team, your organization, your partners, users, and so on).
- As your innovation expands it passes through the five phases of evolution—Metal, Water, Wood, Fire, and Earth—each with its own unique challenges and demands.

The goal of this chapter is to synthesize the themes of the book into an accessible manual for changing the world.

Metal: Discontent

The Metal phase, when properly recognized and embraced, can establish a powerful launching pad for an innovation. To succeed through this phase, consider the following.

Metal: realizing the system is stuck

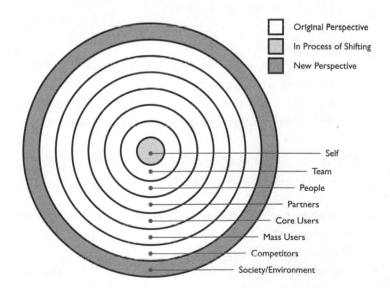

Step One: Identify whether you, or your competition, or your
industry has fallen into a state of rigidity.

All great innovations emerge out of rigidity. They are born when
someone recognizes that the system—the company, the industry,
the country—has frozen and can no longer react to new opportunities or threats. If you can identify where you, your competition,
and your industry are stuck, you can grow your innovation. In the
absence of competitive resistance, you can expand faster, farther,
and with greater ease.

Here are three short exercises to help you recognize points of
rigidity.

Test Prevailing Beliefs:
- What beliefs does your industry currently hold about how
  things work, what does work, what does not work, and what
  constitutes "the way things are"?
- For each belief, what recent evidence exists to support it?
- For each belief, what alternative belief might be held by
  someone who has no related experience; someone who just
  got here?
- Considering in turn each belief, what would be possible if
  this belief were actually not true?

Distinguish Prevailing Stories:
- Look through recent industry articles or think about recent
  conversations you have had.
- Looking particularly at the verbs and metaphors—what stories do people tell about how things got to be the way they
  are?
- Given the past and present of these stories, what is the
  implied future?

Determine Whether Anyone Is Telling One of the Follow-
ing Four Stories:
- "The market won't change."
- "The market may change, but the changes will not affect us."

- "The changes may affect us, but we will somehow survive."
- "We don't have a response and there is nothing we can do about it."

According to these exercises, where are you (or your competitors or industry) potentially stuck?

Step Two: Look for "weak signals" that the environment is changing.

Nearly every significant innovation is born when someone senses that the world is changing in some way. The recognition that baby boomers would soon need to return to college, for example, led John Sperling to create The University of Phoenix and build the largest private college in the country. Nokia was born when it recognized that government regulation and European standardization would create new opportunities for independent telecom companies.

What "weak signals" are quietly calling you and your competitors to an emerging opportunity? Three exercises will help you identify these.

Look for information where your competition is not looking.

- What would it mean to look "deeper" (to look further in the past)?
- What would it mean to look "wider" (to look into other, seemingly unrelated industries or domains)?
- What is going on that people are not looking at?

Look for places where logic is giving you an intuitively incorrect conclusion.

- Review the information you have identified here, but without thinking things through or taking a high-level perspective. What do you intuitively feel is going on?
- If you were talking to a five-year-old, how would you explain what is going to happen?

- In what areas do the logical explanations provided by experts seem overly complex?

Look at what society and the business environment wants.
- If you were the master of the universe with the goal of making sure things work, what situation would be best for society?
- How is this situation different from the current one?
- What would be best for the environment?
- How is this situation different from the current one?
- Therefore, in what direction do you think things will or should move?

Step Three: Use commitment to create a vision.

The first two steps in this section should have revealed a few possible opportunities to cause change. But for your change to succeed, it needs the fuel of a commitment. Without commitment—either personal or organizational—your innovation risks petering out or falling behind someone else's, someone who cares more passionately about it than you do. To help you uncover this requisite underpinning commitment, answer the following questions:

1. What are you personally committed to?
2. What past events do you still remember clearly, and what commitment did they lead you to? (The commitment that eventually led to one of the world's leading software firms, Infosys, occurred when its founder was still a young man and Bulgarian police arrested him for discussing capitalist ideas.)
3. What purpose or passion or belief did your family or upbringing instill in you?
4. If you could change one thing about the world, what would it be?
5. For what purpose do you think you exist?

6. Your innovation will draw greater strength if it taps into the commitment of your entire organization. What is your organization committed to?
7. If every organization exists to serve some purpose, what purpose do you think your organization serves? Why is it still alive? Why should it still be alive ten years from now?
8. What is your organization's formal mission? Is this still what you think the true mission is, as experienced in your and your colleagues' minds?
9. What does your organization's history make it committed to? (Nokia, for example, could transform itself from an old-world industrial conglomerate into a modern telecom company because it had made a commitment to mobile telephony thirty years prior, when it was running a small, relatively unknown telephone division.)

Your answers to the preceding questions will help you tease out what you and your organization are truly committed to. Your innovation is more likely to succeed if everyone involved is committed to the same thing.

"When you look at when the seeds were sown for our most successful products of the last two or three years—for example in mobile phones and digital switching—it was 20 or 25 years ago. That makes you very humble as a manager. What we have done is put a team together that has been successful in exploiting that heritage."

—Jorma Ollila, former CEO, Nokia

Given your commitment and mission, the rigidity of your system, and the opportunity or threat that "weak signals" are pointing to, what vision do you see? Creating a vision based on your commitments and beliefs is an integral part of the innovation process. The following questions will help you clearly define your vision:

- Answer without thinking too much: What do you see could be possible in the future?
- What would it look and feel like?
- If this were a chess game, what would "checkmate" look like?
- When (in how many years) are you committed to having "checkmate" occur?
- If this were a game, how would you keep score? Choose one to three metrics by which you and your organization define success (for example: profit, profit margin, market share, units shipped).
- What would your score be?

Step Four: Define a gap.

Great changes almost always spring from compelling dissatisfaction. To draw the full power from dissatisfaction, take a few minutes to crystallize the "gap" defined by the preceding exercises.

Near-term trajectory: Think back to the stories you identified in the exercises. Given these stories and their related beliefs, where do you think you, your organization, and your innovation will be in the near term (say, one or two years)?

Near-term trajectory measure: Given the score you defined in Step Three, what score would be consistent with this near-term trajectory?

Near-term vision: Now, thinking about the long-term vision you identified (your "checkmate"), what near-term vision would be consistent with that long-term vision? Imagine you are now standing in the near term (one or two years, whatever you decided earlier) and ask, "What would have to be true for us to know that we are on track to achieving our long-term vision?"

Near-term vision measure: Given the score you defined earlier, what score would be consistent with this near-term vision?

Gap: Now compare your near-term vision with your near-term trajectory. What gap exists between these two?

Defining a Gap

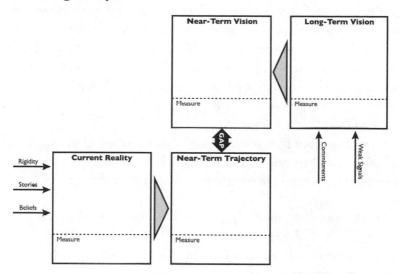

These four steps should move you, your team, and your organization into a state of discontent and reveal obstacles you must tackle. You have established yourself in the Metal phase.

Water: Imagination

Water: enrolling a team with a plan

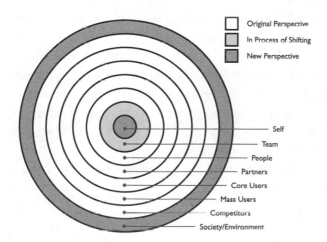

Making the transition from Metal to Water is an important step in the innovation process. In the Water phase you must develop a strategy that propels your vision toward action. By showing how your vision (the immaterial) bridges to clear action (the material) you can gain your believers' support. Here are seven simple steps you can take to move your innovation from Metal into Water.

Step One: Select a team.

It is important that you carefully select a group of people with whom you will co-create your strategy. Keep these points in mind to make sure the people you employ best fit your strategy:

- Ensure the group includes people critical to the strategy's eventual adoption.
- Make sure to exclude anyone who will be too quick to kill off innovative ideas.

Step Two: Assemble your team.

Once you have chosen the people who will help you implement your strategy:

- Review your mission, vision, measures, and obstacles.
- Jointly discuss what you and your team are committed to— your mission.
- Review and, if appropriate, change the vision and measures you wrote down in the Metal phase.
- Discuss what sources of resistance you will face. Who will be your competition? (This may not be obvious, but remember that you are always replacing something, and there are almost always people who prefer the old order of things.)
- Remind yourselves that you are looking for a grand strategy that separates you from the pack.
- Review with your team the difference between a grand strategy, which allows for flexibility, and one that restrains flexibility.

- Go over Sun Tzu's four levels of strategy and agree with your team that you are looking for the "highest form" of strategy: one that your competitors will choose not to resist, that will make your competition obsolete.
- Discuss what it will take to make this strategy development process a performative one, a statement that actually begins changing the world.
- Is there anyone else you should involve?
- How long should this take?
- How much effort should you be investing?

Sun Tzu's Levels of Strategy

Level	Sun Tzu's Wisdom	Implication
1.	"The highest form of generalship is to balk the enemy's plans."	Choose a strategy that your competition will choose not to resist.
2.	"The next best is to prevent the junction of the enemy's forces."	Hinder your competitor's ability to attach (for example, cut off their supply lines).
3.	"Next in order is to attack the enemy's army in the field."	Attack a competitor small enough that you can outmuscle them.
4.	"The worst policy of all is to besiege walled cities."	Attack a large, entrenched competitor.

Step Three: Introduce new metaphors.

Giving your team a fresh perspective on the current situation by supplying them with a new metaphor is a pertinent step in the innovation process. Use these pointers to help organize your team around your new metaphor:

- Sitting together with phones off and doors closed, agree on where you are currently headed (your trajectory).
- Review your long-term vision and your near-term vision to distinguish the "gap."

Now explore together how you might close the gap, looking at this challenge through several different metaphors:

- Look for analogies from other industries.
- Look for analogies from other domains.
- Use five or six metaphors from Appendix A: The Thirty-Six Stratagems.
- Change the implicit metaphors you use to frame the challenge.
- Capture as many ideas as you can without yet considering or discussing them.
- Push your brainstorming further.
- Ask "what players or habits or practices are we assuming can't be changed?" or "How are we defining the boundaries of our playing field?"
- What would be possible if you could actually change these players or habits or practices?
- Again, capture as many ideas as you can without yet considering or discussing them.

Step Four: Create a short-list of ideas.

Now that your team has been assembled and the vision is in place, it is time to generate creativity among your group members. Try the following steps:

- Take a day off from brainstorming; then meet again.
- For each idea, ask how attractive it is. Without gathering data to support your assessment (you will do this in Step Five), imagine you had a magic wand and could make this idea happen. How far would that get you to realizing your vision?
- For each idea, ask how achievable it is. Forgetting for the moment the idea's attractiveness, how easy is it to make this idea happen? Does it cost just a little bit of money, take just a little bit of time, and so on? Again, do not look for facts or data now. You will validate your answer in Step Five.
- Plot your responses on a matrix with two axes: attractiveness and achievability.

- Pick at least five ideas from the matrix that are "crazy" (defined as highly attractive but of low achievability) and brainstorm how you might make these more achievable.
- Review your list of ideas and your matrix again. Pick a manageable number of initiatives (no more than ten) that you want to keep on the table for further analysis, discussion, or execution.
- For each idea, identify what beliefs you must test to convince yourself, and others, that the idea is valid.
- Make at least one team member responsible for each idea. That person should agree to analyze each idea by:
  - Testing any critical beliefs necessary for some to be convinced the idea is valid.
  - Defining the mission, vision, measures, obstacles, and priorities for the idea. These may each be different from, but complementary to, your overall mission, vision, measures, obstacles, and priorities.

Step Five: Define your strategic priorities.

While fostering a successful brainstorming session is important, you must also be able to ground the creativity in fact and reason. Use these tips to do so:

- Have each team member invest time (days or weeks, depending on your time constraints) testing the facts behind the attractiveness and achievability of each idea. Each team member should also define the idea's mission, vision, measures, obstacles, and priorities.
- Meet again.
- Review each other's work.
- Agree on a final set of no more than seven strategic priorities that together represent a clear, compelling path to achieving your vision.

With these processes complete, your innovation should now have built support within your team. You have crafted a credible set of priorities (a strategy) that will lead to your innovation's success. You still have several levels to go, but the gap between your vision and its realization is narrowing. Your vision, which exists in the immaterial world, is now shared by others and therefore is one step closer to becoming real, to transferring into the material world.

Wood: Formation

Wood: enrolling resources

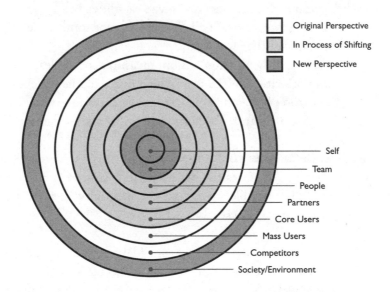

Your innovation is still a dream. Though you and your team may see clearly how you will transform this dream into reality, the innovation lives only in the imaginations and words of a few people.

You must now move your innovation from idea into reality by causing a major shift in the minds of users, employees, and partners. You must take what you and a few close colleagues have in your heads and enroll a larger group of supporters so that your ideas begin noticeably impacting the world.

Step One: Envision the ideal.

"We were looking at trying to build the ideal company in our minds, and then we restructured Puma accordingly."

—*Jochen Zeitz, CEO, Puma*

Without delving too deeply into the logical details, image what your ideal innovation will look like. Think first about the user experience, then work backward to imagine what support would be needed to deliver this experience. Ask yourself what technology you will need, what kinds of people you will need, what skills, capabilities, and habits your organization must have, and so forth.

Step Two: Identify the gaps.

Now mentally place this ideal image against the current reality and list all of the things that need to be removed or added. When Ted Leonsis bought his first sports franchise, he created a long list of everything that needed to be in place for fans to have an outstanding experience. His list included everything from clean bathrooms to comfortable seats. He has been working ever since to close each gap between reality and vision.

Step Three: Prepare for disbelief.

"When you innovate, you've got to be prepared for everyone telling you you're nuts."

—*Larry Ellison, cofounder and CEO of Oracle Corporation*

Each of the gaps you identified will fuel disbelief in your innovation. Each gives a would-be detractor logic with which he or she will convince himself—and then try to convince you and those from whom you need support—that your innovation is flawed.

Take comfort in the knowledge that every innovative idea must necessarily conflict with common logic (accepted beliefs). If it did not, it would not be innovative enough to make a difference. Competitors would quickly copy and dilute your desired change. Remember that the inventor of the Sony PlayStation had to take up offices far away from headquarters because his project would have otherwise been crushed. Remember Michimasa Fujino, an engineer at Honda who is leading a promising project to build a Honda airplane. He was once told by a boss that he was "the stupidest engineer I've ever met in my life." Today the HondaJet is one of Honda's top-priority projects; one they hope will propel the company into a new, burgeoning industry.

Just as athletes pay close attention to pain as a tool for informing their training, look for signs of disbelief as helpful feedback. If you are not getting such feedback, you are not innovating. Also remember that what others believe, and disbelieve, is rooted in the shaky ground of conditioning, perceptions, stories, and selective memory.

Step Four: Plan for the three-front battle.
You must shift the perspectives of three types of networks:

1. Organization: Convincing your colleagues and organization to embrace your innovation, and, if you cannot, seeking or creating a different organization to do so.
2. Partners: Convincing critical partners, including manufacturers, suppliers, and distributors, to cooperate with introducing and supporting your innovation.
3. Users: Convincing customers to adopt and spread your innovation.

For each of these networks, think about where you will receive resistance. Filling out and thinking through this matrix will help you quickly diagnose where resistance will appear. You can then alter your plan to anticipate this in advance.

First, with each of the three networks, identify the key power centers from which you will need support. For example, in the organizational network you may need the support of the marketing department, product development group, and finance. Then think about their existing beliefs, accountabilities, and so on. Note who might resist and what the cause of the resistance might be (write this in the "Cause of resistance" column).

Finally, for every network that may resist, devise a plan for deconstructing the resistance and reconstructing support. Could you, for example, retell their stories so that your innovation becomes the logical next step?

Consider all seven tools:

1. Change their beliefs so they see your innovation as the best choice.
2. Provide them with logic that helps them hold on to the conviction in your idea.
3. Speak so as to resonate with their accountabilities (for example, their moral codes, their societal roles).
4. Introduce distinctions that will focus their conversations on characteristics that give you an advantage.
5. Provide metaphors to give them something to envision that links to what they already know.
6. Retell their stories so that adopting your innovation seems a natural progression of the past.
7. Structure incentives so that they feel better off adopting what you have to offer.

Tools for Deconstructing Resistance

	Organization	Partners	Users
Cause of Resistance			
Beliefs			
Logic			
Accountabilities			

	Organization	Partners	Users
Distinctions			
Metaphors			
Stories			
Incentives			

Great innovators seem able to predict sources of resistance long before they appear. This process can help you engineer similar foresight. If you persist you will eventually reach critical mass and your innovation will take off.

Fire: Takeoff

As you enroll these critical networks into your innovation, each will reach its critical mass at different times. You may have all the partners you need to deliver a product, but not yet have the sufficient core users for your product to take off. You may have enough users calling to buy, but not enough skilled employees to produce the product. Until you have reached critical mass across all three fronts, you will be plodding through the Wood phase.

At some point—and it will seem to happen suddenly—all the pieces will come together. Your formation will be complete. Like a fully drawn bow, you will have achieved *shih* and be ready to let the arrow fly.

The trigger of Fire will shove you into a radically different form of competition. The patience with which you worked through Wood will become a liability. The competition which once dismissed you will now scramble to catch up.

It is now time to revisit and add to your strategy. The complexity of Fire demands a similarly complex set of interconnected tactics that help shield you from competition. Innovators who have successfully navigated the Fire phase offer several lessons to consider.

Fire: managing competitive response

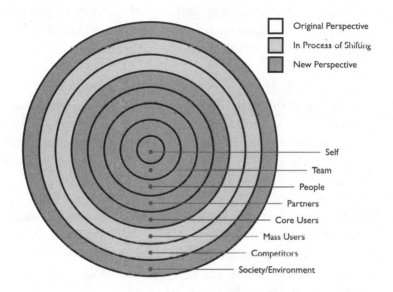

Original Perspective

In Process of Shifting

New Perspective

Self
Team
People
Partners
Core Users
Mass Users
Competitors
Society/Environment

Step One: Choose a path that postpones competitive response.

The longer you can defer competitive reaction, the stronger a foundation you can build. So think now of what decisions you can make to postpone attracting your competitors' attention.

Ask yourself three questions:

1. Who will compete with you? You may not have direct competition taking you seriously yet, but if you are successful, someone will want to own the opportunity you revealed. TiVo, which was the inventor of the digital video recorder (DVR), and Vonage, the company that introduced Internet phone service into the mainstream, both enjoyed brief flickers of Fire while their innovations were young and drew no direct competition of note. But soon after their products took off, cable companies woke up. They realized that by bundling DVRs into cable boxes, and Internet phone service into their customers' phone contracts, they could easily dislodge the innovators.

2. What are they paying attention to? Each of these would-be competitors is watching something—their market share figures, their revenue growth, the number of households they serve. You want to understand what figures or trends they are tracking.

3. How can you grow without affecting what your competition is paying attention to? Gatorade, for example, grew without drawing a reaction from Coca-Cola because Coca-Cola was paying attention to its market share of soft drinks. It did not classify sports drinks into its market and so did not see Gatorade as a threat until it was too late to catch up.

Step Two: Introduce new tactics that play on the mental and moral games of conflict.

"For the great majority of mankind are satisfied with appearance, as though they were realities and are often more influenced by the things that seem than by those that are."

—*Niccolo Machiavelli*

The preceding questions will help you develop a strategy for stepping quietly around the lion without waking it. To bolster this strategy further, you can do things that will confuse your competitor or sap their will to resist you. This is playing on the mental and moral levels that often determine success or failure in conflicts. The idea is to alter your competition's perception so that they do not perceive you as threatening.

There are innumerable ways to play the mental game. You can brainstorm several by again using the metaphors of the Thirty-Six Stratagems in Appendix A. Pick a few and ask yourself how you would use them in order to be to your competitor as Intel was to IBM, as Gatorade was to Coca-Cola, or as Google was to Yahoo! in their early years. How can you implant in your adversary's mind that you are not a competitor?

To play the moral game of conflict, review your mission and vision and ask yourself whether you have chosen to pursue something beyond contention, as Sun Tzu might say. High-growth companies are increasingly adopting missions that reduce resistance and sap the support of people who try to resist them. Whole Foods, for example, has a mission to promote quality foods. GE has publicly placed "making a difference" as a top strategic priority. These missions are more than sweet words to gain public favor. They can provide strategic protection against competition. When customers know that their neighborhood grocery store wants to put Whole Foods—the company that is making the world a greener, healthier place—out of business, they are less likely to provide support.

Step Three: Shorten your decision cycle.

You want to keep your decision cycles shorter than your competition's. This will help you jump on new opportunities and react to emerging threats more quickly than your peers. Each wave of change, then, moves you farther ahead until your lead grows so large others give up.

Innovative companies have implemented several methods to shorten their decision cycles. Some to consider are:

- **Decentralize decision-making.** Analyze what decisions must be made by your entire team and which you can allow team members to make on their own. Try to convert more group decisions into individual decisions.
- **Increase your meeting pace.** Many high-performing teams adopt a series of short, well-run meetings that ensure they share information and make decisions quickly. Consider adopting a daily, weekly, monthly, and quarterly series of meetings.
- **Make small decisions.** Break down large go/no-go decisions into a series of small ones. This way you can try, learn, and adjust quickly rather than investing time in long analyses. Google, for example, has adopted a culture that encourages people to take small financial gambles. It does not punish employees for losing such gambles, as most companies do; rather, by keeping the bets low, Google can use them to try new things while the competition is stuck analyzing.

- **Separate into stand-alone groups.** Break your team into reasonably autonomous groups, perhaps by product category or
by function, such as sales and operations. This keeps meeting times short.

Step Four: Interlock a stream of unorthodox tactics.

To further hinder your competitor's desire to resist you, make
a series of unorthodox decisions that your competition will not
want to copy. These decisions must break away from, even challenge, commonly accepted industry practices. They may seem
minor decisions related to human resource practices or operational
procedures, but because they disrupt your competitor's ability to
respond, they are strategic. Remember, people falsely equate "strategic" with "important." Not everything that is important is strategic. And many choices that may seem unimportant can become
strategic.

Every high-growth, high-profit company that I have analyzed
owes its success in part to unleashing interlocking unorthodox
tactics.

Consider some of Urban Outfitters's decisions (see complete
case study in Chapter 11):
- It adapted each store's décor to the store's location. While
most retailers install and reproduce an identical look and
feel wherever they open a store, Urban Outfitters seeks out
unique spaces and incorporates their features into the store.
Displays may incorporate a tractor, wheelbarrow, antique
tables, or other such distinctive décor.
- The store hired staff that fit the profile of its customers
and looked for a fashion sense that fit Urban Outfitters. It
recruited "right brain," creative people rather than analytical
business-types preferred by traditional merchandisers, even
though such artists may earn higher salaries. It then allowed
employees to make decisions (for example, customizing

displays, choosing what music to play in the store) that other retailers would not.

- Instead of adopting the traditional buyer model, in which experts review trends, go to shows in Asia, and pick lines for upcoming seasons, Urban Outfitters paid young buyers to visit fashionable neighborhoods in the United States, London, and Paris and report on trends.
- It sourced from unconventional places. Even as it grew, it bought and sold used clothing and other vintage goods. Other large retailers have to abandon offering such unique goods because their volume requirements demand sourcing custom-made products.
- It spent very little on marketing and instead focused on creating a store experience that captured people's attention, making each store different.

These four steps will help you customize your strategy to survive the Fire phase. If you are successful, your competition will not know how to defend itself against you; even if they do know how, they will not want to, because doing so is not worth the discomfort or cost.

Earth: Consolidation

Surviving the Fire stage is what most might call success. You have dominated your market, transformed an industry or community, and now are enjoying a place at the top.

But if your innovation is to last, you must now consolidate your gains. This requires yet another major shift: from the fast-paced, unorthodox movement of Fire into an entirely opposite stance. Until now you have been focused on unraveling resistance to change. Now that your innovation has won out, you want to slow down the corrosive threat of change. Before, you fought rigidity; now you want it. Before, you sought to deconstruct the barriers to change; now you want to construct them.

Earth: consolidating your gains

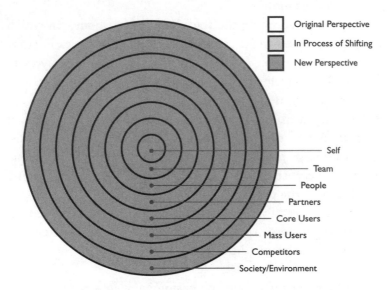

Original Perspective
In Process of Shifting
New Perspective

Self
Team
People
Partners
Core Users
Mass Users
Competitors
Society/Environment

To consolidate your gains you must now shift the source of your advantage. Speed and agility, which gave you success in the past, will not continue giving. As mentioned earlier, innovations that last are able to do one or more of these three things:

1. Lock in clients
2. Lock out competition
3. Lock up resources

To build structures with which you can secure a sustainable advantage, take the following three steps:

Step One: Reprogram your users to lock in clients.

You want users to choose your innovation without thinking. Most of us spend the majority of our day on automatic pilot. We no longer think about on which arm to wear our watch or which way to comb our hair, for example. If you can train users to choose your innovation in the same automatic way, you can achieve one of the three fundamental sources of long-term competitive advantage: customer captivity.

Think about what you can do to move more deeply into your customers' minds, specifically by moving sequentially into three levels of usage.

Conscious choice of the innovation is when your customer considers your innovation, is aware she is doing so, and then, based on mostly logical considerations, decides to give you a try. When Starbucks first launched, for example, its early clients made the conscious choice to buy Starbucks coffee instead of brewing at home or buying from a restaurant.

Automatic choice of the innovation is achieved by getting your customer to repeatedly return until it becomes a habit. Loyal Starbucks customers, for example, might catch themselves stopping automatically when they see a Starbucks logo or find themselves passing other coffee places because they can see a Starbucks logo farther in the distance. Their minds are recognizing the signs of Starbucks and guiding their bodies accordingly.

Subconscious choice of the innovation penetrates one step deeper because it means you have programmed your customer on a subliminal level, reacting to fundamental stimuli like color. When someone sees the color green from the corner of his eye and automatically salivates for a Starbucks coffee, that person is bypassing the need to even see a logo or notice a coffee shop.

Ask yourself:

- At which of these stages are most of my customers today?
- Where do I want them to be in the next, say, three years?
- How can I move them into a deeper stage of choice?

Step Two: De-risk your dependence on clients.

You want to avoid dependence on specific customers. Step One will help prevent customers from abandoning you. Step Two will help reduce the damage caused if Step One fails. Complete the following sequence to see how you can take a proactive approach to de-risk your reliance on specific clients:

1. Calculate what percentage of last year's sales came from your largest client.
2. Do the same for the 10 percent of clients that spent the most with you.
3. Do these percentages scare you? Would your business be at risk if you lost your largest client or if your largest 10 percent of clients significantly reduced their spending?
4. What would you want these percentages to be?
5. What actions can you take to reduce your dependence on these larger clients?
6. How can you sell less to them without damaging your growth rate?
7. How can you increase your average sales to smaller clients?
8. How can you increase the overall number of clients?

Take your time to complete and analyze these findings—you will benefit drastically from understanding the importance of independence from your clients.

Step Three: Shift your ground to lock out competitors.

Sun Tzu describes six types of ground, some of which you can defend and some of which you cannot. Following Sun Tzu's principles, the first step is to look at the chart showing Sun Tzu's six types of terrain applied to modern business in Chapter 7 and identify which ground you presently occupy. If you find yourself on "Accessible ground," "Entangling ground," "Temporizing ground," or at "Positions at great distance from the enemy," think about how you can reach "Narrow passes" or "Precipitous heights."

To shift your ground to "narrow passes," you must seek out niches that you can own. Looking at your current business or market, what niches (customer segments, geographical regions, segments of the value chain) can you build a dominant position in?

What must you do to reposition yourself? How much time do you have to act?

To climb to "precipitous heights," you have to secure your methods for creating a long-term advantage. It means investing more than your competition is willing to spend, for example in research and development, so that you achieve an ability they cannot match. Such investments work when you focus on making incremental improvements rather than radical new innovations. Microsoft, for example, can far outspend its peers in enhancing and refining existing products, but that in itself does not increase the probability of discovering the latest cutting-edge innovation. For this, the company uses a different strategy. Climbing "precipitous heights" requires you to be clear and honest with yourself about what investment will lead to an advantage others cannot luck into.

Step Four: Seek opportunities to lock up resources.

The final fundamental source of long-term competitive advantage is to lock up resources. If you are selling diamonds, you want to control the diamond mine. If you are selling real estate, you want to own the block. The stronger your hold on resources, the greater your competitive power.

To identify opportunities to lock up resources, try the following exercise:

1. List all the resources a competitor would need to compete with you or to offer a similar innovation (do not forget people, capital, and intellectual property as well as raw materials).
2. For each, assess what would be involved in locking up that resource. How much of this resource exists? How much of it does your industry (or market) use? Are you a major user or minor user?
3. For those resources that might be "controllable" to some degree, assess how you could creatively gain control. What strategy does this reveal?

If you have secured one of the three fundamental sources of long-term advantage—locked-in customers, locked-out competitors, or locked-up resources—you have built a wall around your innovation. Your competition will erode your lead only with great cost and effort. The journey is not over, however, because time erodes everything. History "happens" to everyone. You want to use your consolidated innovation as a platform of Earth from which to launch something new.

CHAPTER NINE

LEADERSHIP IMPLICATIONS— UNLEASHING INNOVATION

"When the Master governs, the people are hardly aware that he exists. Next best is a leader who is loved.
"Next, one who is feared. The worst is one who is despised.
"If you don't trust the people, you make them untrustworthy.
"The Master doesn't talk, he acts. When his work is done, the people say, 'Amazing: we did it, all by ourselves!'"

—*Lao Tzu,* Tao Te Ching

"He's the invisible chairman behind the scenes, having absolute power and control."

—*Samsung executive speaking of Samsung chairman Lee Kun-hee*

Leaders of single innovations walk a path of predictable sequence: discontent, imagination, formation, breakout, and then consolidation. But this linearity grows complicated for those whose responsibilities stretch beyond one innovation. Leaders and designers of organizations with lasting aspirations must step back and contemplate how to build an environment that continually fosters innovation in others. How can you free others to successfully drive innovations throughout your organization so that you unleash innovation continually?

Though many of the companies that have produced unusually high growth and profitability over a decade are single innovations themselves—Urban Outfitters is essentially a store concept, University of Phoenix is at its core a new way of educating adults—a few companies have proven themselves able to manage multiple, simultaneous innovations. Samsung, Nokia, Microsoft, Dell, and Vodafone, for example, belong to a select handful of large, multibillion-dollar corporations that have, despite their size, grown at speeds we expect exclusively from small, young, cutting-edge attackers. While most fast-growing companies have ridden one innovation to greatness, these larger companies have been able to ride multiple. They have designed organizations that, at least over the course of a decade, proved able to unleash a roster of new innovations: new products, services, business models.

How do they do it? Is it possible to distill their experiences into some fundamental principles that apply across the board? I believe so. I have studied some amazing companies and interviewed many impressive innovators during my writing of this book. In this chapter I want to share a few lessons harvested from research and interview notes, ideas that may help you as a leader nurture innovations in your company.

Seek Balance

The five phases of change, the model on which this book is based, suggest several interesting, sometimes counterintuitive, considerations. You have probably already realized that its sequence is a simplification. Innovations do not pass cleanly from one state to another, and no company, except perhaps one with a single product, exists in a single state at any one time.

Your company is a symphony of innovations, each at a different stage of evolution. Conducting that symphony so that each individual player, each innovation, has the opportunity to perform brilliantly and all the players blend together in harmony—that's your job, as leader of your organization.

A snapshot would reveal that at any given time there are people in your company looking for emerging needs (Metal), while others are building plans and strategies for new innovations (Water). At the same time, other divisions or product groups are working to pull key resources together to get new businesses into profitability (Wood), while other products have already taken off and are battling for market share with the competition (Fire). Finally, other businesses in your company that reached maturity some time ago are now concerned with maintaining their market share (Earth) and cash flow, which feeds younger innovations. It is your responsibility to see to it that each of these sets of activities are happening at the right level. Let them fall out of balance for long and you are directing your organization toward failure. Being deficient in any of these five will lead to an innovation blockage. It may not be immediate, but it is inevitable. Earlier in this book I described the five phases in depth—what each one looks, sounds, and feels like. Now I would like to show you what it means to be deficient in any one of them. From your vantage point as the leader of your organization, you have the clearest view of the larger landscape and are thus the first to see slippage.

Metal

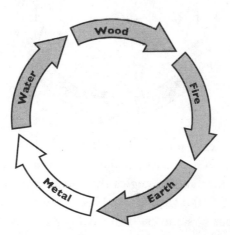

All innovations are born from discontent, when someone realizes an emerging need that the system has grown too rigid to respond to. If your company lacks discontent—for example, if your corporate culture steers people away from uncomfortable conversations—you risk killing off innovations before they can take root.

You risk continuing forever in the same business, selling the same products, until this product passes through its life cycle and dies, taking you along with it.

Insufficient Metal leads to what Warren Buffett calls the "buggy whip" situation, in which you become the best manufacturer of something no one needs any longer. U.S. passenger railroads and, arguably, bus companies are examples to keep in mind. Like frogs in slowly heating water that never notice the rising temperature until it is too late to jump out, such companies never transition away from what made them successful in the past because they fail to reach sufficient discontent to spur change.

Water

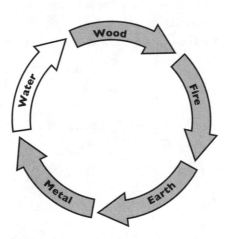

Discontent feeds imagination. Once people grow restless they turn naturally to alternatives. They need the freedom to dream about new visions and strategies that may seem unrealistic using prevailing beliefs and viewpoints. Nearly every significant innovation is born out of someone being willing to dream about something in a way the majority do not. Without sufficient Water your planning may grow too myopic. You become like a chess player who, with an early lead, fails to think forward a sufficient number of moves; or a farmer so concerned with selling today's crop that she does not plant seeds for the next one.

Companies that prove to be able to grow sustainedly make early bets on technologies and businesses that may or may not turn out to work. Most leaders of the analog world, for example, knew that digital technologies might eventually replace analog (they were aware of the weak signals of Metal). But they failed to dream new visions (Water) to plan for this transformation. They took no action, made no early investments in building digital capabilities.

Nokia was one of the first to benefit from worldwide telephone industry deregulation because thirty years earlier this Finnish conglomerate, which ran paper and rubber businesses, had invested in a small mobile telephone business. One reason Samsung closed so quickly on Sony is that Sony, which dominated analog electronics, failed to invest early in digital alternatives.

Wood

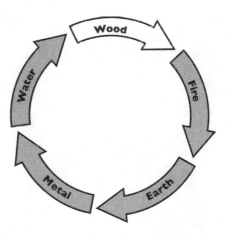

Every innovation passes through a plodding phase in which great efforts produce unimpressive results. You are busy assembling teams, recruiting partners, and building your customer base but your revenue is growing slowly and your profitability persists in negative territory. When your organization can conceive of new ideas (Water) but does not give them the time to form, your innovative thinkers will grow disenchanted and leave. Your partners will abandon you for the competition.

You will recall from Chapter 3 that Xerox created its PARC research lab, staffed it with brilliant innovators, and then bottled up new technologies and breakthrough ideas, never commercializing them. Just as water eventually finds a way around the dam, the creativity generated inside PARC found a way out. It survives today in the computer mouse, graphical computer interface, and other inventions that have significantly changed our lives. But Xerox gained next to nothing from the Water it pooled.

Similarly, Oracle gave birth to two cutting-edge software firms—Siebel Systems and Salesforce.com—in part because their founders left Oracle to do so, when they could not win the internal support they needed to make their ideas happen.

Another common symptom of lacking Wood is a company that cannot align its organization new its strategies. When top management huddles behind closed doors to create a vision or strategy, the people who must execute it often do not understand it. Worse is when employees with good ideas feel they cannot pursue them, and grow discontented. The company becomes like a ship with a captain shouting orders in the wind to a crew who cannot hear or understand him.

Fire

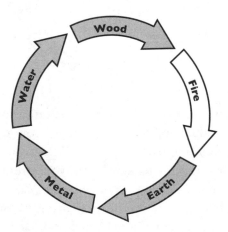

Every successful innovation reaches a distinct takeoff point at which it seems that users suddenly clamor for the innovation, the media wants to talk about it, and the competition wants to take it from you. The Fire phase ushers in an entirely new pace and set of concerns and requires that you rapidly and creatively respond to competitive maneuvers.

Companies that lack Fire conceive of cutting-edge ideas and launch them but are soon eaten up by the competition. If you cannot adopt the fast-paced competitive environment that innovations trigger when they reach breakout, you may find yourself the perennial creator (the company that can conceive of new ideas) but not the innovator (the company that transforms these ideas into reality).

The example of TiVo, the highly creative company that introduced the world to DVRs but lost its innovation to competitors during Fire, was mentioned in the previous chapter. The countless technology entrepreneurs who build new technologies and then sell them to larger firms are similarly more creative than innovative. The difference between Google and countless other technologists (for example, the founders of Skype, hotmail.com, ofoto.com) is that Google successfully navigated Fire while the others did not.

Your company can be successful without navigating Fire (the founders of Skype, hotmail.com, and ofoto.com, for instance, generated impressive wealth), but until you master Fire you cannot reach dominance.

Earth

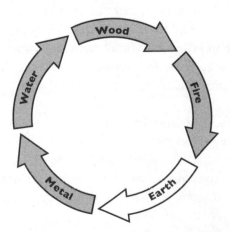

Only a few innovators are able to consolidate their gains after surviving the Fire phase. Those who can do so build walls around the land they claimed during battle by locking in customers, locking out the competition, and locking up resources. Companies unable to move their innovations into the Earth phase find themselves stuck in never-ending battles, always a little bit ahead of or a little behind the competition, always racing and always on the edge of losing. No company I have found has been able to sustain a lead in such a state for long.

Motorola, for example, launched the enormously successful Razr phone, which gave the company a burst of revenue and market share. But Motorola could not root its lead into Earth, could not build a wall around the ground it had captured. In just a few years the competition copied with similar products, prices and margins plummeted, and Motorola found itself once again fighting to stay with the pack.

Maintain a Flow of Continuous Innovation

"Of the Five Phases, none is the lasting victor."

—*Sun Tzu,* The Art of War

To innovate continually and reliably, you must build an organization that exists in all five states at once. Deficiency in any of the five will eventually lead to fizzling out as the innovation that currently feeds you reaches its natural death and you have nothing new to replace it. You must therefore unblock whatever prevents ideas from forming and flowing through this cycle. The companies I have studied and the innovators I have interviewed for this book offer many helpful ideas for unleashing innovation. Here are the twenty-six most memorable.

Advice for Unleashing Innovation
1. Encourage Dissent
Without it, ideas will flow in just one direction, from top to bottom. You already have the world's best marketing resource at your fingertips: your frontline personnel. They interact

with your customers every day, and they are much better judges of what customers want and will accept than those who watch from behind headquarter windows. Bottom-up dissent will carry your customers' voices upward.

2. **Look Where Your Competitors Do Not**

   Innovators appear to see farther ahead only because they see farther to the side. They see change coming because they see it already under way in domains their peers are ignoring. Develop a wide-angle view of the world. Look for trends or themes that cut across multiple businesses; eventually those trends will show up in your business arena as well. Because you have been paying attention to realms beyond your specific industry, you will be able to coordinate and respond more skillfully to your environment.

3. **Exploit Your Heritage**

   Knowledge of your past anchors your innovation more firmly, allowing you to grow it to great height. As former Nokia CEO Jorma Ollila observed, "When you look at when the seeds were sown for our most successful products of the last two or three years—for example in mobile phones and digital switching—it was 20 or 25 years ago. That makes you very humble as a manager. What we have done is put a team together that has been successful in exploiting that heritage."

4. **Know When to Ignore Experts**

   Their know-how works best in familiar situations, but poorly in new territories. The cumulative weight of experience can restrict their perceived options to what they have seen work before. This kills off new ideas before they are given their due. Sony founder Masura Ibuka, for example, was wary of experts: "I have never had much use for specialists. They're inclined to argue why you can't do something while our emphasis has always been to make something out of nothing."

5. **Question the Truth**

   When everyone believes something, their belief will slow them from copying you. They will leave open an unobstructed path for you. Prove their truth is wrong.

6. **Look for an Unfair System**

This is a sign that the system is stuck and will eventually correct itself. You want to already be in position when that happens; awareness presages opportunity. One clear signal that something is wrong: When "those who are doing the work are not earning the money," as Ted Leonsis, the vice chairman of AOL, said. This is a problem looking for someone to solve it.

7. **Create a More Exciting Future**

This will encourage your followers and discourage your competitors. Elon Musk, a cofounder of PayPal, is today seeking an opportunity to build and launch rockets. Why such a dramatic plan? Because, he says, "a future in which anyone can get into space is more interesting than one in which just a few [i.e., a few major aerospace companies] can." He is speaking literally, but the metaphorical implication is just as powerful.

8. **Be the Second Mover, Not the First**

This is a lesson that many smart people find hard to swallow: The early lead rarely lasts. Cable companies are notoriously slow to react to new attackers, but when they wake up they take with relative ease what others gained at great expense. Similarly, in 1995 Microsoft CEO Bill Gates wrote a book on the future of business that famously ignored the Internet. His company seemed far behind early innovators, but it caught up and holds on.

9. **Be Wary of Success**

Because, as Carlos Ghosn, CEO of Nissan and Renault, said, it "breeds complacency and sometimes arrogance." When your company has won one race, celebrate and then move on quickly to a bigger one. For example, as Infosys was realizing its vision of a company that created wealth for all of its employees, it raised the bar by which it judged success. The new goal: becoming a globally respected corporation. Success marks the end of a story and leads us to expect nothing further. Unless you want your story to end, celebrate briefly, then create a new measure of success.

10. **Assemble a "Dream" Team**

Give them just one job: to think about the future. Samsung, for example, staffs its "Creating New Business Group" with visionaries responsible for imagining what living environments will look like five or ten years into the future. Choose people from different corporate backgrounds and at different levels, give them all the tools they need, and then stand back and wait for the magic.

11. **Let People Explore Crazy Ideas**

They are the seeds of innovation. As Jochen Zeitz, CEO of Puma, explained, "We allow people to be creative. We set direction, we set the vision, we set the strategy, but within that framework we allow our people to be as creative as they want to be. There's no idea that can be crazy enough. We just allow that. Of course, we always benchmark it and check if it's in line with what Puma as a brand wants to stand for. But, nurturing creativity, creating creative freedom is important to us."

12. **Build Creative Spaces**

Even the most out-of-the-box people need somewhere to create. Great strategies are born over the water cooler more often than in the boardroom. Do you have a water cooler? Do you have "war rooms" in which your people can brainstorm? If your people wanted to bounce ideas off each other, where would they go?

Google designed its corporate offices (known as Googleplex) taking special care to create creative spaces. Nearly all staff eat at the Google café, which encourages employees to share lunch and ideas with people from different departments. They work in high-density clusters rather than in walled offices. They play Foosball, video games, Ping Pong, roller hockey, and a baby grand piano in facilities provided by Google. Samsung similarly centralizes all research and development activities in one, open-plan building to encourage the fertilization of ideas across product groups, from television to phones to air conditioners.

13. Hold Longer Meetings

Short meetings allow insufficient time for in-depth dialogue, so instead they become reporting sessions. If you want to time to play with ideas, to explore options, to test beliefs, hold just a few meetings but make sure they are longer. Structure them less rigidly to encourage the unexpected.

14. Meet in Smaller Groups

Large groups leave too little "air time" for your discussion to reach any meaningful depth. Everyone in the group feels pressure to contribute, and emerging ideas get trampled as the next person rushes to speak. Allow only three to ten participants in strategy discussions.

15. Turn Your Frontline Managers into Strategists

If they do not participate in creating and evaluating your strategy, they will not fully know it, own it, or act on it. Furthermore, they know, better than anyone, what your users are asking for. If you ignore that precious reserve of marketing insights, your strategy is at great risk of being flawed. Hold your strategy session at frontline locations rather than headquarters. Invite frontline managers to participate.

16. Create a Memorable Name for Your Strategy

This helps people understand and align to it. Nissan's turnaround was called the "180." Beyond the obvious metaphor, the number stood for 1 million more cars, 8 percent gross margins, and zero long-term debt. Similarly, Puma dubbed its turnaround a "fitness program," a phrase all employees, particularly at a sports apparel firm, could understand. When Samsung's CEO wanted to refocus efforts on design, he described Samsung's style as a "balance of reason and feeling," something others could remember and share.

17. Do Not Compete

The highest form of competition is to become so unique that no competitors will consider you a threat. Nearly every firm that made it onto my list of the Most Competitive Companies of the Decade did so by reconceiving themselves as something few viewed as direct competition.

18. **Count Your Deserters**

    If innovative people want to leave, you have blocked your innovation cycle somewhere. We have seen this over and over in American businesses, and always to the companies' profound dismay. Palm Computing, for example, saw two of its founders leave to start a competing company, Handspring. Five years later Palm bought Handspring at a considerable expense.

19. **Write a Legend**

    Nearly every innovative company has a story—or several—that captures, spreads, and reminds people of a companywide value critical to continued success. All Infosys employees know the story of their founders launching the company with just $1,000. Muhammad Yunus is also similarly admired for launching his microcredit revolution with a loan of just $27 to a group of poor families.

20. **Pursue the Long and Short Term Simultaneously**

    No initiative can succeed without hard work in both dimensions simultaneously. When asked the secret to Nokia's success, Jorma Ollila, former CEO, responded, "Our secret? The strong value base, straightforward thinking, fast decision-making and open company culture, which allows for both long-term vision and high flexibility, even in turbulent conditions."

21. **Decentralize Decision-Making**

    Surviving the Fire phase requires you to react quickly to unique developments on the ground. Your competitor in one market may not be doing the same thing in another. If your frontline people must build consensus for the top team before they can act, they will start repeating tactics by rote, over and over again. Several of the most competitive companies of the decade separated their people into stand-alone centers with greater autonomy.

22. **Run Fast and Slow**

    When you are fighting five different types of battles, the slow pace of one (Wood) becomes a liability in the fast pace of another (Fire), and vice versa. Consider running two decision cycles. A leading technology firm, for example, runs two cycles of strategy meetings: an annual financial and operating meeting and a flexible, as-needed series for special projects. A leading pharmaceutical company similarly runs an annual series but overlays it with a series of "new product" meetings every three months.

23. Invoke a Moral Purpose

Not only will it make you feel good, but it has a more practical reason as well: It will make you more competitive. By linking your success to a cause others care about, you strengthen the loyalty of your people and customers while you erode the support of your competition.

24. Be Ready for a Big Change

As Andy Grove, CEO of Intel, said, "There is at least one point in the history of any company when you have to change dramatically to rise to the next level of performance. Miss that moment—and you start to decline." Puma CEO Jochen Zeitz wisely reminds us that "you cannot predict change." But you can learn to recognize it, and be prepared to act when it surfaces.

25. Abandon the Past

It is an anchor that exists only in your people's minds. The past repeats itself only if you let it; if you want the future to look different, you should not hold on to how you got here. By retelling the past, drawing out what will help you get to where you want to go and sending to the background whatever is stopping you, you free your people to move forward.

When Samsung's chairman, Lee Kun-hee, wanted to encourage his people to change, he made a remark that lives in Samsung lore today: "Change everything except your wife and kids." He also held a bonfire at one of Samsung's electronics factories and asked workers to destroy all of their low-quality products. By the end, they had destroyed millions of dollars' worth of inventory. This story symbolizes a clear break from a past when Samsung produced cheap goods.

26. Keep It Simple

In almost every case I can think of, simple thinking overpowers complex analysis. Good ideas originate from the direct experience of an astute individual far more often than from the spreadsheets of an expert. The young CEOs of Urban Outfitters, who turned their personal experiences into a strong retail business, are a perfect example. Detailed analysis can even be dangerous, when it smothers good ideas. What conclusion might FedEx founder Fred Smith have reached if he had permitted a precise calculus on his notion of bringing all packages to one centralized depot and shipping them back out the same night?

The lessons enumerated here outnumber what you can recall (research has shown that humans can store only about seven things in working memory), and yet they are but a sample of what you can learn from studying great innovators. The implication of this is not that you must study and memorize more. That would be a logical approach, but it is not necessarily the right one.

For nearly 5,000 years Taoists have been arguing that humans underutilize their intuition. In recent years cognitive scientists have been approaching a similar conclusion as they explore the surprising power of our intuition as a computational tool. For example, when strategic games such as chess grow too complicated and involve too many moves to consider logically, great players turn on their intuition. They make the right moves but cannot describe how they knew them to be right.

Perhaps, then, rather than memorizing these lessons and studying the hundred or so more you can glean from further research, the right course of action is to turn on the powerful computing power of your intuition. In surprising, magical ways, it will lead you to make the right choices as you open up the blocks that are limiting the creative flow in your organization.

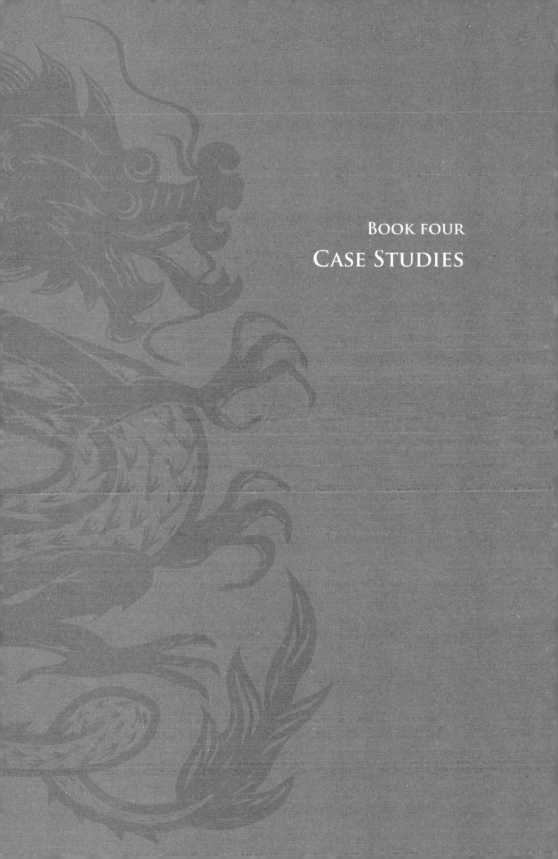

BOOK FOUR
CASE STUDIES

Cases in Innovation

Whether they are transforming companies, communities, or countries, great innovators follow a common path and set of principles. This section guides you through the experiences of eight innovators and the impacts they have had on the world. To illuminate the breadth of situations in which we can apply the same approach to change, I have chosen a diversity of innovations. Six are corporate in nature; two are social. Each has had a significant, even life-changing, impact on the world. Yet each differs from the others in the scale of this impact, the domain in which it dwells, and the position it currently holds in its life cycle.

Corporate Case Studies:
1. Infosys and the rise of software outsourcing
2. The Apollo Group and the rise of for-profit adult education
3. Urban Outfitters—the retailer run by customers
4. Puma and the rise of sports fashion
5. Nokia and the mobile phone revolution
6. Microsoft and the emergence of software

Social Case Studies:
1. Muhammad Yunus and the invention of microcredit
2. Ted Leonsis and the discovery of "filmanthropy"

Each of these case studies will provide insight into the real-world function of innovation. The lessons these corporate and social cases offer can help you become a more skillful leader of innovations in your life and business.

CHAPTER TEN

INFOSYS AND THE RISE OF SOFTWARE OUTSOURCING

Between 1998 and 2004, a relatively small Indian software company grew from $62 million in annual revenue to over $1 billion, an average annual growth rate of 62 percent. Over the same period its peers, even the smaller, fast-growing ones, produced about 20 percent revenue growth. Though the company's primary competitive advantage is that it can deliver programming services at low prices, it did not drive this dramatic growth by cutting profit margins. Indeed the company was nearly twice as profitable as its peers over the past decade and has delivered to its shareholders nearly twice the returns its peers have.

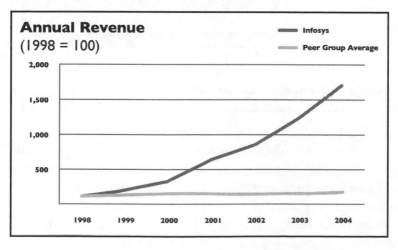

The company is Infosys. It rose from obscurity to become a major global player by skillfully managing and integrating all five phases of innovation. The mental shift that gave the company growth was born in the minds of seven middle-class engineers, then propagated to the world. Their lessons will help you produce similarly outstanding growth.

Infosys in the Metal Phase

Narayana Murthy's modest lifestyle belies his achievements. He lives in a nondescript, middle-class home in Bangalore, India, and reportedly begins each day by cleaning his toilet. Anyone meeting him for the first time would be unlikely to guess that he is one of his country's richest citizens, with a net worth of approximately $1.2 billion.

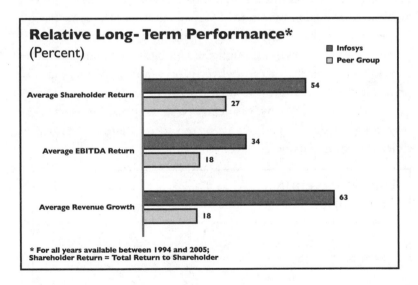

The sixty-year-old entrepreneur gained his wealth by cofounding a new technology company in 1981 and then dedicating over two decades to growing it. But as is the case with most meaningful innovations, the roots of Murthy's innovation precede this time scale by many years. It started in 1974, when Murthy shifted his perspective by making a silent, profound commitment.

Murthy was born into a middle-class family in India. He decided to study electrical engineering and, in 1969, earned a master's degree. He considered himself a strong leftist with a distrust of capitalism. He believed deeply in equality and viewed communism as the best form to ensure this.

In 1971 his job took him to Paris, where he had a chance to see capitalism firsthand. The experience challenged his black-and-white view of the world. He saw some of the benefits of capitalist structures in the quality of life it afforded many of its workers. Three years later, at the age of twenty-six, Murthy felt he had experienced what he needed to of the world outside India and decided to return home. He planned to travel back to India by land, backpacking through all the communist countries he could along the way.

As he traveled through Bulgaria by train, Murthy struck up a conversation with another passenger. They discussed communism and its counterpoint, capitalism. Murthy, still a staunch leftist, was surprised when Bulgarian officials arrested him for the act of speaking about capitalist ideas. He spent three days in a Bulgarian jail without food or water.

The experience proved pivotal. At that moment he proclaimed a deep commitment that would redirect his life entirely. As he later described it, "That was the last straw. My experiences had shaken my faith in communism and I was determined to someday create a venture that embodied the best principles of capitalism and socialism—by creating wealth for all its constituents." Murthy returned to India with a new commitment, one that crossed the boundaries dividing socialism and capitalism.

Red Tape of Rigidity

Murthy's commitment would lie dormant within him for seven years before he saw the opportunity to act definitively. He was working at Patni Computers, an Indian reseller of machines produced in the United States by Data General. The job of selling computers in India was challenging, but not for reasons one would expect. There was sufficient demand; indeed, Indian companies wanted to buy more computers than they were able to. The challenge had to do with regulation.

The Indian government had imposed harsh restrictions on what technology Indian companies could import. Buying a new computer involved a drawn-out, complex import application process that required months of work. The regulations slowed the adoption of new technology by Indian companies. Entire Indian industries were falling behind their foreign peers because they were using outdated hardware.

The situation was unsustainable. The system had fallen into an inefficient state. It would eventually need to change, but a complex web of accountabilities, incentives, and beliefs were preventing the required change.

Rigidity signals opportunity. Murthy and six colleagues at Patni Computers decided to act. They had no clear plan for fighting the regulations or for predicting when things would change. Their assessment that the system was stuck was not something they could incorporate into financial projections. But they knew the system was frozen in a nonoptimal position and that natural laws would somehow eventually force the system to adjust. Regulations would eventually lighten, and Indian companies would ultimately have access to the technology needed to keep them competitive.

Infosys in the Water Phase

We may enjoy the myth of the master strategist who climbs to his mountaintop and designs a brilliant strategy on his own. However, most innovations are not born in the mind of an individual, but are instead co-created in the minds of several. Such was the case for Infosys.

On July 2, 1981, Murthy gathered with his six colleagues to discuss their work at Patni Computers and their personal ambitions. They all agreed that they wanted to make something better of their lives, and so they decided together to start a company. They lacked the experience to run a company and could pull together only $1,000 among the seven of them.

Despite those odds, they jointly created a vision: They would build a company that would generate wealth for all its employees. This vision was clear and compelling. Any Infosys employee could understand it. All would find an interest in Infosys helping them build wealth.

Disbelief of the Vision

As the engineers began offering programming services to multinational companies, they ran repeatedly into the same barrier— no one believed that Indian computer engineers could provide high-quality programming at a low cost.

To counter this belief the cofounders hit on the strategy of traveling to their clients' workplaces and performing the work onsite. Seeing the Infosys engineers every day gave clients a sense of comfort, but it came at great personal cost to the cofounders, who shared inexpensive hotel rooms to keep expenses down, and spent months away from their families.

Their diligence would eventually pay off. By proving and re-proving its work quality, Infosys would slowly replace this initial disbelief with a new understanding that Indian programmers are capable and smart.

The New Metaphor: Programming as Manufacturing

As Infosys was launching its programming services, the concept of outsourcing, in which a company transfers some of its functional work to a third party, was almost unknown. Though contracting foreign manufacturers to assemble goods or produce components was common practice, the idea of contracting an outside company to do nonphysical work was rarely considered. A computer company would be happy to pay an Asian manufacturer to produce its hard drive and another to produce its monitor, but managing logistics or developing proprietary software were considered in-house activities. The word *outsourcing* was rarely used in business and only grew into popularity during the 1980s. Infosys was a critical player in the successful adoption of the concept.

Just as a baby cannot know a ball until it has a concept with which to name it, corporations could not adopt outsourcing until they had something to call it. Infosys became an important contributor to the propagation of the word, and thereby the possibility, of outsourcing.

Infosys did this by introducing a new metaphor, that of programming as manufacturing. In the minds of the Infosys founders, programming shared clear parallels with manufacturing. Both followed a step-by-step process during which components were combined and added to until they became a final, useful product. Both involved line workers (programmers) and supervisors (managers).

Once people view programming as manufacturing, new possibilities emerge. Specifically, if programming is manufacturing and if contracting others to perform manufacturing is commonplace, then contracting others to perform programming seems natural. This metaphor helped Infosys's clients, partners, and employees see outsourcing as a natural progression of a new story.

New Players: The Indian Government

Many innovations are made possible when the innovator chooses not to accept what others take for granted. In the case of Infosys this rule applies to its assessment of government regulations.

Infosys had no direct role in fighting to change the regulations. The current CEO, S. Gopalakrishnan, recalls that "there was no way to predict when regulations would change."

But unlike thousands of other would-be technology innovators in India, the cofounders also did not accept government regulation as a given. While many sought ways to work within the context of tough regulations, Infosys chose to operate in anticipation of regulations lifting.

Infosys in the Wood Phase

The "fuzzy" phase of Infosys's growth evolved between 1981 and 1990 as Infosys patiently put in place what it would need to compete in a deregulated world. It assembled critical resources across three fronts: its own organization, its clients, and its partners.

Organization: Building Shih

During Infosys's first years, hiring employees was not nearly the challenge it is today. India's technology sector produced fewer opportunities than the country's schooling system produced engineers.

Even when Infosys first hired employees in 1982 and recruits worked in Murthy's converted bedroom, which served as the company's headquarters, it was a desirable place to work. The company offered the opportunity to work on interesting projects and possibly to travel abroad. For enough engineers, the appeal of these outweighed the company's inability to guarantee stability.

Building organizational *shih* was not Infosys's top challenge in its early years. Acquiring customers was more difficult. As the company grew, however, its ability to attract and excite good people became its number-one priority and the fundamental source of its advantage.

Clients: Winning Over Critical Mass

Infosys went through four distinct phases of evolution. First, it recognized it needed to create acceptance for the company and for Indian programmers in general. This involved replacing the belief that Indian programmers produced lower-quality output. Through persistent delivery of high-quality work, Infosys slowly changed minds. Reebok signed on as one of Infosys's first multinational clients, trusting the company with a significant project.

The second phase of Infosys's evolution was perhaps more difficult. After it proved that Infosys and Indian programmers produced high-quality work, it needed to build acceptance for the outsourcing model. The company had been flying programmers from India to Europe and the United States to do their work at their clients' sites. The cofounders knew this was not the most efficient model and were also personally drained from the amount of travel it demanded. The right answer was to convince large multinationals to trust Infosys to perform its work in India. To do this, Infosys used three critical tools: logic, distinction, and stories:

1. Logic: Infosys adopted ISO and other internationally accepted quality standards to prove to its customers that it could be trusted to deliver high-quality output. It was the first Indian company to completely embrace such standards.

2. Distinction: As already mentioned, Infosys helped introduce and drive the adoption of the new business concept of outsourcing. As this word entered the business lexicon it became something investors and board members began accepting, and so it was something management companies increasingly had permission to consider.

3. Stories: Infosys needed to show clients that the idea of outsourcing was not entirely new, and that it was indeed a natural progression of an accepted story. It did this by relating programming to manufacturing and framing itself in a compelling story.

This is the story: When Great Britain colonized India it snuffed out many of the country's fragile industries. It forced Indian cotton mills to stop production and instead required Indians to buy their cotton from Scotland. Mahatma Gandhi's famous march to the ocean to extract salt from the sea was in direct opposition to a similar British policy, which required Indians to buy salt produced in England. As a result of these policies, India never experienced the Industrial Revolution. That India's manufacturing sector was relatively underdeveloped had not to do with India's skill at organizing but rather its colonial legacy. Had India developed independently, it might have been a major manufacturer for the world.

Fast-forward to the 1980s and you can see that computer programming is much like manufacturing. You can ship raw material (base code and requirements) to India, have it produced (programmed), then shipped back for packaging and distribution. From this perspective it makes sense for India to be the programming hub of the world.

The use of these tools worked. Throughout the 1980s Infosys shifted the perception of its clients. It built trust, told its story, and proved its ability. By 1993 the company had worked on projects for GE, Nestlé, Holiday Inn, and other major multinationals.

Today, both the company (Infosys) and the concept (outsourcing) are broadly accepted. The company's next challenge on the client front is to convince clients to trust the company with more complex, higher-value-added work.

Partners: Infecting Their Minds

The final front of Infosys's Wood phase was to enroll partners. Infosys's outsourcing model requires that it depend little on partners. With foreign marketing and sales outposts feeding work to Indian development centers, it can provide its full breadth of services with minimal outside support.

However, one partnership provided a critical step in Infosys's U.S. expansion. While working for a client in late 1985, Infosys met members of an Atlanta-based consulting firm, Kurt Salmon Associates (KSA). Infosys recognized that it needed credibility and a local presence to expand in the United States and that KSA could provide this. So in 1987 it launched a joint venture called KSA/Infosys.

By partnering with a known U.S. brand, Infosys was able to more quickly shift clients' perceptions about what Infosys could do. Most who knew KSA felt the brand could be trusted. Those who did not at least felt comforted by its Western-sounding U.S. name and roots.

The partnership was in place for eight years, until 1995, when Infosys established its own marketing office in the United States. By then, of course, Infosys had engineered sufficiently broad acceptance of its name and model.

Infosys in the Fire Phase

As described in Chapter 6, the cofounders of Infosys nearly gave up on their vision in 1989. Indeed, all but one said he was ready to quit. But because Murthy remained committed, in the end the group held on.

In 1992 their willingness to hold on paid off. That year, the Indian government lifted its regulations on the importation of computers into India. This was the trigger Infosys needed. It set off a surge in local demand for IT servicers. As Indian companies tried to rapidly close the technology gap between their companies and their international competition, Infosys's programmers and services found themselves in high demand.

Shift from Strategy to Tactics

The trigger was followed by rapid growth. In 1993, Infosys issued stock (an IPO) in India. In 1996 it opened offices in Europe and the United Kingdom and, one year later, in Toronto. By 1999, just seven years after the lifting of government restrictions, Infosys reached $1 billion in annual revenue.

As it grew, Infosys responded rapidly and creatively to emerging challenges. It unleashed a series of "firsts" that kept the competition off-guard and maintained Infosys's distinct position. For example, it was the first Indian company to place the value of its human resources and its brand equity on its balance sheet. It considers these the most important sources of value, and so wanted to communicate this value to shareholders.

It was also one of the few Indian companies to issue stock on the U.S. NASDAQ market. It was the first to launch an employee stock option program and the first to embrace fiscal transparency. While most Indian companies allow their founders to use company assets (such as the company car) for personal purposes (for example, to run an errand), Infosys made a radical break from tradition. Not even the CEO can do this.

By unleashing a stream of interconnected, unorthodox tactics, Infosys was able to navigate itself through the fast-paced Fire stage without losing its character or momentum. It emerged a truly unique organization.

Playing the Moral Level of Conflict

Central to Infosys's mission is its founders' original goal of creating wealth for its employees. Sun Tzu would have called this purpose "beyond contention," as to oppose it is also to oppose a fundamental, broadly accepted value. Competitors cannot attack Infosys on its purpose.

Infosys in the Earth Phase

Infosys became great by positioning itself at the center of the emerging Indian outsourcing trend, by proving to the world that Indian programmers could do high-quality work at low prices. As the company emerged from obscurity, it struggled most with clients who did not trust Indian programmers or did not yet embrace the concept of outsourcing.

De-risking in Clients

But as is the case with most sustained innovations, the source of struggle and the source of advantage for Infosys shifted. Clients came more easily. And by implementing a de-risking process in 1997 (see Chapter 7 for more detail), Infosys removed its dependence on big customers. The percentage of its revenue that came from its five largest clients declined from 43 percent in 1997 to 35 percent in 1998, and 29 percent in 1999.

Infosys's key competitive advantage is not related to locking in clients. Rather, it requires locking up resources—specifically, people.

Locking up Resources

Of the three sources of sustainable advantage—locking in clients, locking out competition, and locking up resources—Infosys depends most on the last one. We might say its strategy is essentially to sell IT work where the prices are high and perform it where the prices are low.

But just as DeBeers generates wealth by having superior access to diamonds, Infosys's wealth depends on its ability to attract and retain talent. To that end, it has launched innumerable initiatives that make Infosys a more attractive place to work than the competition, such as:

- Mandatory retirement at age sixty—which even the CEO must comply with. For this reason Murthy recently retired. This ensures continued upward opportunity.
- No nepotism. The founders' children are not allowed to take over the company. In a country where most conglomerates are run like kingdoms by their founders' family members, this makes Infosys an attractive place to begin a career.
- Access to day care centers with trained teachers, and a gymnasium with tennis and volleyball courts
- A fully staffed medical center
- A cafeteria with high-quality food
- Sleeping facilities for employees who work late
- An open-door policy held by all senior management
- Employee committees that make many management decisions; for example, a committee of employees decides what should be on the cafeteria menu

To copy Infosys, competitors would have to abandon many of the entrapments, beliefs, practices, and habits common to India's largest corporations. As long as these entrapments hold, Infosys can enjoy one of the most powerful sources of sustainable competitive advantage: preferential access to their industry's most critical resource—people.

CHAPTER ELEVEN

URBAN OUTFITTERS— THE RETAILER RUN BY CUSTOMERS

"We weren't taught ways of doing things so we did things differently from the outset."

—Dick Hayne, CEO, Urban Outfitters

What started as a homework assignment has become one of the fastest-growing, most profitable retailers in the United States. The rise of Urban Outfitters—a difficult-to-categorize retail store that serves college students—to over $1 billion in annual revenue offers a compelling reason to resist the pull of conformity.

Urban Outfitters in the Metal Phase

One lesson great innovators teach through their example is that simple thinking overpowers complex analysis. The recognition that the system is stuck comes more often from the direct experience of an individual than from the spreadsheets of an expert.

That was the case for Scott Belair and Richard Hayne, two college roommates, who after graduation found themselves together again, in Philadelphia, on the campus of the University of Pennsylvania. Belair was studying business at the Wharton Business School; Hayne was studying anthropology.

Commitment to Pass a Class

The commitment that led Belair and Hayne to see the opportunity that would lead to forming their company was not dramatic. Unlike other innovators featured in this book, neither drew on a significant childhood experience that drove them to retail. Indeed neither knew much about the industry as they embarked on their journey. What they had was a class assignment. Belair needed to conceive of a business for an entrepreneurship class, and Hayne agreed to help.

Rigidity and the Unmet Need for Scented Candles

Research shows that entrepreneurs rarely see new opportunities until they have the intention (make the commitment) to start a business. Belair's class gave him this intention, and he and Hayne brainstormed what business they might start.

Instead of researching industry growth rates and structures, the two asked a simple question: "What do we need that we can't get?" This led them to thinking of products that students like them would like to be able to buy but that retailers near the Penn campus were not selling. They came up with a list of items such as vintage clothing, scented candles, Indian fabrics, interesting T-shirts, and ethnic jewelry.

This simple exercise revealed to the would-be entrepreneurs that the system, at least in some small way, was stuck. There were things students wanted to buy but that retailers were not selling.

Their idea was compelling enough to earn Belair a good grade and to convince the two to actually start their store. They pulled together $5,000, rented a 400-square-foot space near campus, and launched a store called Free People, selling an odd assortment of inexpensive used clothing and other items that they themselves, as students, would want.

Urban Outfitters in the Water Phase

Their Water phase shows all the elements you would expect of a successful innovation. They created the strategy together; it was not the sole brainchild of one person. They faced disbelief, most helpfully by other retailers who did not take Free People as a serious threat. Because they were not retailers, they did not limit themselves in the way other retailers automatically do. For example, they sold used clothing and new products together, while most serious retailers avoid selling used merchandise.

But the root of their success was the metaphor the friends originally used to conceive of their business. From the first, they thought of themselves as customers. When they launched the store they maintained this perspective. They were creating a store run by customers. As Hayne later explained, "I was the market. Everyone associated with the store was the market."

At the outset this metaphor—a store run by customers—seemed insignificant but would have a profound impact on the company's future success. This metaphor represents a challenging shift for traditional retailers, most of whom think of their stores as outlets or distribution points from which their employees sell or "push" goods to customers. The store run by customers challenges this view. Urban Outfitters made stores places where customers—some working for the retailer, some visiting—convene. For its founders, there was no boundary between the workers and the customers; the two were the same.

This view would flower into numerous unorthodox decisions over the next two decades. Those decisions would help the company evolve into a unique innovation that traditional retailers would resist defending against. This situation—which occurs when you make decisions that your competition will not bother to defend—is what Sun Tzu called "taking whole."

The Free People store was a hit on campus, so much so that while Belair graduated and launched a career on Wall Street, Hayne stayed in Philadelphia to continue running the store.

Urban Outfitters in the Wood Phase

The Urban Outfitters Wood phase would last about fifteen years, as the two novice entrepreneurs put in place the essential pieces needed for growth. During this period they would add and remove elements across three fronts:

1. They refined the concept to attract customers (users).
2. They built their team in order to have the right people in place.
3. They secured critical partners.

Over the first few years of operation Belair, the Wharton student, worked on Wall Street while Hayne was successfully growing the business. Hayne's progress was significant enough to attract Belair from a promising financial career, and in 1976 he returned to Philadelphia to help his friend get the Free People store off the ground.

They immediately started shaping their small store into the image of a large retailer. They changed the company's name to Urban Outfitters and officially incorporated.

How They Attracted Their Users

On the customer battlefront, Urban Outfitters had already proved successful. Their concept was working. They hired college students and gave them the freedom to shape the store as they would like.

Their challenge was not to get more shoppers into the store but to put more stores in front of shoppers. They needed to open new locations. Four years after Belair returned, the original store had grown to $3 million in revenue and was generating enough profit to open a second store. Sticking to their successful formula—putting stores near campuses—the two chose Cambridge, Massachusetts, as their next target. They built their second store within reach of several colleges there in 1980.

Getting the Right People in the Right Places

To continue its store growth the company needed funding, but to get funding the company needed more professional financial records and practices, something neither founder had the background to ensure. So in 1987 Urban Outfitters hired a CFO, who institutionalized professional financial practices and introduced new controls to better manage shoplifting.

Meanwhile, the founders put intense focus on making sure they had the right employees in the stores. They were careful to hire people who represented the Urban Outfitters customer, who had fashion sense, and who came from the community that the particular Urban Outfitters store intended to serve.

Partners and Their Importance

The company had little difficulty securing supply partners. With one store generating over $3 million in revenue and a second store opening, promising yet more revenue growth, Urban Outfitters was an attractive client to the suppliers the company cared about.

Financial partners were the key block to the company's growth. But Urban Outfitters's CFO had put in place the measures banks would want to see before lending. He helped the company borrow $3 million to open six new stores over the next three years.

With its management team rounded out, loyal customers in Philadelphia and Cambridge, and the banking partners willing to underwrite the costs, the company was ready to grow. After fifteen years it had assembled a platform from which to expand.

Urban Outfitters in the Fire Phase

The company would grow at an explosive rate over the next ten years, opening stores across the United States. It would follow the approaches that have helped other fast-growing companies maintain their advantage in the face of increased competition. It would stick to its formula, preempt competitive resistance by launching a series of unorthodox tactics, and shift more quickly than the competition to stay ahead, to stay inside the competitors' decision-making loop.

The excitement of rapid growth tempts many companies to change their formula, which risks shortening their Fire phase and potential. But even if Urban Outfitters's founders felt a temptation to alter their formula, they had less power to do so relative to traditional retailers, because they hired college students and gave them unusual freedom to shape the look and feel of their stores.

The company would remain true to its mission: serving the needs of local college students.

Unleashing Unorthodox Tactics

This unique management philosophy, grounded in the company's underlying metaphor of a store run by customers, also led Urban Outfitters to launch a series of unorthodox tactics that would collectively immunize the company from the competition because traditional competitors would resist copying Urban Outfitters's business innovations. Consider a few of the company's unorthodox decisions:

- It adapted each store's décor to the store's location. While most retailers install and reproduce an identical look and feel wherever they open a store, Urban Outfitters seeks out unique spaces and incorporates their features into the store. In Philadelphia, for example, Urban Outfitters opened a store in a former bank building and used the bank's safe as a product display room. Other stores were established in old theaters, a stock exchange, and even a former Woolworth's store. Each time the building's unique characteristics became part of the look and feel of the store.

- The store hired staff who fit the profile of its customers and looked for people with a strong sense of aesthetics ("sensory merchandisers" as Haynes calls them). This allowed the company to trust its employees in ways other retailers would not. For example, staff decided what music to play and even brought their own tapes and CDs to work. All department managers were given freedom to create the look of their section. As one manager explained, "It's the only place I've worked where you can bring an old crate to work, make something out of it, and [the bosses] love it."

- As mentioned in Chapter 8, Urban Outfitters paid young buyers to visit fashionable neighborhoods in the United States, London, and Paris and report on trends, and it sourced from unconventional places such as used clothing stores.

- It spent very little on marketing and instead focused on creating a store experience that captures people's attention. Each store is different, with displays that may incorporate a tractor, wheelbarrow, antique tables, and so on.

Walk through each of these business decisions and ask yourself, "If I were a traditional retailer (for example, the Gap, or Laura Ashley), would I copy this innovation?" Almost entirely across the board your answer would be "No," or in the most provocative stance, "Let me think about it some more." In the resulting competitive vacuum, Urban Outfitters grew.

Note that the central theme that makes all of these ideas possible is that Urban Outfitters sees its stores as being run by its customers. This is a fundamental shift in perspective. The result is a set of interlocking tactics that traditional retailers will hesitate to adopt because they require changes in deeply held beliefs and habits.

Looking at Customers Rather Than Products

Urban Outfitters has also been able to offer a great variety of products at a more rapid pace in a way that Sun Tzu and John Boyd would admire. The company often surprises its competitors by offering products that others do not foresee will work.

This happens in part because the company is not oriented to its business the way most companies are. Most retailers take a product perspective; they see themselves, for example, as a clothing store or a sports apparel store. Urban Outfitters pays less attention to its products. By focusing instead on the Urban Outfitters customer and lifestyle, the retailer is ready to offer almost anything a customer might want.

As Hayne explains, "We have this concept where we have a unique and singular group of people that we are trying to service and we have a concept that emphasizes the lifestyle approach to servicing these customers. The product category to us is not particularly important, as long as we can make money, but the lifestyle is incredibly important."

Beyond Geographic Growth

As its growth accelerated into the 1990s, Urban Outfitters seized two new growth opportunities. First, it recognized that it made more margin selling its own brands than selling others' brands. So it decided to begin selling more of its own brands.

From the traditional retailer perspective, the way to do this is obvious: Create a brand, commission products, and have the buyers incorporate these products into the mix. But since Urban Outfitters is run by customers, it could not force buyers to use its own brands.

Instead, the company created Urban Wholesale in 1990 to design, produce, and sell products under three different labels. What is interesting about this arrangement is that Urban Wholesale has to actively sell its goods to Urban Outfitters stores. They are not guaranteed sales.

The company's second significant nongeographic growth opportunity appeared two years later. Recognizing that its nonclothing products were unexpectedly popular, Urban Outfitters launched a new store concept: Anthropologie.

The first Anthropologie store was opened in a renovated auto dealership in Wayne, Pennsylvania. It was designed to target older shoppers living in the suburbs. Though it did sell clothing, it put more emphasis on "hard goods," including furniture, books, picture frames, and soaps.

Shifting to Earth

By 1992, the company's sales reached $59.1 million, a 34.7 percent growth for the year. It was large enough and growing quickly enough to tap the public markets, which it did in 1993. The IPO raised $13 million, which was used to fund the opening of more stores.

Reaching a sustainable Earth phase in retail is difficult. Only retailers who innovate on the operational side (such as Wal-Mart) seem able to sustain their advantages. Whether Urban Outfitters can consolidate its gains is unclear. The company is still relatively small; at $1.2 billion in annual revenue the company belongs in the middle tier of retailers, with the likes of Abercrombie & Fitch and Bebe Stores Inc. Also, since it is still growing at 20–30 percent per year, seeking to consolidate its gains is perhaps premature.

To sustain the innovation that Urban Outfitters has unleashed on the world would mean shifting from its traditional source of advantage to something that will either lock in customers, lock out competitors, or lock up resources. To date the company has excelled on the customer front. But if history's lessons prove applicable to this innovative retailer, it will need to begin succeeding on the second source: To hold on to its gains, it will need to establish competitive barriers and start climbing precipitous heights.

With the company's unique perspective on retail (a store run by customers), it could certainly devise distinct operational practices that would solidify its gains.

CHAPTER TWELVE

PUMA AND THE RISE OF
SPORTS FASHION

In 1993 one of the world's most recognized sporting brands was on the brink of collapse. Puma AG had grown from a small German shoe factory into a large family-owned company, then into a fully independent, publicly traded corporation.

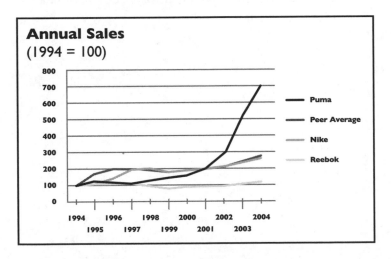

Annual Sales
(1994 = 100)

But recent years had been trying. The firm started losing money, year after year. In 1991, a Swedish conglomerate, Proventus AB, bought all of Puma's publicly traded stock. The next year, Proventus gave its new company a badly needed capital infusion. But even this was insufficient. The company continued its long, steady decline, posting its eighth straight year of profit losses in 1993.

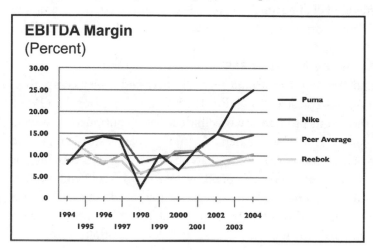

The company appeared to be stuck in a no-win situation. It was attempting to sell athletic footwear in a stagnant market. Product cycle times were accelerating, requiring companies to invest ever higher amounts in research and development and on new-product launches to remain on the cutting edge. But since Puma was the smallest of its peers, it could not win this spending race. Reebok and Nike could easily outspend whatever Puma could afford to invest.

So Puma tried what everyone else was trying. It tried to abandon the low-end, low-margin market and start selling higher-end, higher-margin sneakers. Nike and Reebok, however, were pursuing the identical strategy and there was insufficient room for so many players in the high-end market. Puma found itself squeezed; market share and sales declined still further.

In 1993, Puma appeared a lost cause. Ten years later, however, it emerged as the industry's idol. It is the fastest-growing, most profitable company in its industry. Industry leaders such as Nike and Reebok that once scoffed at the company are attempting to emulate its success. For this reason, Puma is one of the 100 most competitive companies of the decade ending 2005.

How did Puma engineer such a dramatic change of fate? By creating a new metaphor for its business and then managing the five stages of change until everyone—customers, partners, employees, competitors—saw things the way Puma did.

Puma in the Metal Phase

Around the time that Puma seemed at its end, a key competitor, Reebok, was also struggling. But Reebok was far larger than Puma and, though its profitability was in decline, it continued delivering some profit to its shareholders. As such, Reebok's discontent did not reach the depths of Puma's. Reebok saw hope in copying the same strategy of its peers—spending heavily in R&D and marketing, shifting from the low end to the high end—because it was large enough to theoretically survive such a game. Puma, however, was too small to smell the cheese at the end of that maze. Their only hope was to do something radically different.

Discontent Leads to a Bold Move: A Thirty-Year-Old CEO

Puma's owner, Proventus, replaced the CEO with one of its proven executives. But when an internal shakeup removed this new CEO, Proventus—perhaps out of desperation for a radical change—made a bold move: It handed over control of Puma to a thirty-year-old marketing executive, Jochen Zeitz. At that time, he became the youngest CEO of a publicly traded German company.

Zeitz's resume was short but impressive. After earning his MBA, he worked for Procter & Gamble, where he refined his marketing skills. When a headhunter called him about joining a relatively small German shoe manufacturer, German-born Zeitz decided to head back home. He felt a small company would offer more opportunity. A few years later his bet paid off for him, in the form of a CEO role. But would this bet pay off for Puma?

The First Water to Wood Cycle: Solving the Financial Crisis

Most corporate turnarounds consist of two distinct cycles. First, the company acts quickly to get out of a financial crisis; then it pursues growth. This makes sense—without stable financials and access to sufficient capital, a company will be attempting to grow from a shaky foundation.

Entering the Water Phase: Introduce a New Metaphor— the Corporation as Athlete

Zeitz's first challenge was to pull Puma back from the brink of failure and prepare it for growth. He and his team would not work on growing until they had implemented an extensive restructuring program, optimizing the global organizational structure. To do this, they introduced a new metaphor, that of the company as an athlete. Just as an athlete must train before a game, Puma needed to get in shape. The team introduced a strategy they called the "fitness program." This metaphor communicated concisely a complex mass of information. It communicated, for example, that the company was not dying but was just out of shape (it retold the past to create a better future); getting in shape would require some pain but it was a worthwhile, healthy thing to do that would lead to a better quality of life; and that just as each muscle in a body needs to exercise, so every part of the Puma organization would need to get in shape itself for the organism to be ready.

This program involved rigorous cost-cutting and deep reorganization. Inflexible structures were changed (for example, Puma merged the purchasing and product development departments), several warehouses were replaced with a central distribution center, and all departments were converted into profit centers.

Shifting to the Wood Phase: Getting People and Investors on Board

Puma faced a battle on three fronts: its people, users, and partners. However, during this phase, Puma did not worry much about customers or even partners; it put all its focus on its people.

The biggest barrier for Puma's turnaround was that the company had been restructured so many times before that people had grown cynical about the process. They had adopted a "story" about restructuring that went something like this: Puma faces trouble, it restructures, but the restructuring does not work, so we remain in trouble. They had seen how the restructuring story ends and so were not easily enrolled in what Zeitz and his team were undertaking.

Zeitz had to replace this story, so he focused on pushing through all of the planned changes quickly and simultaneously. In just six months Puma implemented all the necessary changes, "from reengineering to cutting costs, closing production facilities, warehouses, and so on and so forth. We just streamlined the entire organization without compromise."

The results of this first cycle of change were impressive. In 1993, the first year of Zeitz's leadership and of the turnaround, Puma showed a profit. This was the first profit in eight years and it signaled to employees and investors that a new story was about to begin—they were not repeating Puma's history of failure. The "fitness program" lasted about three years. In 1996 Puma gave the first dividend to shareholders since the company went public in 1991. By 1996 the company posted its highest three-year sales record in corporate history.

These facts, points in the new story line of Puma, created a new picture for investors, who now began changing their perception of the company and, more important, the way they would project Puma's future financial performance. This new story created an opportunity Puma had been waiting for. In order to fuel future growth, there was one critical resource that Puma needed: funding. The newfound appeal of the company allowed Puma to offer stock on the Frankfurt and Munich exchanges in June 1996 in an amount that reduced the share of its parent company, Proventus Handels AB, to 25 percent. A few months later Proventus sold half of its stake (12.5 percent) to Monarchy/Regency, an American movie production and distribution firm.

The first Water-to-Wood cycle of Puma's turnaround put the company in an enviable position. While before it was privately held and 100 percent controlled by one company, now it was publicly held with no shareholder controlling more than 12.5 percent of its stock. It was also profitable and growing. Its people grew excited about the company's future. The critical pieces for growth were in place.

The Second Water-to-Wood Cycle: Growth

Cost-cutting alone would not be enough for Puma to survive. The company remained one of the smallest in its industry and still faced the dilemma of an impossible strategic choice. If it focused on the low-end market, its margins might decrease to the point of nonprofitability again. Moving into the crowded high-end market would require more investment than Puma could afford. When your perspective reveals no acceptable solution, you must change your perspective. This is what Puma did.

Enter the Water Phase: Fashion for Fans

In 1997 Puma launched what it called "Phase II of the Corporate Development Strategy." Puma took on a bold transformation in how it defined itself. Since its founding in the 1920s, Puma had been a shoe company. But since this perspective no longer offered an acceptable future, Zeitz and his team reconceived Puma as a fashion company. They turned industry priorities upside-down. While its peers prioritized sport as primary and considered fashion secondary, Puma decided to prioritize fashion and de-emphasize sport, to be the first sports brand to merge sport and fashion and thereby become a "sports-lifestyle" brand.

This reconception seems minor, but it had profound implications for how Puma would operate. Today, for example, Puma offers lines of shoes and sports clothing created by designers such as Lamine Kouyate and Amy Garbers, a vision that's incompatible with a company focused solely on sports shoes.

Like other successful innovators, Zeitz's new metaphor left room for others to participate. He and his team did not fully define what this new strategy entailed, and they did not direct from above a new set of detailed priorities. Rather they left room for experimentation.

Zeitz gave a twenty-one-year-old skateboarder named Antonio Bertone control over a new Puma division called "sport-lifestyle." This division was responsible for creating and launching new fashion projects. Bertone was given the freedom to experiment, keeping the new vision for Puma in mind. He collaborated with the German fashion designer Jil Sander to create a new line of fashionable shoes that combined elements of Puma's classic 1960s soccer cleat with new materials (such as suede) and modern colors.

These new shoes were released in 1998. They were met, as is usually the case for new ideas, with disbelief. Industry experts dismissed Puma's fashion experiments. Puma's core customers wanted the company to stick with what they knew Puma for: soccer shoes. New ideas like these almost always meet a skeptical audience because, as all ancient schools that have studied the human condition have found, human beings dislike change.

Despite this initial skepticism, Puma's new shoes took off. Fashionable customers created so much demand for them that retailers had to create waiting lists in anticipation of new shipments. This experiment was the pilot that would transform the entire company. "It took a while—and from my perspective, a lot of energy—to protect this new little child [the lifestyle group] of Puma from getting killed," said Zeitz. "Eventually, it became the entire company."

Transitioning to Wood: Enrolling Partners and Consumers

Puma had already won the minds of its people and investors. Now it had to win over users and partners. Over the next few years the company focused its attention on penetrating the minds of its customers and its marketing partners, enrolling a critical mass of them into its new innovation: Puma as a "sports-fashion" brand.

Puma took particular aim at the United States. The United States was the world's largest sporting-goods market, yet Puma generated only 4.5 percent of its sales in the country. With just a 1 percent market share, Puma felt it faced great opportunities with U.S. consumers.

In Puma's business, the key to penetrating the minds of consumers is to find the right, influential partners. So Puma moved quickly to put in place the pieces (the Wood) it needed to reconstruct U.S. consumer perceptions of its brand. It first bought Puma North America and the Puma trademark from Proventus. It signed a long-term contract with the Women's Tennis Association (WTA), through which Puma became the official supplier of shoes and textiles for the WTA tour. It bought a 25 percent share in Logo Athletic, a company that was the leading provider of sports apparel to American professional sports leagues.

As is always the case during the Wood phase, Puma faced a lag between effort and sales. But it was assembling the critical pieces it needed to be competitive in the United States. Once it had compiled what it needed, these Wood elements began interacting. Tennis sponsorships fueled further marketing efforts, which combined with the credibility derived from being a leading provider to sports teams. Together these spurred the awareness and then adoption of Puma products by consumers, triggering Puma's Fire phase.

Puma in the Fire Phase

As the Puma brand began taking off through the United States and the world, Puma maintained a rapid pace, keeping its decision-cycle times short, enabling it to keep inside its competitors' cycles. It launched a series of creative tactics that kept the competition off-guard. Some of these tactics were even more powerful because they were moves that the competition would choose not to copy:

- It organized itself into a "virtual company" with three headquarters instead of just one; each headquarters took responsibility for different corporate functions. Puma hires people for different functions in different countries and enables them to connect and collaborate through technology. Its product development function, for example, is divided among three locations; certain functions take place in Germany, others in the United States, and others in Hong Kong. This is a radical organizational design decision, and one that its larger adversaries would find too expensive to duplicate and would resist adopting themselves.

- It launched a broad array of products far beyond the bounds by which its competitors define their business. It produced, for example, a cutting-edge bicycle that cannot be stolen because its frame's integrity is held by a lock incorporated into the bicycle itself. It launched a line of driving shoes and racing suits and is today the main producer of these items for both Formula One and NASCAR.
- To feature its broad product offering, it launched concept stores in key cities such as Athens, New York, Paris, London, and Tokyo. These stores give customers an experience of everything Puma does and offers, an experience Puma can't deliver through retailers who only buy a limited set of products.
- Perhaps Puma's most important strategic move was to adopt an "open" design model. The company contracts with people such as France's Xuly Bet, Japan's Yasuhiro Mihara, and model Christy Turlington to unleash an ever-expanding, ever-changing line of products, even incorporating new categories of products. Companies that define themselves as sports shoe companies or, even in the broadest sense, as athletic apparel companies (Nike, for example) would find this kind of idea too difficult to copy. Their businesses' R & D efforts are based on proprietary development of performance technology. An "open" model is countercultural.

These are not tactics Puma's competitors cannot copy. Indeed if Puma continues its rise, competitors will likely embrace many of these innovative approaches. But they are choices competitors will hesitate to adopt. In the gap of this hesitation, Puma will grow. As Puma continues unleashing such unorthodox tactics, it can extend this competitive gap to prolong its unfettered growth.

Puma in the Earth Phase

Has Puma consolidated its gains? It has at least proven itself not a fad. It is not L.A. Gear Inc., which sparked with a hit line of footwear and then collapsed almost as quickly as it rose. Puma's innovation persists.

But the competition is beginning to wake up to Puma's new model. Converse has teamed up with John Varvatos, Vans with Marc Jacobs, and Adidas with Stella McCartney to design products. The company can probably continue to compete in the Fire phase. Zeitz believes, for example, that Puma has become an automatically changing organism that constantly evolves. It can, in other words, stay ahead of the competition during Fire.

But to consolidate its gains it must achieve one of three things: (1) It must lock in customers, (2) it must lock out competition, or (3) it must lock up resources.

iDoing the first is difficult. Puma has certainly built brand loyalty, but such loyalties, unsupported by more concrete barriers, always erode with time. They are not permanent.

Locking up resources is a challenge because Puma's "open" model makes such a strategy almost impossible. The product innovativeness on which it depends derives precisely from not locking up its inspiration.

But Puma appears to hope it can achieve the second form of consolidation, blocking out competitors. It seems to be seeking economies of scale (or to climb precipitous heights higher than the competition would think to follow) by merging with one of the world's largest fashion companies.

In early April 2007, Puma's shares jumped 10 percent. Then on April 10 the French retailer Pinault-Printemps-Redoute (PPR—owner of the Gucci brand) announced it had acquired a 27 percent stake in the company. This positions PPR for a takeover of Puma. Puma management supports this takeover as being good for the company and for investors. If this acquisition succeeds—as it appears it will—Puma may find a home on the precipitous heights its peers, Nike and Reebok, would find too costly to follow.

CHAPTER THIRTEEN

NOKIA AND THE MOBILE PHONE REVOLUTION

In December 1988, things were looking so bleak for the Nokia Corporation that its chairman committed suicide. Founded in 1865 as a forestry business located near the river Nokia in Finland, the storied company had evolved into a sprawling conglomerate, one of Finland's largest companies. It commanded businesses in industries ranging from rubber footwear and tires to cable operations and consumer electronics to paper goods. But for the decade, profits had been declining, pulled down by the company's consumer electronics division.

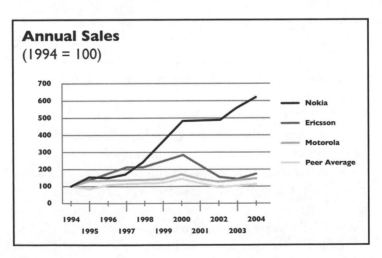

In the 1980s, going into consumer electronics had seemed like a good idea. The company had been fairly successful in data processing and industrial automation. It could probably leverage these technical skills into competing with TVs and radios. Between 1980 and 1988, Nokia's consumer electronics business took off, growing from 10 percent of Nokia's sales to 60 percent over the period.

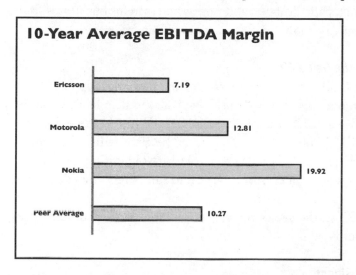

From the outside—seeing only its infrastructure and employees—Nokia appeared a diversified company. But with more than half of its revenue derived from one business area—consumer electronics—Nokia's survival depended heavily on the price of TVs.

Nokia in the Metal Phase

The problem was that as the 1980s came to a close, TV prices were dropping, pulled down by a new crop of competitors. Low-cost Asian producers were undercutting established Western producers, bringing down prices and margins, as they pushed what was once a high-margin business into the realm of commodity. Between 1989 and 1990 Nokia's profits began dropping, and by 1991 the company posted a $102 million loss.

It was this dramatic turn, when a 125-year-old company was brought to its knees in just three years that led Nokia to the depths of discontent from which great innovations spring.

After the chairman took his life in 1988, Nokia put in place a new CEO to launch a restructuring. He divided the company into six business groups and divested several old divisions, exiting the flooring, paper, rubber, and ventilation systems businesses. But Nokia needed a more dramatic change of direction.

Enter the New CEO

Jorma Ollila spent eight years working for Citigroup in various European offices. He was eventually posted to help launch a Citigroup office in his home country, Finland. While there, he decided to leave Citigroup and join Nokia, at the time still a diversified conglomerate. In 1985 he took a role in Nokia's finance department. A few years later he was tapped to run Nokia's mobile phone division.

In 1992, at the age of forty-one, Ollila was asked to take over as CEO of Nokia.

Weak Signals

Ollila had been with the company for six years and knew its businesses fairly well. He was trained as an economist and so looked at Nokia's environment as an economist might. His assessment revealed three weak signals that pointed to a significant opportunity:

1. Governments across Europe, and the world, were deregulating the telecom sector. Businesses that had previously been served by protected, national telecom monopolies were now open to independent competition.
2. Analog communications technology was slowly giving way to digital technology. This transformation would allow phone operators to offer a host of new services and thereby expand telecom markets around the world.

3. Unlike the United States, Europe had agreed on and adopted one common phone network standard a year before Ollila took over. This would enable European telecom companies to compete across borders with technological ease.

Ollila sensed that these three weak signals would lead the telecom industry into a very different competitive arena. Whereas in the past telecommunications services were defined by country and provided by protected government operations, competition in the future would be waged by more innovative, dynamic, private companies without regard to borders. Ollila decided he would move into this world quickly, before the competition.

The Institutional Commitment

Great innovations almost always reach back to an event that at the time seemed without clear purpose. For entrepreneurial innovations, this event usually seems to be one in which the innovator experienced something meaningful and made a profound commitment. Corporate innovations also reach back, but the commitments they draw on seem less personal. Perhaps this is because the CEO of a large company can wield a longer lever by seeking beyond him- or herself and finding some commitment the entire company holds.

In the case of Nokia, this commitment occurred in the 1960s when the company decided to expand into communications systems. At the time, this seemed a tangential offshoot only loosely related to its industrial automation and consumer electronics businesses. But this offshoot proved pivotal to Nokia's turnaround.

The commitment to communications systems led Nokia into telecommunications. By the time Ollila took over as CEO, Nokia had nearly thirty years of telecommunications experience. As Ollila puts it, "Nokia had a background in telecommunications since the early 1960s—so we were not totally new in this business area."

With the three critical elements of discontent in place—weak signals revealing rigidity meeting a commitment—Ollila had the platform from which to launch a change.

Nokia in the Water Phase

Ollila devised a vision for a "new Nokia." The company would cease to be a conglomerate and instead would become a company that was, as he says, "clearly telecoms-oriented." He prepared a memo for Nokia's board, outlining his new vision and his plans for achieving it. He wrote that he planned to divest Nokia of nearly all its nontelecom businesses and put in place the pieces needed to realize the new Nokia: Nokia as a telecom company.

It is unclear how much resistance or disbelief Ollila faced. Perhaps the board members had reached sufficient discontent that they were open to such a radical turn of direction. Perhaps they resisted at the time but now, enjoying the unambiguous success of the decision, cannot clearly recall their initial doubts. Whatever the reaction, Ollila prevailed and won support for his new vision.

Nokia in the Wood Phase

"In every block of marble I see a statue as plain as though it stood before me, shaped and perfect in attitude and action. I have only to hew away the rough walls that imprison the lovely apparition to reveal it to the other eyes as mine see it."

—Michelangelo

As with most corporate transformations, the Nokia turnaround occurred in two distinct cycles. The goal of the first was to carve away what did not fit Ollila's new vision for Nokia; of the second, to put in place or grow what was missing.

Ollila spent his first two years removing what no longer fit. He immediately replaced Nokia's top team with a crop of young managers. Nokia Data had been sold off the year before and Ollila wanted to do the same with the company's consumer electronics business. But he could find no buyers, so he cut its work force by 45 percent, shut down factories, and consolidated operations to reduce overhead costs.

In 1994 Nokia sold its power unit, and the following year sold its television and tire businesses. Ollila merged the businesses that remained into three divisions: telecommunications (which produced infrastructure for fixed and mobile telephone systems), mobile phones (which made handsets), and electronics and cable (which would concentrate on products closely related to telecom).

Around 1995, Ollila had substantially carved away what he needed to. Nokia was slim and focused exclusively on one industry: telecom. As he described in a 1995 interview, "When you look at the task we set out three years ago of creating a company clearly telecoms-oriented, we are pretty close to what we have to do—and we have been able to implement the changes faster than we expected."

From Carving to Building

During this carving period, Nokia made no acquisitions and entered no joint ventures of note. It had made one important strategic investment before Ollila took over: in 1991 it bought a U.K. company, Technophone Ltd. That proved a critical piece in Nokia's ability to excel in mobile phone R & D. But around 1997, as the company's growth began to pick up steam, Nokia entered into numerous deals with which it expanded its telecom capabilities. It formed a global partnership with IBM, for example, to accelerate the growth of the wireless Internet. The two companies worked together to develop technology that would enable customers to extend e-business from the desktop onto mobile phones. Nokia partnered with RealNetworks to develop technology for delivering Internet audio and video content to mobile devices. It even partnered with Whirlpool to develop network solutions for the home. Nokia was winning over all three stakeholders most critical during the Wood phase: people, partners, and customers. Its people were excited because Nokia had stopped losing money and was now growing. Nokia became one of the most desirable companies to work for in Finland. Partners were embracing Nokia as a firm that could help them move into the mobile Internet. And customers were buying Nokia's phones in increasing numbers. It was not until 1998, however, that customers would pass their tipping point and pull Nokia into the leagues of its larger competitors, Motorola and Ericsson.

Nokia in the Fire Phase

In 1998, Nokia launched the 6100 handset phone. It was a major breakthrough. It was small (about the size of a pack of cigarettes), lightweight, and had an impressive battery life. Nokia first introduced the phone in China but it quickly took over the world. The 6100 contributed to a banner year for Nokia. In 1998 the company sold nearly 41 million phones overall and produced a 50 percent jump in revenue, to $15 billion from $10 billion. Its operating profits increased 75 percent and its stock shot up more than 220 percent, delivering a 250 percent total return to its shareholders that year. Nokia had caught fire. The next year, 1999, sales jumped another $6 billion to $21 billion while the company delivered shareholders a 490 percent total return. Nokia was still smaller than Motorola ($30 billion in revenue) and Ericsson ($26 billion), but it was catching up quickly.

Innovations that are sustainable are rarely driven by product alone. Products can trigger the Fire phase and raise public awareness that a company is doing something interesting, but products are too easy to copy. Nokia persisted through the Fire phase by following what John Boyd advised his pilots: cycling faster and producing more creative responses than did the competition. For example, in 1998 Nokia decided it needed to protect its business from Microsoft, which was making inroads into the software that runs mobile phones. It did not have the scale or expertise to compete with Microsoft in the game Microsoft knows best (software), so Nokia devised a creative strategy to simulate Microsoft's size. It convinced its rivals Ericsson and Motorola to join a new alliance they would call Symbian. Together these rivals developed and continue developing their own mobile software.

Toward the end of 2000 the telecom industry experienced a sudden, painful crash. At the time, Ollila and his wife were refurbishing a 200-year-old mansion outside of Helsinki. Ollila and Nokia had already proven themselves. They could have reacted as most of their peers did by focusing the company on its core business of handsets, retrenching from the riskier bets such as software and mobile Internet technology. But Ollila did exactly the opposite.

He pushed Nokia ahead against Microsoft with still heavier investments in software. In 2003 Nokia increased its stake in Symbian to 32 percent from 19 percent. This bet paid off for Nokia quickly as the market for mobile software exploded.

In 2001, Nokia's market share eclipsed that of Ericsson. Ironically, back when Nokia was in deep financial trouble it narrowly missed being taken over by this Swedish rival. In 2002, Nokia toppled Motorola from its position as the largest mobile phone manufacturer in the world. Between 1998, when Nokia entered its Fire phase, and 2004, Nokia more than doubled its revenues to $36 billion from $15 billion.

Nokia in the Earth Phase

The question for most investors now is whether Nokia will sustain its dominance and how it will do so. Mobile phones are transforming into multimedia devices luring in new breeds of competitors. Apple, for example, is currently pushing its sophisticated handheld device, the iPhone. Traditional mobile devices are commoditizing, with inexpensive Asian manufacturers selling phones at ever-lower prices. The situation bears some uncomfortable resemblance to Nokia's consumer electronics business in the 1980s, when the company fell deep into loss. But Nokia is showing signs of resilience. By 1995, arguably the point at which Nokia exited the Fire phase, the company had a worldwide market share of 35 percent. As of 2007 it has sustained this share even in the face of strong competition. Of the consolidation options—lock in clients, lock out competition, or lock up resources—Nokia appears to be seeking to lock out competition. As one of the three biggest players in its market it can afford to invest more than most contenders. The more it invests, the more difficult it becomes to follow. This is what Sun Tzu would call climbing precipitous heights. Ollila describes Nokia's key to success as "the constant and vigorous investment in research and development—around 10 percent of group sales—as well as design and changing the product portfolio by simplifying the technology and allowing economies of scale in production." If we draw the boundaries of analysis traditionally, around

Nokia's direct competitors, this strategy has been proven to work. Only one other company, Motorola, is targeting the same high-end market Nokia serves, so Nokia may not need to concern itself with Sony, Samsung, and LG Electronics, which are focused on the lower end. With fifteen manufacturing facilities in nine countries and R & D facilities in twelve countries, Nokia has scale few could rival.

But significant innovations disrupt giants because they come from unexpected places. With the mobile phone morphing into the territory of computer firms and music-device companies, and attracting the attention of countless other industries, it is difficult to discern from where Nokia's next threat will strike, and therefore against whose measure we should judge how far Nokia has climbed precipitous heights.

CHAPTER FOURTEEN

MICROSOFT AND THE EMERGENCE OF SOFTWARE

By 1995 Microsoft had already achieved what most ambitious companies aspire to. Since its founding twenty years earlier it had grown from a two-man partnership into a $6 billion firm that dominated its market with an 85 percent market share. It had established itself as the largest software company in the world, the best-known software brand, and secured itself at the hub of a fast-growing global industry. Examining Microsoft's rise to this Earth state offers valuable lessons for outmaneuvering the competition.

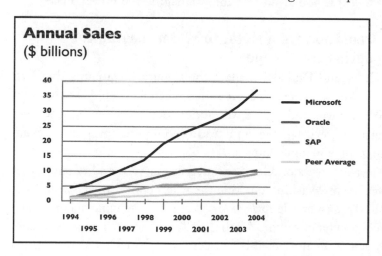

What makes Microsoft unique is not its sprint to greatness. Nokia, Puma, Infosys, the Apollo Group, and other companies analyzed in this book all produced similar rises. What makes Microsoft unique is what happened next.

Most companies would be content to have won such a worthwhile race, allowed its leaders to cash out their gains, and then shifted its attention to protecting its ground. In other words, most companies would have reached the accepted inevitable mark of maturity, the "plateau."

But Microsoft achieved what few others have attempted. It took no rest after its sprint. It broke through the finish tape and kept running. From selling $6 billion in 1995, by then far larger than its peers, the company multiplied revenues more than six times, reaching $40 billion by 2005. Microsoft not only broke away from the pack by passing through Metal, Water, Wood, and Fire more quickly, but it has managed the mature Earth phase with unprecedented success. Only Samsung, Vodafone, and Dell have managed to reach such size and maintain such high growth rates.

Business strategists will be analyzing ingredients of the Microsoft story for many years to come, but what it especially offers to readers of this book is insight into managing the Earth phase.

The Transition from Metal to Water: Laying the Foundation for Change

Bill Gates and Paul Allen spent their youth in pursuits that left most of their peers puzzled. At a time when few people knew what a computer was and even fewer understood its potential, the two youngsters were writing and testing computer programs, even earning some income doing so.

After high school, Gates enrolled at Harvard and Allen at the University of Washington. But their academic careers would be cut short by an article in *Popular Mechanics* magazine about a new microcomputer called the Altair. Reading that article, the two suddenly saw immense potential for converting their passion for programming into something bigger. Almost in an instant, what had been a hobby was transformed into a compelling, burning calling.

They each quit college and formed a partnership, named "Micro-soft," to write software for the Altair. In 1975, Micro-soft's first year of operation, the company posted $16,000 in revenue.

While Gates and Allen were running their two-man company, a young New Yorker, working at an electronics firm called the Ampex Corporation, was building a database for the Central Intelligence Agency. During this project he came across a research report on relational databases; what he read convinced him that corporations were overlooking a tremendous opportunity. He and some partners "realized there was tremendous business potential in the relational database model." So in 1977, Larry Ellison left his job to start his own company, with the intent of commercializing the technology for building relational databases. He invested $2,000 of his own money in the new venture, which he named Software Development Laboratories. A few years later he changed the company's name to Oracle, the code name given to his CIA project.

As the 1970s came to a close, both young software companies were positioning themselves to ride a wave they believed would transform the world. And both had their sights fixed on IBM, the company that led the computer revolution.

Microsoft in the Wood Phase

In the beginning, Gates and Allen focused on creating new pro-gramming languages and winning over users to sell them to. They first developed BASIC, which they licensed to Radio Shack and to Apple Computer, a much larger company at the time, for $21,000 in 1977. That same year the company, now called Microsoft without a hyphen, developed FORTRAN and then, in 1978, a version of COBOL. The company's customer base grew, and by 1978 Micro-soft was generating $1 million in revenue and employed 13 people.

Winning Over Partners

The year 1980 was pivotal for Microsoft, though no one could have predicted just how important it would be. That was the year Gates and Allen signed a contract with IBM to develop an operating system for IBM's breakthrough product, the personal computer.

Microsoft was not IBM's first choice. It had pursued a far larger, more established firm, Digital Research, but could not negotiate an acceptable arrangement. So IBM turned to Microsoft. Because Microsoft had no operating system to offer (it had only been working on programming languages), it bought an operating system from a Seattle firm for $75,000, modified it, and renamed it MS-DOS.

The IBM partnership would become the pole that vaulted Microsoft into dominance. IBM's PCs gained acceptance in offices and homes nationwide, and every one of them carried with it Microsoft's MS-DOS. The company would grow, substantially under the radar screen of large corporations who were paying more attention to hardware—computers and mainframes—than to the software they ran.

Oracle, meanwhile, was enjoying even greater success. Its programmers were working to simplify databases and show corporations why and where to use the technology to manage information. It was building a strong sales force and was slowly pushing the Shift—the realization of databases' potential—into the minds of corporate decision-makers.

Microsoft in the Fire Phase

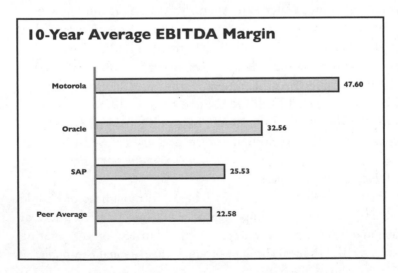

10-Year Average EBITDA Margin

Motorola	47.60
Oracle	32.56
SAP	25.53
Peer Average	22.58

I will touch only briefly on the Fire phase because Microsoft's most valuable lessons have to do with managing Earth. Both Microsoft and Oracle were poised to benefit from a transformation that the computer and its software would impose on the world. Throughout the 1980s both companies reacted to a fast-changing market by releasing a series of new products in rapid succession (for example, Microsoft released new versions of MS-DOS; a graphical user interface called Windows; computer mice) and forming a network of alliances. To erode IBM's PC monopoly, Microsoft formed alliances with Compaq, Hewlett-Packard, Texas Instruments, and Digital Equipment Corp. In the mid-1980s both companies went public: Oracle in March 1986, raising about $30 million, and Microsoft in 1987, raising $61 million. These issues coincided with a wave of other high-tech offerings from companies that included Sun Microsystems and Adobe Systems.

By 1990 Oracle was generating more than $500 million in revenue and Microsoft became the first software company to reach $1 billion in annual revenue. Oracle reached the Earth phase by securing its position as the leading database management software firm; Microsoft achieved the same by dominating the operating system space.

The parallels between the Oracle and Microsoft stories are astounding. Founded within years of each other, both hitched rides on the PC bandwagon initiated by IBM, both dominated their chosen domains, and they went public within a year of each other. But their stories diverge as they entered their mature Earth phases in 1990. Oracle would continue to grow at a rate comparable to that of its industry. But Microsoft would consolidate from its gains a set of advantages that would springboard the company far beyond the reach of even its most aggressive peers.

Microsoft in the Earth Phase

In 1990 Oracle booked its first quarterly profit loss. Investors, angry because they had been led to expect rapid growth, sued the company for giving misleading earnings forecasts. This upset forced the company to restructure its leadership team, consolidate operations, and lower earnings forecasts.

In March of the same year in which Oracle was losing investor confidence, Microsoft gave its shareholders a 100 percent stock dividend and split its stock. A few months later the company reported it had generated a record $1.18 billion in annual revenue. What was behind this sudden divergence in performance? I believe this is a compelling illustration of how one company brilliantly managed the Earth phase, and one did not. Microsoft was adjusting its tactics to adopt a more stable, mature competitive stance. What Microsoft had depended on for advantage up to this point—quick reaction to emerging needs of computer users—was not what would ensure its continued success. Instead the company abandoned old tactics and embraced those demanded by the Earth phase of competition. Those who deride the company for being slow to market (it is rarely the first to launch a new product) or weak on initial product quality (it often introduces lower-quality products and slowly improves them over time) are misunderstanding where advantage comes from in the Earth phase. Microsoft grew from $6 billion to $44 billion precisely because it stopped trying to be fast and agile. John Boyd's rapid airborne maneuvers may help you win the war, but they offer little help in governing your domain. Such governance requires a new approach. Microsoft understood this.

Let's analyze how Microsoft has built a sustainable wall around its innovation by looking at the three most important sources of long-term competitive advantage:

1. Locking in customers
2. Locking out competition
3. Locking up resources

Most companies seek to sustain their innovations by seizing one of these three, but Microsoft holds all three simultaneously and has assembled them in such a way that each reinforces and strengthens the others.

Locking in Customers

Central to Microsoft's advantage is that the company holds a 90 percent market share of operating systems. By convincing IBM to use MS-DOS, Microsoft came to own the de facto standard operating system for all computers—*all* computers.

Therefore, when Microsoft offers a new product it is selling to existing customers who would prefer something guaranteed to work with the underlying software of their computers. If you could buy two spreadsheet programs of approximately equal quality, you are more likely to choose Microsoft's because it carries less risk of being incompatible with your computer's operating system. Microsoft leveraged this fact to make Windows the de facto standard graphical user interface and to become the dominant provider of productivity software (word processing, spreadsheet, presentation, and so on). From these strongholds Microsoft has expanded to dominate new, related areas. For example, its Windows NT operating program has successfully pushed Microsoft into the market of large corporate clients (the enterprise market) and dislodged the hold Unix and other mainframe operating systems had traditionally had on large corporations. As well, Microsoft was late to the Internet browser business, but with the patient application of its customer-captivity advantage managed to knock Netscape from its dominant position.

The power that captive customers give Microsoft is significant. It has, for example, invited innumerable lawsuits and even efforts from the U.S. government because this position gives the company a highly unfair advantage. Whether the unfairness of this advantage makes it illegal is the central question of these lawsuits. One reason Microsoft has been able to lock in customers more successfully than Oracle can be traced to the Buddhist five aggregates. Because Oracle sells high-ticket products, it has been unable to make such purchases automatic. Each time a corporation makes a decision on whether to purchase an Oracle product, it does so consciously: It has the IT or finance department analyze costs and alternatives. Each time Oracle makes a new sale, it brings customers into the conscious level of analysis.

This is dangerous. When your customers choose consciously, you risk losing them.

Microsoft, on the other hand, has moved more deeply behind its users' consciousness. It has done this by adopting the right pricing and distribution strategies. It sells products that simply cost far less than Oracle's products. Windows, for example, might cost hundreds of dollars, while an Oracle database costs millions. Just as you think less about which pen to buy than you think about which car to buy, because the former costs a tiny fraction of the latter, by choosing to sell lower-ticket products Microsoft can remain under the radar while Oracle must contend each time with conscious analysis. Microsoft is additionally able to convince users to automatically choose Microsoft by adopting an indirect distribution strategy. Instead of selling its products directly to end users, it sells them to computer manufacturers. When you buy a Dell computer, for example, you buy it with Microsoft Windows preinstalled. So you never consciously ask yourself, "Do I want Microsoft Windows on my new Dell computer?" Instead you are thinking about hard-drive size, processor speed, memory, display size, and so on.

All told, Microsoft has achieved a level of customer captivity most companies only dream of. It has become the de facto standard, carefully crafting a strategy to remove itself from the scrutiny of conscious choice. Microsoft's two core sources of cash flow—operating systems and productivity software—benefit from automatic customer choice. People buy Microsoft's products without even thinking.

Locking Up Resources

While locking in customers can lead to the long-term sustainability of your profits, Microsoft links that advantage with a second one: locking up resources. Before MS-DOS became the accepted standard operating system, programmers (like the young Bill Gates writing programs for the Altair microcomputer) faced a high-risk decision. They had to decide what platform to write their programs for because computers used different operating systems.

If you chose to write your programs for the Altair, for example, they would not necessarily work on a different computer. This limited your market (you could only sell to Altair users) and also forced you to bet your product's success on one computer (what if the Altair turned out to be a flop?).

MS-DOS was a useful innovation for programmers. If all the computers in the world would run one type of operating system, a programmer could develop a new product that would work on any computer in the world. They did not need to worry about whether Dell or HP would become the most popular computer brands because their program would work on either machine. This usefulness factor—having just one, common operating system—helped MS-DOS emerge as the standard. It also gives Microsoft a continual advantage.

Today, computer programmers can choose to develop software for any number of applications, but because Microsoft has the largest user base for many of them, programmers would be better off developing software for Microsoft-based applications. Let's say, for example, you wish to develop a new add-on for word processing. You must decide whether you will design this software to work with Microsoft Word, WordPerfect, or any number of other word-processing programs. Regardless of which platform you choose, developing your software will require six months of work. What are the chances you will invest those six months to develop your product for WordPerfect—a program that just a small percentage of computer users write with? Your six-month effort has a far greater potential payoff if instead you write it for Microsoft Word. This is why software developers like RealPlayer first launch new versions for the Microsoft Windows platform and only later create versions for the Mac or other operating systems.

The result is that independent programmers around the world are developing software to work with Microsoft's applications. Few are dedicating themselves to work with Microsoft's competition. Just as video game consoles win or lose on the number of independent game developers they convince to design games for their platforms, independent programmers are a critical resource that determines the competitiveness of software. As the preferred choice of this critical resource, Microsoft has a powerful advantage over its competitors.

For similar reasons, Microsoft is able to lock up a second critical resource: distribution. Computer manufacturers, for example, have a better chance of selling their products if they preload a Microsoft operating system (such as Windows) than if they use a less-well-known alternative. Their analysis of which system to load is straightforward. They can target their $1,000 computer with Microsoft Windows to the 90 percent of computer users who are already using Windows, or they can load it with an alternative and try to sell it to just 10 percent of the market. Either way they are selling it for $1,000. Either way it costs them, say, $800. No question why they will naturally prefer to distribute Microsoft's products.

In the corporate sector Microsoft has put in motion a similarly salutary dynamic. Systems integrators, who typically learn to install programs from many providers, will inevitably come across Microsoft products. Their customers' desktops will almost inevitably be running Windows, for example. So as integrators choose which solutions to become licensed in, they may or may not choose Oracle, they may or may not learn to install SAP, but they have a strong incentive to somehow learn and therefore represent Microsoft.

Locking Out Competition

Finally, Microsoft can afford to spend more on research and development than any of its competitors. It can afford to lose more money launching a product than anyone else can. From its enormous capital base, it has climbed precipitous heights. Its research efforts are focused not on cutting-edge technologies, but rather on the safer investments of improving existing ones. It is possible to come up with a brand-new product class that Microsoft has overlooked, as Google has. But to beat Microsoft at improving an existing product (accounting software, for example) would require entering an investment race that Microsoft can always win if it chooses to.

Microsoft can afford to outspend others not just because it has a larger wallet but also because it spreads its investment over a far larger user base. This is what corporate strategists categorize as "economies of scale" applied to R & D. Its resources also enable it to be more patient than others. When Microsoft launched Internet Explorer to compete with Netscape, for example, most Internet industry experts dismissed its attempts as too late. Internet Explorer was not an immediate success, and the chants of disbelievers grew. But each year Microsoft improved its product, distribution, and marketing. Slowly its market share grew. Where a smaller competitor would have given up and relegated the browser market to Netscape, Microsoft persisted because, more than any other potential contender, it could afford to. The ending of this battle is not unlike those of countless other Microsoft forays. Through its patient, sometimes plodding, effort, Microsoft eventually won. So Microsoft leverages its size to block out the competition by outspending and outwaiting any company that puts itself in contention.

Bringing It into Harmony

The magic behind Microsoft's advantage is not just that it enjoys all three sources, when most companies struggle to achieve just one, but that all three exist in self-reinforcing harmony. Microsoft's captive user base attracts more programmers and distributors. Its programmers and distributors help Microsoft reach and retain more users. Its captive user base also generates more profits, which enables Microsoft to reach higher economies of scale. Its economies of scale in turn enable Microsoft to spend more on R & D to build better products for its users and thereby keep them captive. Finally, its economies of scale attract programmers and distributors by offering more support, in the form of R & D spending and distributor incentives, than the competition can.

All of this, however, is built on the captive base of Microsoft
users who automatically buy Microsoft's operating system. If this
root were cut, it is possible the entire dependent structure would
shrivel. Today there are several technological trends that are putting this root at risk. Companies such as Google and Salesforce.
com, for example, are attempting to bypass Microsoft's operating
system altogether by delivering software as a service directly to
consumers via the Internet without requiring them to install anything on their hard drives. Such an offering removes much of the
incompatibility risk that has traditionally kept customers tied to
Microsoft. Whether Microsoft will continue its dominance over
the long term is not guaranteed. It never is. But Microsoft has
engineered a run that no other company in recent history has been
able to match. It has done so by managing the Earth phase brilliantly, putting all three sources of competitive advantage into a
self-reinforcing lock.

CHAPTER FIFTEEN

MUHAMMAD YUNUS AND THE INVENTION OF MICROCREDIT

In the 1970s a poor woman who lived in a developing country and had neither skills nor a steady job almost always had to choose from two dead-end options. To feed her children and give them cover from the rain, she could either beg or borrow. Begging meant walking through richer areas of town asking for handouts. Some days she might return with enough for her children to eat, other days she might not.

Alternatively, she might borrow some money and use it to purchase raw materials that she could transform into something she could sell. She might, for example, borrow money for some straw, weave this into a basket, and sell it later that day for a small profit. But since she was too poor to borrow from a respectable bank, she had to turn to loan sharks whose interest rates might exceed 10 percent per day, more than she could hope to earn from her finished products.

With the borrow option, at the end of each day she would owe more than she could earn. After a few iterations of borrowing, weaving, and repaying more than her profit, she would find herself trapped in a debt spiral. Eventually her few possessions—her roof, her home, her pots—would fall into the hands of moneylenders, leaving her worse off.

The best hope, then, was to beg.

Today this woman has a third option. She can borrow a small amount of money, say $5, from a respectable bank at a fair interest rate. She can invest this in straw, weave a basket, and sell it for a profit that covers her interest payments and still leaves money to buy food for her children. Today this woman has access to the same fair financial options that people who are not poor take for granted. She has this access because an economist in Bangladesh successfully changed the world by introducing an innovation known as "microcredit."

Today over 250 institutions in more than 100 countries regularly make small loans to poor people like this woman because Muhammad Yunus proved this radical model of banking possible. His journey started in 1976, with a loan of $27 to 42 toolmakers. From that he has built an organization that as of 2006 has provided over $3.8 billion to over 2.4 million families in rural Bangladesh. In 2006 he was awarded the Nobel Peace Prize for his efforts. His story shows how, by managing the five phases of change, we can transform the world.

Microcredit in the Metal Phase

The potential for change arises when three conditions coincide. The system grows rigid, unable to respond to emerging needs or opportunities. Weak signals reveal this rigidity. And someone with a long-held commitment realizes these facts.

Yunus's Personal Commitment

Yunus grew up in a small village in one of the most densely populated and poorest countries on earth, Bangladesh. From a young age, he learned to care about the poor. His mother, whom he considers the strongest influence on his life, regularly saved money for any poor relative who might visit from other villages. Though his father was a relatively successful businessman, he strictly limited the allowance he gave his children.

Out of a context in which money was conserved yet shared with the needy, Yunus developed an interest in economics and social reform. He studied hard in school, won a Fulbright scholarship to study in the United States, and, through this, earned a Ph.D. in economics from Vanderbilt University in 1971.

When he returned to Bangladesh in 1972, Yunus brought with him the same two interests that led him abroad: social reform and economics. He first took a senior position with the government's Planning Commission but soon found the work uninspiring, so he resigned to head the economics department of Chittagong University.

As is the case with most innovations, Yunus's journey will soon seem preordained. It seems that his commitment coincided precisely with a moment when the universe needed change that the system would not accommodate.

Recognizing the Rigidity of a Stuck System

Yunus returned to studying the economics of poverty in an academic context. His position as department head afforded him access to conferences, papers, and peers who put him at the cutting-edge thinking of his field. What he discovered, however, was that "brilliant theorists of economics do not find it worthwhile to spend time discussing issues of poverty and hunger. They believe that these will be resolved when general economic prosperity increases. These economists spend all their talents detailing the processes of development and prosperity, but rarely reflect on the origin and development of poverty and hunger. As a result, poverty continues."

Chittagong University was located in a rural area far from Bangladesh's capital city. Beyond its walls, behind which Yunus taught and studied poverty, the villagers of Bangladesh were starving.

While economists studied poverty in a way that avoided the details of the individuals who lived it, banks who attempted to address it were similarly misdirected. Bangladesh had created a special bank to assist the rural poor, but it focused on farmers. While farmers might be poor, they were landowners and still far better off than the majority of the poor whom Yunus felt needed support.

Additionally, banks in general had adopted practices and rules that prevented them from addressing the needs of the very poor. As we will see later, they chained themselves within a network of norms that prevented them from making loans to the illiterate (as most poor Bangladeshis are) or in amounts small enough to be of relevance to the poor.

Weak Signals: Realizing the System Would Not Respond

Sufiya Begum proved to Yunus that the system was stuck.

One day Yunus was conducting firsthand interviews of the poor in the nearby town of Jobra. He approached a hut in which a young woman was weaving bamboo stools. Bangladesh is a Muslim country, and many people, particularly in rural areas, look down upon a woman speaking to a male stranger. So Yunus was careful not to enter the hut or jump quickly into his interview. But after some gentle respectful chitchat, Yunus convinced the young basket weaver to tell her story.

Her name was Sufiya Begum. She was twenty-one years old. To buy her bamboo she needed about 22 cents. Because she did not have 22 cents, she borrowed her bamboo from middlemen and sold the stools back to them for a profit of about 2 cents. With just 2 cents per day in income, Sufiya was barely holding on.

She could earn a more respectable profit if she had the cash to buy the bamboo herself. However, the only people who would lend her the 22 cents were moneylenders who would charge between 10 percent and 50 percent interest per week. She knew this option would drive her into debt, just as it did most who deal with moneylenders.

As Yunus listened it dawned on him that an investment of just 22 cents could liberate this woman from the trap of poverty to a state of self-sustainability. The realization left him "angry, angry at myself, angry at my economics department and the thousands of intelligent professors who had not tried to address this problem and solve it. It seemed to me the existing economic system made it absolutely certain that Sufiya's income would be kept perpetually at such a low level that she would never save a penny and would never invest in expanding her economic base. Her children were condemned to live a life of penury, of hand-to-mouth survival, just as she had lived it before them, and as her parents did before her."

At that moment Yunus reached the state of discontent required for significant change to occur. The three critical ingredients of innovation were present:

- His long-held personal commitment was met.
- A system was stuck, unable to react to a problem (poverty).
- Weak signals showed the problem could be solved.

Now it was time to transition from the rigidity of the Metal phase into the fluidity of the Water phase.

Microcredit in the Water Phase

Yunus lived in two worlds. On one side he rubbed shoulders with bankers and people who studied the banking system. Every year he attended conferences around the world with people who, like him, studied issues of money supply and demand, interest rates, and fiscal policy. He was the friend to economists and bankers who were preoccupied with issues such as loan repayment rates, interest spreads, and treasury operations.

At the same time, his experience growing up in a small village and his current academic position near the rural town of Jobra implanted him in a different life in which illiteracy, starvation, and poverty showed their personal, human faces. This was a world inhabited by social workers, aid agencies, philanthropies, and non-governmental organizations.

The New Metaphor: Banking for the Poor

It is perhaps no surprise then that Yunus approached the problem of poverty from a unique perspective. Bankers viewed poverty as rooted in macroeconomic issues, such as land ownership and GDP growth rates. Social workers looked at the social aspects of poverty; for example, the social status of women and the adoption of new agricultural approaches.

The issues we focus on are determined by the tool we hold. Give a child a hammer, for example, and everything looks like a nail. Yunus approached the problem of poverty with a unique set of tools. By viewing the poverty problem at the human level of social workers but with the perspective of a banker, Yunus saw a fundamental issue that others had not.

When Yunus thought about Sufiya he did not see a complex web of social issues or macroeconomic relations. He saw something much, much simpler: She needed to borrow 22 cents at a fair interest rate. If Sufiya and the millions of poor like her had access to small loans, they could escape the cycle of poverty.

Facing Disbelief: "The Poor Do Not Repay"

Yunus asked his assistant to go into town and compile a list of people like Sufiya who were dependent on middlemen for their supplies. That produced a list of forty-two people who collectively needed a total of $27 (USD) to extricate themselves from traders and moneylenders and become financially independent.

The sum was laughably small. But when Yunus asked the local bank to lend the forty-two families the money they needed, he was given a lesson in one of the many cold realities of banking: Bankers believed the poor did not repay loans.

As Yunus discovered later, banks had adopted a web of practices and rules that left them incapable of lending to the poor. Central to this web was the belief that repayment rates were correlated with income. The rich knew how to manage money and, because they would continue to need financing throughout their lives as they started and expanded businesses, they were motivated to pay on time. The poor, however, had nothing to lose. They could take a loan, spend it, then disappear.

Refused but not deterred, Yunus personally lent $27 to the forty-two families. He reacted on impulse but his decision would later prove important, because those forty-two families repaid their loans more reliably, with a lower default rate, than one would expect of even wealthy borrowers.

The experience laid the foundation of Yunus's new vision in which the poor could access extremely small loans at fair interest rates from responsible financial institutions. He began envisioning a new type of banking: banking for the poor.

Other elements of Water are present in Yunus's story as well. Yunus "expanded the game." While other social causes tended to accept banks and their protocols as given facts of the environment, Yunus's vision was to transform them. In addition, he devised a strategy beyond contention. He did not aim to replace banks with a new one, but instead envisioned a new type of banking that he hoped to enroll all banks into. His strategy was one of inclusion.

Microcredit in the Wood Phase

During the fuzzy phase of Yunus's strategy, few could visualize his intention clearly. He spent the next decade enrolling the key resources and supports he would need to realize his vision.

Partners: Deconstructing Banks

His greatest challenge was to deconstruct the beliefs, logic, and stories that constrained the traditional banking industry into rigidity. When he met with bankers to tell them about his program and encourage them to lend money to the poor, he consistently bumped up against five key logical objections:

1. The poor did not repay loans.
2. The poor did not have collateral, so lending to them was too risky.
3. It was too expensive to service very small loans; the paperwork on a 22-cent loan, for example, could easily cost more than the 22 cents itself.
4. Most poor were illiterate, so they could not fill out loan papers or read enough to know their balances and payment records.
5. The poor had trouble traveling into town to do their banking.

Much of Yunus's struggle was to deconstruct these five entrapments and construct new beliefs. He did this first by personally guaranteeing every loan, so that from the bank's perspective they were lending to a respectable borrower with collateral. He completed the initial loan papers himself; after six weeks of processing he could begin underwriting loans to the poor in Jobra. But he had to sign papers for every loan. So when he was out of the country, at a conference for example, the process seemed untenable. However, he fixed this by having the bank fax papers to his hotel room, which he would sign and mail back.

His initial effort provided data to disprove the first two, most critical, beliefs. A phenomenal 98 percent of his loans to the poor were repaid. This showed that the poor do repay even without collateral. Yunus had always believed the poor would repay at a higher rate than the nonpoor because they had more to lose. The inability to borrow again did not just result in the loss of their business, it threatened their survival.

Evidence and logic are two of the most compelling tools for challenging beliefs. Now Yunus had both behind him. However, even evidence and logic combined are insufficient to overcome entrapped beliefs. People assume their beliefs are rooted in logic, but this itself is a false entrapment. When people are invested in false beliefs, even logic and data will not guide them free.

Yunus needed to solve the full set of issues before banks would be willing to begin lending to the poor in an institutionalized manner. He adopted several unique organizational solutions to the remaining problems:

- To reduce the cost of servicing very small loans, Yunus lent to groups of borrowers who self-policed repayment. Typically five women would form a borrowing group and agree to jointly borrow and repay the entire amount. This realized two economies. First, the borrowing amounts were larger. Second, the structure required less bank oversight since the women met regularly to help each other and ensure prompt payment.
- Because the poor were illiterate, Yunus's people helped borrowers complete required forms and used a network of representatives in the field to keep track of payments. A typical representative might be the owner of a local shop, who would maintain a ledger of payments.

- Since the poor had trouble traveling into town to do their banking, Yunus's program came to them. Its bankers did not sit behind desks but instead walked long rural roads visiting borrowers.

To broaden support among partners—other banks, national and local governments, the international community—Yunus introduced a new distinction he named *microcredit*. People do not understand something until they can name it, and an innovation certainly cannot grow through media or word of mouth without a name. By introducing microcredit, Yunus gave his innovation a vehicle in which it could propagate.

Yunus improvised and adjusted his model as his program grew. By creating a proven set of new, unorthodox banking practices, he would eventually convince bankers that they could profitably do what they initially thought impossible.

Building Shih to Promote Organization

At the organizational level, Yunus battled with an entirely different set of entrapments. His primary dilemma grew from an important strategic choice he made at the very beginning: He decided his program would target women rather than men.

He believed this to be the right choice for two reasons. First, women were the best avenue for impacting poverty. Women supported children and maintained homes at a greater rate than men. Improving the lives of women would actually improve the lives of many more people. Second, women were significantly underserved by banks. Muslim traditions required that men, not women, do the working and the banking. Conforming to this, bank loans went almost entirely to men.

However, this strategic choice created a problem for Yunus. Women borrowers were more comfortable talking to women bankers, especially in a traditional Muslim country like Bangladesh. But when Yunus tried to hire women bankers he bumped against the same tradition that required he hire women: The families of his would-be bankers did not want their daughters to work.

Roadblock after roadblock was put in front of Yunus. If people were not objecting to his employment of women, they objected to the fact that his bankers walked rural roads rather than sitting behind desks.

Yunus persevered. He went through great effort to build an organization that young people would want to work for. He was careful in how he hired and compensated people. But perhaps his most powerful tool for building his organization was accountability.

When new bankers first joined Yunus's program, they would go into the fields to meet borrowers, and there they would hear the stories of Bangladesh's poor. As an example, consider Mufia, a mother who lost one child shortly after birth and two more before they reached term. When her husband died, she was left to beg on the streets for money to pay her rent and feed her remaining three children. A new Yunus employee would visit Mufia several times to get to know her. She would be there when Mufia came home to find that her landlord had sold the tin roof on Mufia's house because Mufia did not pay rent. She would be there as Mufia racked her brain wondering how she would keep her children dry.

By the end of this experience, Yunus's bankers made a deep, profound choice. They did not choose Yunus's program, necessarily, but chose to help their poor countrypeople. He helped establish in them a deep accountability to their people. In this way Yunus built organizational *shih*.

Users: Winning Over the Critical Mass

As with most innovators, Yunus fought a three-front battle. It was not enough to win over partners and employees; he also faced numerous barriers among users, the poor women who would borrow the money. He implemented all seven of the tools for winning over customers.

Challenge accepted beliefs. Poor Bangladeshi women had generally developed a justifiable distrust of lenders. Independent moneylenders and middlemen faced no competition or regulation, so they could freely raise interest rates to the critical point at which the poor could earn just enough to survive. The generally accepted belief was that people who lent money were usurers. So to recruit a new borrowing group, Yunus and his people attended numerous meetings with interested women to explain the program and address their concerns. The most common questions centered around why a "bank" would want to lend money at such low rates. What was the bank really after?

Provide logic. At these meeting Yunus and his people detailed the program's objectives and why the "bank" was doing what it did. They also needed to explain the logic behind their group-borrowing model, payment procedures, rules of conduct, and why all of these made sense both for the borrower and the "bank."

Give choice to build accountability. The program only lent money to small groups, usually between five and eight borrowers, mostly women. In this way they established accountability not just from borrower-to-lender but between borrowers themselves. If one woman missed a payment, the other four would hold her accountable to making it up.

Introduce a new distinction. Yunus named his program the Grameen Bank, which in Bangla means "rural bank." Through this he introduced a new concept, that of a for-profit bank with a social mission of serving the rural community.

Change metaphors. Yunus merged his metaphor's two key components—social service and banking—wherever he could, in his organization's name, logo, and messaging.

Retell stories. Since Grameen Bank now serves millions of poor families, each with a unique story, it has a rich source of storytelling to transform conceptions. By telling of people who transformed their story of poverty into an ending of liberty, the bank can effectively retell the ending that its would-be borrowers normally expect. Poor borrowers who believe they are destined to continued poverty begin seeing an alternative future, one in which they can triumph, as others have, over their situations.

Change incentives. Finally, as we will see shortly, Grameen Bank introduced an innovative structure for its loans to help poor borrowers move away from the behaviors that lead most poor into further debt.

Microcredit in the Fire Phase

In the three years after Yunus loaned his first $27 to forty-two families in 1976, his program grew more than tenfold; by 1979 there were 500 borrowers. Yet his program still paled in scale to established banks, who generally dismissed Yunus and his efforts as "nothing, only a flyspeck compared to the big national banks we manage," as one elderly banker told Yunus after a lecture.

But at some time in the following three years, Grameen Bank reached the Fire phase. By 1982 its membership of borrowers had grown to 28,000. What triggered this and subsequent growth?

The Trigger: The Tangail Pilot

In 1979 the Bangladeshi government gave Yunus an opportunity to prove his concept on a large scale. The beauty of this opportunity was that it drew encouragement from both his supporters and opponents. The former hoped he would succeed; the latter hoped to reveal Yunus's idea as just the "flyspeck" they believed it to be.

Yunus was given a two-year leave of absence from his university and took over as the head of the Grameen Bank Project in a rural district called Tangail, just outside Bangladesh's capital, Dhaka.

Rather than build new offices, the government worked with participating traditional banks to leverage existing offices. Grameen Bank, which had operated out of one branch in Jobra, grew overnight to an organization with twenty-five branches (co-located in branches of existing banks spread throughout Tangail).

It was this project that Grameen Bank would use to prove its concept on a larger scale. It also thrust the program into rapid growth mode (Fire), which required the swift, creative design of new tactics.

The Shift from Strategy to Tactics

As Grameen Bank exploded, it faced a rapid succession of new challenges to which it needed innovative responses. The end result was a set of operating procedures that would make Grameen Bank a truly unique organization.

Because Grameen did not want to depend on what it viewed as the unreliable staff of its national banking partners, it tried to recruit young talent as quickly as it could. Grameen maintained high standards, turning down most applicants, but turned to an unusual source for talent: former revolutionaries. The Gonobahini were underground fighters who had taken up arms to liberate their country. Grameen Bank gave former Gonobahini a new weapon with which to help their people, and they in turn responded by channeling their hard work and dedication to Grameen and its borrowers.

Traditional bank loans require borrowers to make regular monthly payments, or sometimes only monthly interest payments and then one large balloon payment at the end. For the poor, such structures complicate their efforts at fiscal responsibility. When a poor borrower has cash, she finds it difficult to set it aside for a future payment when pressing needs are always present. So Grameen bank structures every loan as a weekly annuity. Borrowers make a fixed payment every week until the loan is paid off. This helps poor borrowers keep their loans in budget.

Because Grameen wants its bankers to appear as different as possible from traditional ones, it gives them no office and very little in the way of forms and procedures. They are not allowed to accept gifts. They must pay for their own room and board. When in the field, some Grameen bankers even find shelter in abandoned houses or schools.

Combine these practices with the Grameen group model—in which borrowers must form groups of five to eight members—and the limitation that it only makes very small loans, and you find a bank that truly stands out among others. The entire Grameen system is built to support a holistic set of strategies that no traditional bank would find it easy to duplicate. These tactics prevent the

Grameen innovation from being copied incompletely and watered down by traditional banks.

Moral Conflict

At the core of the Grameen Bank strategy, of course, is its uncontestable social mission. Although the bank is profitable, its model is built around a singular social purpose. It is designed with just one customer segment in mind, the very poor. As such, any financial institutions that resist the bank find themselves eventually isolated by the international community. The principle at work here is precisely what John Boyd (Chapter 6) describes in his theories of moral conflict. By choosing an objective of higher moral value, you can overcome even more powerful adversaries. They will eventually find themselves isolated, unsupported, in their resistance.

The pilot project in Tangail did not fully unleash Yunus's innovation. He proved his model but still had to struggle with powerful people who found reasons to discount it. Grameen continued to experience the Fire phase, outmaneuvering opposition, for several years as it expanded still further into rural Bangladesh. But soon after the Tangail pilot, the innovation became self-sustaining. It grew because it attracted notice, and attracted notice because it grew. This growth cycle fed itself as the bank moved into new countries.

Microcredit in the Earth Phase

Assessing the Earth phase for a social innovation is somewhat complicated. Yunus does not view his competition as other banks. Indeed, his mission is to convince traditional banks to embrace his model. So when Yunus seeks to block out the competition, it is not banks he worries about but rather any forces whose actions might slow or erode the growth of microcredit. He must, for example, shield microcredit against governments who might introduce laws preventing it or against programs that might mismanage their microcredit schemes and tarnish the concept's reputation. That's why the ownership structure helped land Yunus's innovation in the Earth phase.

When Yunus finally convinced the Bangladeshi government to accept Grameen Bank as an official financial institution, he was named the bank's head. That meant he became a government-appointed bureaucrat and could be removed at any time for any reason. This made the bank vulnerable to potentially capricious government interests. After some patient effort, Yunus was able to adjust governance structure to remove this risk. He had the rules changed so that the Grameen Bank managing director was appointed by a board of directors, not by the government. Just as for-profit companies do not want to depend too heavily on one client, Grameen Bank did not want to depend too heavily on one supporter—in this case, the government.

In addition to the ownership and dependency issue, the bank simultaneously undertook the efforts most traditional companies do when grounding themselves in the Earth phase. It streamlined and institutionalized operating procedures, for example. It built arguments and procedures that aligned it with traditional Muslim laws. It packaged its formula so that organizations in other countries could easily introduce microcredit programs. With all this, Yunus successfully navigated the Earth phase.

CHAPTER SIXTEEN

TED LEONSIS AND THE DISCOVERY OF FILMANTHROPY

You cannot see global warming. You cannot taste it or smell it or touch it. Yet scientists and politicians debate it as passionately as they argue about anything.

Global warming is a classic example of social construction. Its name represents a trend in our environment that may or may not be happening and may or may not lead to better or worse conditions in the future. But because we can name it, we can efficiently debate something that would otherwise be too complex for most of us to develop an opinion of. The ability to debate this concept is critical because, depending on your viewpoint, the debate could lead to the demise or rescue of the planet and all the life on it.

What is amazing about this debate is how quickly and dramatically our beliefs around it have changed. In 2000 a meaningful majority of opinion leaders held the view that global warming was not actually occurring, or at least that its significance was unclear. As President George W. Bush said during a presidential debate on October 11, 2000:

"Some of the scientists, I believe, haven't they been changing their opinion a little bit on global warming? There's a lot of differing opinions and before we react I think it's best to have the full accounting, full understanding of what's taking place."

Bush's stance was shared by many well-regarded scientists, and he was speaking for a large percentage of the U.S. populace.

But by 2007 the debate had changed dramatically. In just seven years, the seesaw tilted completely the other way, as public and scientific opinion changed from disbelief or confusion to conviction that global warming was a serious threat. The scientists who once questioned whether the globe was warming grew quiet. Even George W. Bush reconstructed his position. On May 31, 2007, during a Group of Eight summit, he said in a speech:

"The United States takes this issue [of global warming] seriously. My proposal is this: By the end of next year, America and other nations will set a long-term global goal for reducing greenhouse gases."

Something deconstructed and reconstructed the opinions of the public, the scientific community, and politicians between 2000 and 2007. Many factors played a role in the change, but one in particular stands out: a documentary narrated by former vice president Al Gore titled *An Inconvenient Truth*.

By all measures *An Inconvenient Truth* was a breakthrough film. The documentary drew audiences in numbers even traditional movies would envy. It won two Oscars in 2007, including Best Documentary. It won numerous awards from movie festivals and organizations throughout the world. It birthed a companion book that reached first place on the *New York Times* bestseller list and stayed there for months. The movie is one of the three highest-grossing documentaries of all time.

In terms of its impact on the global warming debate, the film has been a definitive success, turning the public debate on its head. But the movie's success points to another emerging trend of equal significance: filmanthropy as a tool for changing the world.

The term *filmanthropy* was coined by Ted Leonsis, vice chairman of AOL, who has been mentioned several times in this book. Leonsis, who has successfully transformed businesses across several industries, believes the *Inconvenient Truth* phenomenon points to wide-scale change in how people affect their worlds. Investigating how he came to this conclusion, and how he is using filmanthropy to change the world, provides insight into how successful innovators think.

Leonsis says he "stumbled upon" filmanthropy, and is pursuing its possibility using the same steps that have led him to countless highly profitable ventures. He recognized rigidity (Metal), introduced a new metaphor (Water), assembled the needed resources (Wood), drove for acceptance (Fire), and worked on consolidating his gains (Earth).

The Filmmaker in the Metal Phase

The journey that led Leonsis—a high-tech entrepreneur and sports franchise owner—to film began with a very innocuous event: On a yachting vacation with his wife, he ran out of reading material. At port in St. Bart's he looked everywhere for a bookstore. The one store he found only sold books in French, a language Leonsis does not read. Desperate, Leonsis pleaded with the shop owner for something, anything, in English. The best she could scrape up was forty-five days' worth of old *New York Times* newspapers.

With nothing else to do, Leonsis read every newspaper from cover to cover, including sections he would normally pass over, like the obituaries. This act of looking where he usually would not was the beginning of a new adventure. Innovations seem to begin when someone looks where others are not looking, when someone combines two domains that others do not usually mix.

In the obituaries, Leonsis came across one for Iris Chang, the author of *The Rape of Nanking*, a bestselling book about the Japanese occupation of China in 1937, when Japanese soldiers killed 300,000 Chinese living in Nanking. The news captured his attention. After finishing all forty-five editions of the *New York Times*, Leonsis threw the stack of papers in the garbage. Serendipitously, the obituary featuring Ms. Chang landed on top.

Later that evening as he and his wife were leaving for dinner, Leonsis walked by the stack of papers, looked down, and again saw the obituary. This planted a vague idea in his head. Just before disembarking, Leonsis felt he needed to turn around. He was not yet sure what his mind was working on, but the story of Ms. Chang was calling to him somehow. He asked his wife to wait while he returned to save the article from the trash heap.

Back home after the vacation, Leonsis started to investigate the Nanking story further. He bought three books on the topic, including *The Rape of Nanking*, read them carefully, and arrived at a deep state of discontent. The story of Nanking was important. It was nothing short of a holocaust, but it was one that few people knew about. It angered him that the lives of the 300,000 victims at Nanking went substantially unremembered and that the Japanese government refused to acknowledge, let alone apologize for, the atrocity. He decided he wanted to let people know about this, and set about figuring how to do so.

The Filmmaker in the Water Phase

People needed to know about the Nanking story, but what would be Leonsis's strategy for helping them understand? Most of what had been written about the episode was in books which few people had read. Leonsis wanted to use a different, more vibrant medium, and decided his best bet was to create a film that told the Nanking story.

The Filmmaker in the Wood Phase

Just as he did when he transformed AOL from an Internet company into a media company, Leonsis set about putting in place what he needed to create a successful film. He turned to Creative Artists Agency (CAA), a group of people who perhaps know more about what it takes to create a film than anyone else. He shared what he wanted to do and asked two questions: "Am I crazy?" and "If not, tell me what I need to do."

CAA told him that the critical central component is to have a well-regarded director buy in to the project. CAA introduced Leonsis to Bill Gutentag, a successful documentary filmmaker. Gutentag flew to visit Leonsis, was persuaded by Leonsis's passion, and signed on to be part of the project.

With the director and CAA secured, the remainder of what Leonsis needed fell more easily into place. He hired researchers to find Nanking survivors and the families of the people who helped these people survive. He then recruited well-known actors including Woody Harrelson to provide dramatized narration in character.

As the project advanced—filming survivors, getting government approval—Leonsis added other critical elements to his puzzle. He approached potential investors and distributors, and prepared to submit to key movie festivals.

The Filmmaker in the Fire Phase

Nanking, Leonsis's first film, was a success by many counts. It was accepted into the prestigious Sundance Film Festival, a feat with tougher odds than an application to Harvard University.

His film won the award for Documentary Film Editing at Sundance. It went on to win the Humanitarian Award for documentary at the Hong Kong International Film Festival. It was the first Sundance film to be screened at the 2007 Tribeca Film Festival. And it was awarded inclusion into the 2007 SilverDocs Film Festival in Washington, D.C.

By consciously choosing the message to ensure it appealed to several niche demographics, Leonsis has drawn a large audience. One of his key targets was the Chinese-American community. However, his main characters also resonate with Germans (one of the main heroes in the story is a German) and Americans (several of the other important heroes are American). Most important for Leonsis, however, is that the film raised awareness, and sparked a discussion, of the Nanking tragedy.

The Filmmaker in the Earth Phase

Most would be satisfied with Leonsis's film success. He has many other important projects demanding his time, and no one would question it if he called his movie a worthwhile experience and moved on to new things.

But Leonsis sees an opportunity to make a longer-term impact by encouraging young people throughout the world to embrace what he calls "filmanthropy." He believes the time is ripe for a revolution in documentary filmmaking. He believes this because the five stages of change tell him so.

Leonsis is now well positioned to make this emergence of filmanthropy real because his documentary *Nanking* has changed how people recognize him. Before making the film, Ted Leonsis was known as many things—an executive with AOL, an entrepreneur, a sports franchise owner—but not as a filmmaker. Now the film has constructed a new identity for Leonsis. When people introduce him, they now call him a filmmaker. With this identity in place, Leonsis has the potential to lead the change he wished to see in the world. He is already executing his plan to the third phase of change.

Filmanthropy in the Metal Phase

"When I see an industry's value chain is broken, when the system is not fair, I see an opportunity."

—Ted Leonsis

Like Infosys, Nokia, Microsoft, and other corporate innovators mentioned in this book, Leonsis sees opportunity when the system is stuck. Leonsis believes the film industry is stuck. He bases this view on the fact that there are thousands of talented filmmakers who are not getting chances to share their work. According to Leonsis's calculations, there are 25,000 documentary filmmakers. Of these, only 5,000 submit their work to film festivals like Sundance, of which only a handful have their films accepted. And only a fraction of those will get a distribution deal, the critical contract needed to get a documentary film to the mass audience.

Leonsis believes there is immense creative talent bottled up, wasted because it cannot squeeze through the tight lock that traditional gatekeepers have on which movies are produced. The system is stuck, or, in his words, "the value chain is broken" because the people with ideas who are doing the real work are not afforded opportunities or are not receiving a fair share of the money that movie companies bring in. As he puts it, "The people doing the work are not the people making the money."

He also sees several weak signals that indicate this nonoptimal state will soon unlock and reorganize into a more efficient state. He specifically sees four trends:

1. Self-expression is becoming the new focus of youth. In the 1970s the most sought-after college grads wanted to get into advertising. In the 1980s investment banks and Wall Street were pulling graduates. In the 1990s the brightest young minds looked to the high-tech industry for intellectually challenging and financially rewarding jobs. Today, youth are looking for opportunities to express themselves. The rise of YouTube and similar Web sites is one small example of this trend.

2. Technology advances are dramatically reducing the costs of producing a film. With a good computer and the right software, anyone can simulate the ability of even large, well-established studios. So it becomes affordable to produce movies that reach smaller and smaller audiences. Not every film needs to be a blockbuster.

3. New distribution options are opening. There are 1 billion Internet users, yet media companies are still relying almost exclusively on distribution media that ignore most of these users at any given time. There are only about 500 theater owners who carry documentaries and just 25 distributors who might sell to these theater owners. Media companies are overlooking an emerging opportunity to distribute movies online. YouTube is one sign of this idea's potential. Leonsis thinks YouTube's stellar success is just the first sign of a trend that will continue.

4. New ways of earning money are evolving. These trends are strengthened by the appearance of new business models that make it possible for even small, independent filmmakers to collect money for their work without needing to negotiate expensive deals with theater chains or invest in large-scale business teams. It is increasingly common to sell advertising space on a site that allows people to see your video free or to charge subscription fees to users. You can turn on such revenue-generating models with a few clicks of your mouse.

These weak signals point to the understanding that the existing players in the media industry are stuck. Their practices and approaches are acting too slowly to change. This is perhaps because the traditional distribution method—from production company to distributor to theater—generates higher profits than does online distribution.

Filmanthropy in the Water Phase

Recognizing that the system is stuck, Leonsis is launching a new effort to help would-be documentary filmmakers succeed. One of his first steps was to create a metaphor for the phenomenon that he felt would capture people's imagination and help them immediately understand what he was talking about. He combined *film* and *philanthropy* into a new word—*filmanthropy*.

His vision is to make *filmanthropy* as common as *documentary* or *global warming*. He imagines building a central service that will help independent documentary filmmakers efficiently launch new films that have philanthropic intentions. He would like young creatives to have a place where they can find funding (for example, through an online auction to would-be investors), get distribution (to television channels and other large players), and immediately tap revenue (such as advertising or subscriptions).

This filmanthropy model would open the floodgates of the millions of talented, creative people with something to say. It would transform what would otherwise be a certain failure (even a successful documentary will lose money if it pursues traditional distribution) into a feasible social venture (his model would enable such a filmmaker to make a profit and thereby continue to expand).

Filmanthropy in the Wood Phase

Leonsis is now building. He gives speeches to introduce the concept of filmanthropy. He is assembling the pieces needed for his vision: the technology, community, financing, and the rest.

Will Leonsis succeed in his next, new-change effort? Only time will tell. But his track record at recognizing an opportunity (Metal), thinking of a way to seize it (Water), assembling the needed pieces (Wood), managing the competition (Fire), and consolidating his gains (Earth) is impressive. If he says he sees a dramatic change underway, we would be wise to listen.

THE THIRTY-SIX STRATAGEMS

More than 2,500 years ago, military and political minds in China began to debate how to make a science of strategy by distilling their collective knowledge into a few universal principles. The process took more than a thousand years, and it produced a catalog of thirty-six strategies for gaining, expanding, and retaining power: the Thirty-Six Stratagems.

For the past decade I have been using these stratagems as brainstorming tools to help executives devise creative options for outthinking their competition. By viewing your challenge through three to five of these ancient metaphors, you may find a winning move that you would otherwise have overlooked. Simply answer these two questions for each stratagem: What would it mean to apply this tactic to your situation? How would you translate this move, described here in the flowery language of an era long past, into a solution to your modern problem?

1. **To Catch Something, First Let It Go.**
   Do not attack your adversary; rather, let him go, and follow close behind.
2. **Exchange a Brick for a Jade.**
   Give your adversary something on which you place relatively little value in exchange for something you value much more.

3. **Invite Your Enemy Onto the Roof, Then Remove the Ladder.**

   Entice your adversary to enter your area of control and then cut off all escape routes. This forces your adversary to fight where you hold the advantage.

4. **Lure the Tiger Down from the Mountain.**

   Lure your adversary out of his stronghold onto an open field where he has no advantage. Then attack him or take his stronghold.

5. **Befriend the Distant Enemy to Attack the One Nearby.**

   Ally yourself with a distant, or indirect, competitor to jointly attack a nearby, or direct, one.

6. **Kill with a Borrowed Knife.**

   Use a third party to attack your adversary.

7. **Besiege Wei to Rescue Zhao.**

   Have an ally attack your adversary. This will force your adversary to disengage from his conflict with you to defend himself. He must then fight on two fronts.

8. **The Stratagem of Sowing Discord.**

   Find someone your adversary depends on, lure him to work in your favor, and thereby topple a critical relationship on which your adversary depends.

9. **Trouble the Water to Match the Fish.**

   Create confusion around your adversary to blind him and hinder his ability to understand your intentions or see your approach.

10. **Remove the Firewood from Under the Pot.**

    Rather than engage your adversary head-on, attack his supply line or cut off a critical resource he needs to attack you.

11. **Shut the Door to Capture the Thief.**

    When your opponent is weak, divided, or dispersed, surround him, prevent his escape, but avoid direct attack.

12. **Replace the Beams with Rotten Timbers.**

    Attack the key support structures on which your adversary's advantage depends.

13. **The Stratagem of the Beautiful Woman.**
    Identify your adversary's key weakness or need and use this
    to encourage him to act in a way counter to his benefit.

14. **Beat the Grass to Startle the Snake.**
    Launch a false, small-scale attack to encourage your enemy
    to reveal his plans. Then plan your real attack with this new
    knowledge.

15. **Loot a Burning House.**
    When trouble strikes, look for your adversary to freeze or
    retreat. Capitalize on his inaction or retreat to take action
    and build power.

16. **Sometimes Running Away Is the Best Strategy.**
    Rather than fight a more powerful adversary, retreat to pre-
    serve your power and apply it somewhere else or at some
    other time.

17. **Seize the Opportunity to Lead the Sheep Away.**
    Look for a moment when your adversary fails to act (for
    example, because he is distracted), and attack where he will
    not defend.

18. **Feign Madness But Keep Your Balance.**
    To avoid being perceived as a threat, appear crazy or incapa-
    ble. When your adversary puts down his guard, take him.

19. **Watch the Fire on the Other Shore.**
    When your adversary is engaged in conflict internally or
    with his allies, refrain from acting. An attack might cause
    unification. Allowed to continue, the internal conflict will
    damage him.

20. **Let the Plum Tree Wither in Place of the Peach.**
    Allow your adversary a victory on one front to preserve,
    even strengthen, your competitiveness on another front.

21. **The Stratagem of the Open City Gates.**
    Openly reveal your strength, weakness, or strategy. This
    will encourage your adversary to call off his attack because
    he fears your strength, no longer considers you a threat, or
    believes he understands your strategy.

22. **Await the Exhausted Enemy at Your Ease.**
Identify the next battleground, set up a defendable position there, and wait for your adversary. When he arrives, use your superior position to defeat him.

23. **Exchange the Role of Guest for That of Host.**
Encourage your adversary to accept you as an unthreatening guest. Incrementally build power over him and eventually take control.

24. **Borrow the Road to Conquer Gao.**
Look for someone who has better access to your objective, and create an alliance with him to gain passage.

25. **Shed Your Skin Like the Golden Cicada.**
Create a façade and make your adversary think it is the real thing; then move the action somewhere else.

26. **The Stratagem of Injuring Yourself.**
When your adversary's suspicion hinders your success, injure yourself to either win your adversary's trust or avoid appearing to be a threat. When your adversary accepts you or lets down his guard, advance.

27. **Borrow a Corpse for the Soul's Return.**
Adopt a forgotten or abandoned model, idea, or technology to differentiate yourself and build power.

28. **Point at the Mulberry But Curse the Locust.**
Rather than attack your adversary directly, aim your attack at a different target. This will send a covert message that will alter his behavior.

29. **Clamor in the East; Attack to the West.**
Feign an attack the defense of which exposes your enemy to a different attack. Launch your true attack and defeat your adversary.

30. **Openly Repair the Walkway, Secretly March to Chen Cang.**
Focus your adversary, or let your adversary focus on, a direct, orthodox attack while you launch an indirect, unorthodox attack to take him by surprise.

31. **Fool the Emperor and Cross the Sea.**
    Take actions that appear normal, ones that appear everyday, to lull your adversary into complacency. By the time he realizes your actions constitute a threat, it is too late.

32. **Create Something Out of Nothing.**
    When your direct attack (one using existing players) is ineffective, create a new player or entity to catch your adversary off-guard.

33. **Hide a Dagger Behind a Smile.**
    Because a direct attack would generate resistance in your adversary, choose an approach that is, or appears to be, friendly. When your adversary lets down his defenses and welcomes this approach, take him with a secondary attack.

34. **Deck the Tree with Bogus Blossoms.**
    Combine and coordinate independent elements within your environment to become a much stronger whole, then overpower your adversary.

35. **To Catch the Bandits, First Capture Their Leader.**
    Focus your attack on your adversary's leader or leaders. By influencing them you can direct your adversary with less effort. This is like leading a horse by directing its head.

36. **The Stratagem of Linking Stratagems.**
    Rather than concentrating on just one, execute multiple strategies, either simultaneously or in succession. If one strategy is not effective, the next one is. If the next one is not effective, the following one is. This eventually overwhelms your adversary or catches him in an impossible situation.

A Note on How the Discussed Companies Were Chosen

To test the theories presented in this book I analyzed the histories of twelve outstanding companies. To identify these companies, I gathered fundamental performance data on more than 7,000 publicly traded firms, from all major stock exchanges, for which at least ten years of financial data was available.

I screened out companies with less than $1 billion in annual revenue to focus on companies with meaningful scale. Then, for each of the 2,300 remaining companies I calculated a "competitiveness score" based on the company's ten-year average annual sales growth, profit margin (earnings before interest, taxes, depreciation, and amortization), and total return to shareholders.

From the 100 companies with the highest competitive scores (the most competitive companies of the decade), I chose twelve for which I could gather a sufficiently large amount of historical data (including analyst reports, books, and journal articles) regarding the company and its peers. From these secondary sources, and interviews I conducted with leadership of several of the companies, I tested my core hypotheses. The results are sprinkled throughout this book.

Cases for six of the twelve are provided in Book Four of this text (along with analyses of two innovations that are not part of this list because they are social innovations and not centered around a publicly traded, for-profit corporation). I would have provided case analyses of all the cases I studied were more space available.

The twelve companies I analyzed, in order of their calculated "competitive score," were:

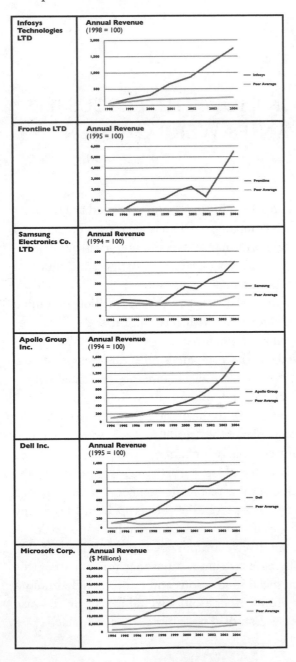

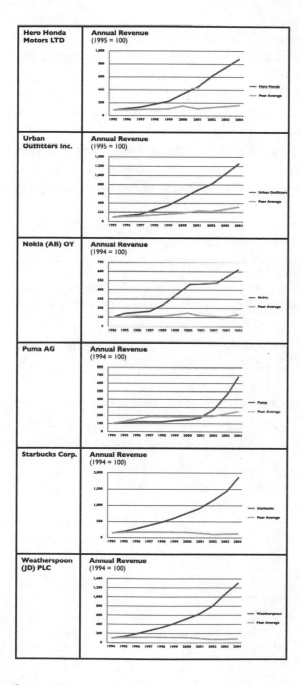

Revenue is in thousands of dollars except where noted.

These twelve companies not only grew faster than their peers but did so while maintaining competitive, often superior, profit margins. They also delivered higher returns to their shareholders than did their peers. Few companies in the world (indeed, only 100 out of more than 7,000) have achieved comparable performance over an extended period of time.

The following table summarizes the ten-year average performance of each of the twelve companies compared to that of its peers. It also provides the names of some of the key peers used in the comparison.

10-Year Financial Performance*

	Total Return to Shareholders	Sales Growth	EBITDA Margin	Key Peers/ Competitors
PUMA	47.24	23.29	13.57	Adidas, Reebok, and Nike
Peer Average	19.75	6.89	10.17	
Difference	27.49	16.41	3.41	
DELL	72.16	33.21	9.44	Apple, Gateway, and Lenovo
Peer Average	32.25	20.61	6.83	
Difference	39.90	12.60	2.61	
CISCO	32.69	37.34	31.78	3Com and SonicBlue
Peer Average	(14.34)	1.78	(13.30)	
Difference	47.03	35.56	45.07	
SAMSUNG	69.44	21.49	24.67	LG Corp, Philips, and Sharp
Peer Average	14.35	4.02	9.55	
Difference	55.10	17.46	15.12	

	Total Return to Shareholders	Sales Growth	EBITDA Margin	Key Peers/ Competitors
NOKIA	29.24	21.45	19.92	Ericsson, Motorola, and Qualcomm
Peer Average	19.31	7.02	10.73	
Difference	9.93	14.43	9.19	
HERO HONDA	56.25	27.50	13.80	Harley-Davidson and Yamaha
Peer Average	19.09	7.20	14.78	
Difference	37.15	20.30	(0.98)	
FRONTLINE	60.65	25.21	47.95	A.P. Moeller-Maersk, Evergreen Marine, and Mitsui O.S.K. Lines
Peer Average	18.91	9.57	16.18	
Difference	41.74	15.65	31.77	
URBAN OUTFITTERS	66.28	32.35	12.89	Gap, American Eagle Outfitters, and H&M
Peer Average	35.14	15.43	11.52	
Difference	31.14	16.93	1.37	
WEATHERSPOON	28.69	35.40	19.19	Whitbread
Peer Average	8.24	(1.18)	16.48	
Difference	20.45	36.58	2.71	

	Total Return to Shareholders	Sales Growth	EBITDA Margin	Key Peers/ Competitors
STARBUCKS	32.56	34.48	15.38	McDonald's, Outback Steakhouse, and Wendy's
Peer Average	15.28	13.21	14.81	
Difference	17.28	21.26	0.57	
INFOSYS	54.06	62.99	33.83	Cap Gemini, CSK Holdings, and LogicaCMG
Peer Average	31.37	24.21	12.49	
Difference	22.69	38.78	21.33	
MICROSOFT	31.07	23.51	47.60	Computer Associates, Oracle, and SAP
Peer Average	15.59	14.09	16.85	
Difference	15.48	9.42	30.75	
APOLLO GROUP	37.75	30.69	23.50	Devry Inc. and ITT Educational Services
Peer Average	27.59	19.24	17.84	
Difference	10.16	11.44	5.66	

*For the decade ending 2005.
Source: Compustat and Global Vantage.

INDEX